Mothers as the Image of God

Mothers
as the Image
of God

JULIANN BULLOCK

RESOURCE *Publications* · Eugene, Oregon

MOTHERS AS THE IMAGE OF GOD

Copyright © 2022 Juliann Bullock. All rights reserved. Except for brief quotations in critical publications or reviews, no part of this book may be reproduced in any manner without prior written permission from the publisher. Write: Permissions, Wipf and Stock Publishers, 199 W. 8th Ave., Suite 3, Eugene, OR 97401.

Resource Publications
An Imprint of Wipf and Stock Publishers
199 W. 8th Ave., Suite 3
Eugene, OR 97401

www.wipfandstock.com

PAPERBACK ISBN: 978-1-6667-5834-4
HARDCOVER ISBN: 978-1-6667-5835-1
EBOOK ISBN: 978-1-6667-5836-8

NOVEMBER 16, 2022 9:32 AM

Scripture quotations marked ESV are from the ESV® Bible (The Holy Bible, English Standard Version®), copyright © 2001 by Crossway, a publishing ministry of Good News Publishers. Used by permission. All rights reserved. The ESV text may not be quoted in any publication made available to the public by a Creative Commons license. The ESV may not be translated into any other language.

Scripture quotations marked NASB are taken from the (NASB®) New American Standard Bible®, Copyright © 1960, 1971, 1977, 1995 by The Lockman Foundation. Used by permission. All rights reserved. www.lockman.org

Scripture quoted by permission. Quotations designated NET are from the NET Bible® copyright ©1996, 2019 by Biblical Studies Press, L.L.C. http://netbible.com All rights reserved.

Scripture quotations marked NIV are taken from the Holy Bible, New International Version®, NIV®. Copyright © 1973, 1978, 1984, 2011 by Biblica, Inc.™ Used by permission of Zondervan. All rights reserved worldwide. www.zondervan.comThe "NIV" and "New International Version" are trademarks registered in the United States Patent and Trademark Office by Biblica, Inc.™

Scripture quotations marked NLT are taken from the *Holy Bible*, New Living Translation, copyright ©1996, 2004, 2015 by Tyndale House Foundation. Used by permission of Tyndale House Publishers, Carol Stream, Illinois 60188. All rights reserved.

For Mum,

who extended God's motherly love to me even before my birth, and continues to do so to this day.

Thank you for giving me a beautiful experience of God's image.

And for Kristin,

a spiritual mother and midwife for my soul.

CONTENTS

Abbreviations | viii

1. God and Motherhood | 1
2. Birthing Imagery | 19
3. Breastfeeding Imagery | 33
4. Jesus, Motherhood, and the Kingdom of God | 63
5. Motherhood in the Old Testament | 94
6. Motherhood in the New Testament | 162

Bibliography | 191

ABBREVIATIONS

BDAG: Danker, Frederick William et al. *A Greek-English Lexicon of the New Testament and Other Early Christian Literature*. Chicago, IL: University of Chicago Press, 2000.

HALOT: Koehler, Ludwig and Walter Baumgartner. *The Hebrew and Aramaic Lexicon of the Old Testament*. Translated and edited by M.E.J. Richardson. Leiden: Brill, 1994–2000.

NIDOTTE: VanGemeren, Willem, ed. *New International Dictionary of Old Testament Theology & Exegesis*. Grand Rapids, MI: Zondervan, 1997.

1

GOD AND MOTHERHOOD

In the Image of God

In the image of God he created them, male and female he created them. (Gen 1:27, NET)

I think we were in the third mile of our seven-mile run, with more than half of the workout still ahead of us. It was a cold autumn day; not the bright, crisp kind but the damp, soggy, gray kind that seeps into your bones. As usual, my cross country teammate and I were deep in an interesting conversation. When you run with someone for hours and hours, there is almost nothing you don't end up talking about at some point. I don't remember the topic or flow of this particular conversation, but I will never forget the moment when my friend said, "Well, you're made in the image of God, aren't you?"

Was I? I was surprised by my own doubt. Nobody had ever told me that I wasn't made in God's image, and yet somehow I wasn't sure. I knew that men were made in God's image . . . but was I? I tried to sound nonchalant, in spite of the rising emotions within me as I responded lightly, "Am I?" My friend laughed kindly, and told me the reasons why she knew that we, too, were created in the image of God—reasons I no longer remember though I will always remember the joyful relief that erupted in my chest as she spoke.

Why was I not more sure? Both of my parents valued and affirmed my worth as a girl and then as a woman, and I never believed that I was in any way inferior because of my gender. I had not consciously considered myself to *not* share in the image of God. Where did that shadow of doubt outside my consciousness come from?

Almost twenty years later, my own daughter pointed me towards the answer. In the middle of one of her frequent, meandering monologues my tiny daughter declared emphatically, "But God's a boy." I'm sure I never told her that God was a boy, but that was the message she had absorbed. And if God is a boy, how can a little girl (or a grown woman) be made in God's image?

Is God a boy? Jesus is obviously a man, but is the Godhead essentially male?

When God created humanity, we are told two things: humanity carries the image of God, and that image is carried by two types of people—male and female. Both male and female humans do fully and equally reflect the image of God, and yet it's so important not to project our own ideas about masculinity or femininity back on God. It's not that God has a masculine side and a feminine side and was therefore constrained to reflect the image of God in masculine and feminine humans. As a spirit, God transcends gender, and is neither male nor female, nor both! God just is. Nevertheless, because God did decide to reflect God's image in two very different types of people, I believe that men and women *together* can give us a fuller, more robust picture of God's nature than either gender could alone.

Many of God's attributes are reflected similarly in both genders, but men and women are not the same, and we are not interchangeable, so it seems that unique aspects of God's nature must be highlighted in each gender. Some attributes tend to be showcased more clearly in men, and others more clearly in women. Before Eve's creation, it was not good for the man to be alone, and not just because the man was lonely or had unmet needs. It was not good for creation for the man to be alone, because the full image of God was not reflected in the man alone. Nor would it be reflected in a woman alone. The truest reflection of God's glory and character is seen in both genders together, living in unity and harmony as we were meant to live.

So what aspects of God's nature are most clearly displayed in women? When Adam was alone in the garden, a good but incomplete reflection of God, what was missing? What kinds of things did God choose to tell us about Godself through the creation of Eve, and all of her daughters?

These questions are not merely philosophical. They are intensely practical, especially for women, because their answers will also answer the question, "Who am I?" As human beings, our deepest identity is rooted in our identity as God's children, children *made in God's image*. Children (usually) look like their parents, and God's children are no different. We look like our heavenly FatherMother, and that is who we are. But if we view God as a predominantly male figure, then it becomes difficult for women to see clearly how we look like God. How can we be deeply rooted in our identity as daughters of God, daughters who look like their Mother, if we are not sure whether the most feminine parts of our nature do look like God? My desire in these reflections is to nourish us with the confidence that we, as women, profoundly reflect the image of God.

Avoiding Stereotypes

Most of God's attributes are reflected to some degree in both men and women. I hesitate to even talk about "God's feminine attributes" versus "God's masculine attributes" because it tends to be dangerous, difficult, and unproductive to attempt to nail down what makes a woman feminine and a man masculine (apart from the obvious physical and biological differences). So many "gender differences" are rooted entirely in culture or tradition, and many others are actually shared by both genders, even if they tend to appear more obviously in one gender than in the other. It's also important not to reflect our own ideas about masculinity or femininity back on God. We must remember that it is we who are like God, not God who is like us.

Nevertheless, since God is the one who invented gender, I believe it is worth muddling through and exploring what it means to be a woman in the image of God. As I reflect on the ways that I, as a woman, have seen womanly aspects of God's nature reflected in my own life, please bear in mind that I am not attempting to define a theology of gender differences. I am not suggesting that all women and only women portray these aspects of God's nature, while all men and only men portray others. It's much more complex than that, and there is a great deal of overlap between the genders. So please accept these reflections with a healthy dose of salt.

Having said that, there is one experience that God has gifted exclusively to women: motherhood. Again, there is a great deal of overlap between mothers and fathers, and much of God's beautiful love for God's children is similarly reflected by both mothers and fathers. I am not suggesting that none of God's motherly nature can ever be reflected by men. However, the experience of pregnancy, childbirth, and breastfeeding is a profound one that men are biologically unable to share. I'm not sure that men actually have any such experience that women are completely unable to identify with but, not being a man myself, I won't try to speak authoritatively on that topic. What I do know is that there are particular aspects of God's love and care that are vividly displayed in the process of motherhood. Even if these aspects of God's nature are reflected to some degree in all of humanity, they are highlighted in mothers, showcased if you will. And I believe that they can be displayed just as beautifully in women who are spiritual or adoptive mothers as they are in biological mothers. We don't have to have biological children in order to beautifully reflect God's motherly heart to the spiritual children God has put in our lives.

Do We Need a Mother?

Given that most of God's nature is reflected to some degree in both genders, and that both fathers and mothers similarly reflect much of God's love for God's children, do we need to see God as a mother? God loves me, provides for me, protects me, teaches me, leads me, comforts me, has compassion on me, and so do *both* of my parents! Does it really matter if I view God primarily as a father rather than a mother? Absolutely.

Children who grow up with only one parent suffer from that, regardless of which gender is absent. Our earliest experience of God's love was meant to come to us through our parents, and God intended God's image to be reflected in a man and a woman *together*. If a child grew up with a wonderful, loving father, but she had no memory of her mother, that child might tell you that she felt no need for a mother. Having had no experience of her mother's love, she would have no way of identifying what she was lacking, or even that she was lacking anything. Her father had always met her felt needs. The same might be true of a fatherless child with a wonderful, loving mother.

Spiritually, I believe we are that child. We have only ever known God as Father, and we have grown accustomed to seeing God meet all of our needs as a father, and a perfect one at that. Having never allowed ourselves to experience God's motherly love for us, we do not even know what we are missing. And yet, lacking a gender in our experience of divine parenting must have even more significant repercussions than lacking a gender in our experience of human parenting. We need to be mothered spiritually as surely as we needed to be mothered physically.

But Is God Really Our Mother?[1]

When I was very young, I once heard adults talking about a couple who had left a church because they felt that the church was no longer being faithful to the Bible. The only detail I remember about the supposedly unfaithful church was this comment, made in a shocked and disdainful tone of voice: "They were calling God, 'Mother'!"

I processed this tidbit of information and concluded that thinking of God as a mother must be very bad indeed, a conclusion that was subtly confirmed by many churches I have attended. But here's the rub. If God is, indeed, exclusively (or even primarily) our father, rather than our mother, then fathers offer a clearer, more accurate reflection of God's relationship with us than mothers do.

As a child I managed to ignore that logical conclusion, but as I became a mother myself I could not escape its implications. If fathers were a clearer reflection of God's love for God's children than mothers, that would mean that my children could see God's love for them more clearly in my husband than in me. If that was the case, was I truly created in God's image to the extent that my husband was? Was I not somehow a lesser picture of God?

So I began investigating these rumors about God self-revealing as a father rather than a mother. And it's true that God never specifically says, "I am your Mother." But it's also true that the Bible is full of vivid maternal imagery about God, imagery that is only meaningful if we allow ourselves to think of God as a mother as well as a father.

As a child, I was taught that my father's love for me was meant to be a picture of God's love for me. God's love remains perfect even when earthly fathers utterly fail to love, but for me God's fatherly love was easy to grasp because my dad was an amazing guy who loved me well. My mom was just as amazing and loved me just as well, and I was taught that motherhood was one of the most important jobs on the planet, which I

---

1. This article first appeared in CBE's blog, *Mutuality*, on 10/28/20. https://www.cbeinternational.org/resource/article/mutuality-blog-magazine/god-my-mother

still believe it is. But I didn't grow up consciously seeing my mom's love for me as a reflection of God's love for me, and I continued to believe that it would somehow be sinful to think of God as a mother. I heard people say that God chose to self-reveal as our father, so we ought to respect God's wishes and view God as Father, not Mother.

As I investigated this idea, I discovered that God first refers to Godself as a father in Deuteronomy 32:6: "Isn't [God] your Father who created you?" (NLT). The first time that a name, title, or description is used often sets the tone for its use later, so the first time God calls Godself a father is a good thing to pay attention to.

This introduction of God as Father is even more significant because it occurs in the "Song" that God told Moses to teach to all the Israelites so that it would "never be forgotten by their descendants" (Deut 31:21, NLT). This Song is God's own words about who God is and how God wanted to be remembered by all the future generations of Israelites. Yes, God wanted to be remembered as their father. But what follows is fascinating. Immediately after referring to Godself as a father for the very first time, God goes on to describe Godself with three distinctly maternal images. Let's look closer at how God is described in the "Song."

First, in Deut 32:10–11 God is described as an eagle caring for her young: "He found them in a desert land, in an empty, howling wasteland. He surrounded them and watched over them; he guarded them as he would guard his own eyes. Like an eagle that rouses her chicks and hovers over her young, so he spread his wings to take them up and carried them safely on his pinions" (NLT).

When it's time for a baby eagle to fly on its own, the mother eagle forcibly pushes it out of its nest high on a rock and allows it to fall. The first time this happens, the baby would likely fall to its doom if the mother did not rescue it—so she does. She hovers nearby and, when it's time for the lesson to end, she swoops under her baby and carries it, on her wings, back to the nest.[2] This is what God did for Israel, hovering near them through the wilderness and, each time they fell too far into thirst, hunger, despair, or sin, swooping down to rescue them and carry them along.

From the eagle metaphor, God flows seamlessly into the next image and says that God has also cared for Israel like a woman breastfeeding a baby. Deut 32:13 in the NLT says that God "nourished them with honey from the rock," but the verb there can be translated "to breastfeed." It's

---

2. Christensen, *Deuteronomy 21:10—34:21*, 797.

not a complicated word, and it doesn't have a lot of different meanings. It just means to breastfeed a baby. This verse could also be accurately translated as, "God breastfed them with honey from the rock," and this translation would emphasize further the motherhood imagery. God self-describes God's relationship with Israel as that of a nursing mother.

But, says God in verse 18, "You forgot the God who had given you birth" (NLT). Not only is God like a father, and an eagle caring for her young, and a woman breastfeeding a baby, God (in God's own words) is also like a woman giving birth. The verb used in this phrase carries the connotations of painful labor[3]—God says that God is the person who gave birth to Israel through a painful delivery. Only one person can give birth to a child, and that is the child's mother. By definition, your mother is the person who gave birth to you. "The God who has given you birth" is your mother as surely as "your father who created you" is your father. Both descriptions are metaphors, and both are equally true about God.

All those people who told me that we needed to respect God's wishes and view God the way God was revealed in the Bible—they were right. We do. But it turns out that the Bible does not describe God as only a father. The first time God calls Godself "father," that description is immediately followed by not one but three maternal descriptions: God is also portrayed as an eagle caring for her young, a woman breastfeeding a baby, and a mother who has given birth through painful labor. If we truly want to respect God's wishes, we must embrace God in the way that God says God wants to be remembered by future generations—and this includes viewing God as a mother.

As I have discovered these facts and allowed them to sink into my soul, these truths have set me free to relate to God as both my father and my mother. The freedom to think about God as a mother and talk to God as a mother has dramatically deepened and vitalized my relationship with God. Not only that, but it has also given me a deep sense of joy and purpose in my own role as a mother. Knowing God as my mother has given me the confidence that I, as a mother, do indeed have one of the most important jobs on the planet—the job of giving my children glimpses into the amazing love and care of their Heavenly Mother.

3. *HALOT* 310.

More Than a Father

Many conclusions have been drawn based on the fact that, while the Bible refers to God specifically as a father, Scripture never explicitly uses "Mother" as a title for God. It's easy to get the idea that the Bible is overflowing with fatherly references to God but has few (if any) motherly references. However, many commentators agree that "'Father' is not a frequent name or title given to God in the Hebrew Bible,"[4] and "the address to Yhwh as the people's father is very unusual in the Old Testament."[5] In fact, "this attribute, which seems so natural, is of relatively rare occurrence in Israel of the biblical period."[6] "The appelation 'our father,' for God is rare in the OT, appearing only here [twice in Isaiah 63:16] and in 64:7."[7]

A thorough search reveals that the word 'father' is directly applied to God only twelve times in the entire Old Testament.[8] Some English translations supply the word 'father' to passages like Deut 1:31, but it is not in the Hebrew text.

Furthermore, there are many passages in which a masculine description of God would have been fully sufficient for the point being made, but God goes on to offer parallel feminine imagery. Consider the following examples:

- Even if my *father and mother* abandon me, the Lord will hold me close. (Ps *27:10*, NLT)

- We keep looking to the Lord our God for his mercy, just as servants keep their eyes on their *master*, as a slave girl watches her *mistress* for the slightest signal. (Ps *123:2*, NLT)

- The Lord goes out like a *mighty man*. He shows himself mighty against his foes. [He will say,] "Now, like a *woman in labor*, I will cry and groan and pant." (Isa *42:13–14*, ESV)

- What sorrow awaits those who argue with their Creator. How terrible it would be if a newborn baby said to its *father*, "Why was I

---

4. Smith, *Isaiah 40–66*, 681.
5. Goldingay, *A Critical and Exegetical Commentary on Isaiah 56–66*, 404.
6. Blenkinsopp, *Isaiah 56–66: A New Translation*, 262.
7. Watts, *Isaiah 34–66*, 902–3.
8. Deut 32:6; Isa 63:16 (twice); 64:8; Jer 3:4, 19; 31:9; Mal 1:6, 2:10; Pss 68:5, 89:26; 1 Chr 22:10

born?" or if it said to its *mother*, "Why did you make me this way? (Isa *45:9–10*, NLT)

Of course, God is neither male nor female, but when described in human terms God is pictured as both man and woman, both father and mother. The Bible may not use "Mother" as a title for God, but God is often described with explicitly feminine images of birth and breastfeeding.[9] Some of these feminine allusions to God have been obscured by English translations, but they are unavoidable in the Hebrew text. If, therefore, Scripture is to be the guide for the language we use to describe God, we must not describe God as an exclusively, or even primarily masculine being.

Calling God "Mother" [10]

I was a new, young missionary in the middle of my field orientation course. We had hiked out to a remote Papua New Guinean village where we would be spending the night, and we were enjoying the warm hospitality of the people who lived there. It had been raining for quite a while, and the absence of electricity or indoor plumbing meant that, sooner or later, we would need to venture out with our headlamps to find the outhouse. This is not something I enjoy at the best of times, but on this particular evening I was dreading it even more than usual because the rainflies had hatched.

Every once in a while, during a heavy rain, a new generation of these large flies hatches all at once, and hundreds of flies instantly cover every exposed surface. They are particularly attracted to light, which made a trip to the outhouse with a headlamp a daunting prospect. As my friend and I approached the outhouse, trying to work out how to have enough light to not fall into the outhouse hole, while also minimizing the areas of ourselves that would inevitably be covered in rainflies, my Australian friend exclaimed, "I want my mum!" I wanted my mum too, but mine was in Texas and hers was in Australia, so we bravely carried on without them.

Not being Australian myself, I had never called my mom "Mum" before, but when I later told her about that experience, I referred to her

9. Deut 32:13, 18; Job 38:8–9, 29; Ps 90:2; Isa 42:14, 49:15, 66:13

10. This article first appeared in the Fall 2021 issue of CBE International's *Mutuality* magazine. https://www.cbeinternational.org/resource/article/mutuality-blog-magazine/rainflies-canoes-and-god-our-mum

as "Mum" and have often used that name for her ever since. Even though she had never referred to herself that way, I felt no need to ask her permission to call her something different—in fact, having a new and special name for her expressed my love for her and the unique bond I felt with her even while I was on the other side of the world.

Do we have a similar freedom with God? Although the Bible is full of vivid maternal descriptions of God, many people are still uncomfortable using the word "mother" to talk about God or to talk to God, because the Bible never explicitly uses "mother" as a title for God. But does this make it wrong for us to call God "mother"? Are we free to address God in ways that are not explicitly modeled in Scripture?

There are many situations in which it would be inappropriate to "invent" titles for someone. The President's staff are not free to call him whatever they want. They are required to stick to the prescribed title and call him "Mr. President." If you found yourself speaking to the Queen of England, it would be advisable to address her as "Your Majesty" and avoid inventing your own title for her. But her children probably have a lot more freedom than that.

The underlying question is this: what kind of a relationship does God want with us? Does God want us to speak to God as we would speak to a president or a monarch, being careful to use only the prescribed, preapproved titles that are explicitly used in Scripture? Might God want to have an intimate, parent/child relationship with us, in which we are free to express our love for God with any title, even our own unique title, as long as it accurately expresses the reality of who God is, as revealed in Scripture?

Let's see what God has to say about this:

- *So let us come boldly to the throne of our gracious God. (Heb. 4:16, NLT)*

- *You are my friends if you do what I command. I no longer call you slaves, because a master doesn't confide in his slaves. Now you are my friends, since I have told you everything the Father told me. (John 15:14–15, NLT)*

- *For all who are led by the Spirit of God are children of God. So you have not received a spirit that makes you fearful slaves. Instead, you received God's Spirit when he adopted you as his own children. Now we call him, "Abba, Father." (Rom. 8:14-15, NLT)*

The Supreme Ruler of the universe calls us "friends," adopts us as sons and daughters, and tells us to "come boldly" before God's throne. God does not want us to relate to God as fearful slaves, scared to use a title that has not been preapproved by the master. God wants us to come as beloved children, and beloved children have the right to express their love for their parents through intimate titles—titles like "Abba," "Daddy," or even "Mother."

Many people have used Rom 8:15 to argue that God is telling us to call God "Father" rather than "Mother." But the context makes it clear that gender is not the point here. God is making a distinction between calling God "Master" and calling God "Daddy."[11] The point is that, as God's children, we have the privilege of relating to God on intimate terms, such intimate terms that we are free to use familiar titles like "Daddy." Or "Mum."

Acknowledging the Reality of Who God Is[12]

Of course, any title we use for God must be consistent with God's nature as revealed in Scripture. The language we use to talk about God should accurately express the reality of who God says God is. Here's how the Bible describes God:

- Deut 32:18 describes God as the one "who had given you birth."
- Isa 49:15 compares God's love to the love of a nursing mother.
- Deut 32:13 says that God breastfed the nation of Israel.
- Job 38:29 suggests that God "gives birth to the frost" and is "the mother of the ice."

These passages indicate that maternal titles for God are certainly consistent with the way God's nature is revealed to us in Scripture.

Titles do not create reality, but accurate titles acknowledge a reality that already exists. Refusing to use a title can be an attempt to deny the existence of that reality, but it does not make the reality any less true.

---

11. Aldrege-Clanton, *In Whose Image?*, 36.

12. This article first appeared in the Fall 2021 issue of CBE International's *Mutuality* magazine. https://www.cbeinternational.org/resource/article/mutuality-blog-magazine/rainflies-canoes-and-god-our-mum

For example, the person responsible for managing a group of employees is often given the title of "manager." If someone were doing all the work of a manager, but was not given the title, then their employer could potentially avoid paying them the salary that a manager deserves. The title would accurately describe the reality of that person's work, but withholding the title would allow the employer to deny that reality when writing the person's paycheck.

Another example is that when I use the title "Mother" to refer to my own mother, I am acknowledging the reality that she is the woman who gave birth to me. This would be true whether or not I used the title, but every time I call her my mother, I am affirming the reality of my relationship with her. Not only that, but I am also expressing a desire to relate to her as a daughter. If I were to refuse to call my mother by any maternal title, I would be communicating to her that I either did not think she was fulfilling the role of a mother in my life, or that I did not wish to fulfill the role of a daughter in her life.

If we refuse to use maternal titles when referring to God, we are refusing to acknowledge that God fulfills any type of maternal role in our lives. Since Scripture is full of maternal language about God, a refusal to acknowledge that reality is a refusal to accept all of who God says God is. Calling God "Mother" as well as "Father" affirms the reality of who God is—as revealed in the Bible—and acknowledges our desire to relate to God in a way that is consistent with *all* of God's self-revelation.

The Incarnation of Language

I once asked someone whether they thought we should relate to God as a mother as well as a father, and they replied, "Clearly, the Scripture does not ever refer to God as a mother. There is no 'goddess' language in the scriptures." In this person's mind, thinking of God as our mother would require God to be female in some way, and would therefore make God a "goddess." Since Scripture never talks about "Goddess," and we know that God is not actually female, their conclusion was that God could not function as a mother.

What if we used the same logic on the title "Father"? Does calling God "Father" require God to be male? If we believe that God is not actually male, just as God is not actually female, doesn't calling God "Father" imply masculinity just as much as calling God "Mother" implies femininity? Is it more acceptable to imply that God is masculine than to imply that God is feminine?

Many people who would agree that God is neither male nor female still think that it is, indeed, more acceptable to use masculine language for God because that is the language used in Scripture. This is a valid point, but we must remember that *any* language used to describe God limits God in some way. Being described by language at all is a type of incarnation. When the Word became flesh, God humbled Godself and consented to live within the confining parameters of a human body that could never possibly reveal all of who God is. And when the Word was written, God consented to be represented within the confining limits of human language, which (even with over seven thousand unique languages) can never possibly reveal all of who God is. This is why the words written by people like Ezekiel and John, who actually saw God, are so astounding and confusing. They were doing their best to describe the indescribable, and found that words utterly failed them.

God has humbled Godself and condescended to be described within the limitations of human language because God wants to be known by us. But we must not make the mistake of thinking that God could ever be defined by language. Language can give us but a glimpse into the nature of God; it can never offer a complete picture of all that God is.

> *Now we see things imperfectly, like puzzling reflections in a mirror, but then we will see everything with perfect clarity. All that I know now is partial and incomplete, but then I will know everything completely, just as God now knows me completely.* (1 Cor 13:12, NLT)

Any language that we use to describe God is, at best, like a fuzzy reflection in a dirty mirror. God is infinitely more than any of the language used in Scripture, and while God has condescended to be described by our words, God will never be completely defined by our words—not even our masculine pronouns.

Markedness

Language cannot define God, and the Bible's use of masculine language does not require God to be more male than female. So why does Scripture use masculine language? To answer that question, we need a quick lesson on Hebrew grammar and the linguistic concept of *markedness*.

In linguistics, an "unmarked" word, pronoun, tense, or gender is more general and less specific. According to the Oxford Reference, "The unmarked form . . . is often used as a generic term while the marked form is used in a more specific sense."[13] For example, in English *lion* is unmarked because it could refer to any lion—male, female, young or old. *Lioness*, on the other hand, is marked, because it refers specifically to a female lion. In both Hebrew and Greek, masculine pronouns are unmarked, which means that they can refer to a person generally without specifically implying that that person is male. Feminine pronouns, however, are marked, and always specifically refer to a female. Similarly, masculine relational words like "father" and "brother" are also unmarked in both languages, while their feminine counterparts are marked. In Hebrew and Greek, "fathers" and "brothers" can mean "parents" and "siblings," while "mothers" and "sisters" always refer specifically to female relatives. Therefore, in either of the biblical languages, feminine language about God would be marked and would imply that God was actually female and not male. Masculine language is used for God in Hebrew and Greek not because God is male, but because God transcends gender and unmarked language is therefore more appropriate.

For example, when Jesus taught his disciples the Lord's prayer in Luke 11:1–4, if he had addressed God as "Our Mother who is in heaven," that would have been very marked, and it would have implied that God was in some way actually female. To refer to God as "Father," on the other hand, was unmarked, and allowed the focus to remain on the intimate, parental nature of God's relationship with us, without requiring God to be one gender or the other.

Still, if God doesn't want to be defined by masculine language, why was Scripture inspired in gendered language? Why did God not inspire Scripture to be written in a language with a nice, clearly neutral pronoun? Does the fact that God chose Hebrew to be the original language of Scripture mean that God *wanted* to be revealed in a masculine way?

Unfortunately, God has not revealed a list of reasons why Scripture was originally written in Hebrew and Greek, so we don't know the answers to those questions. What we do know is that it's very dangerous to speculate about *why* God did things and draw theological conclusions based on those speculations. It's a large assumption to say that if God doesn't want to be viewed as masculine, surely God would have inspired

---

13. Oxford Reference, "Markedness," lines 3–4.

Scripture in a language with a neutral pronoun. Maybe God wants us to use our brains and figure out that masculine in Hebrew is unmarked! We could use the same line of speculative reasoning to say that if God was against slavery, surely the New Testament would have been inspired in a culture without slavery, thus avoiding problematic passages like 1 Tim 6:1–4. In fact, the nineteenth-century American church did use that reasoning, with catastrophic consequences.

Instead of speculating about why or why not God used Hebrew and Greek as the original languages of Scripture, our job is to work to understand those languages as well as we can, in an effort to see God as clearly as possible in the fuzzy mirror of language. Since masculine is the unmarked gender in both Hebrew and Greek, it's important to recognize that God was using the less specific gender within the parameters of the Biblical languages. For a God who transcends gender, of course the less specific gender is the more appropriate choice.

What About in Our Language?

In the original languages of the Bible, masculine language was unmarked, or less specific, so it did not always imply masculinity. In modern American English, however, it does. While masculine pronouns have traditionally been unmarked in English, they are now just as marked as feminine pronouns for the generation of children learning English today. I was reading *The Emperor's New Clothes* to my three-year-old and when we got to the page where the naked emperor was proudly parading his new clothes but nobody wanted to admit that they couldn't see the clothes, the text read, "No one wanted to look stupid or bad at *his* job." My daughter pointed to a group of women in the picture and said, "Mommy, why does it say that they're all 'him' when they're not all 'him'?" In her mind, that masculine pronoun implied that everybody there was a man, even though the picture showed her that they were not all men.

It's not only three-year-olds who think that masculine pronouns can no longer be used neutrally in English. The Modern Language Association encourages the use of the pronoun *they* "'as a generic third-person singular pronoun to refer to a person whose gender is unknown or irrelevant to the context,' as the seventh edition of the *Publication Manual of the American Psychological Association* attests (120)."[14] The MLA also

---

14. MLA, "How Do I Use Singular *They*?" lines 9–11.

states that "for generic uses, writers should not use *he* or *she* alone or alternate *he* and *she*."[15] In other words, according to one of the leading English style guides, it is now an improper use of the English language to use masculine pronouns generically. In modern English, masculine pronouns always mean that the person being referred to is a male.

English Bible translators fifty years ago made the sound decision to translate unmarked pronouns as unmarked pronouns. At the time, masculine pronouns were unmarked in English, as they were in Hebrew and Greek. That is no longer the case. Now we find ourselves translating unmarked pronouns as marked pronouns, thereby adding a required meaning of masculinity that was not in the original text! Masculine pronouns in the Bible communicate to modern readers that God is, in fact, a male being. Translation is complex, and language will never offer a perfect or complete description of God, but we must make every effort to avoid misrepresenting God, which is what exclusively masculine language does in English today. May the Spirit continue to guide the language we use to describe our indescribable God.

The Father of Jesus

> *Jesus replied, "My Father is always working, and so am I." So the Jewish leaders tried all the harder to find a way to kill him. For he not only broke the Sabbath, he called God his Father, thereby making himself equal with God. (John 5:17–18, NLT)*

One of the objections that is sometimes raised to the idea of relating to God as both mother and father is the fact that Jesus consistently referred to God as his father, never his mother. However, we must remember that we are not Jesus and that, being God himself, Jesus' relationship with the other members of the Trinity is not the same as our relationship to the Trinity.

Theologically, it's both significant and necessary that God was Jesus' father and *not* his mother, because his mother was a human being. Had God somehow been both the father and the mother of Jesus, Jesus would have been God, but he would not have been fully human as he is. Neither would he have qualified as the offspring of the woman promised in Gen 3:15, who came to crush Satan, sin, and death forever. Hundreds of pages

---

15. MLA, "How Do I Use Singular *They*?" lines 23–24.

have been written explaining why Jesus had to be both fully God *and* fully human, and this would not have been possible if God had been his mother as well as his father. So we should not be surprised that Jesus addresses God as his father!

We, however, are not Jesus. We are not fully God, or even a little bit God, and our relationship with the Trinity is nothing like the relationship Jesus has with the Father and the Holy Spirit. It was Mary, a human woman, who gave birth to Jesus, but when we enter God's Kingdom we are told in John 3:6 that it is the Holy Spirit who gives birth to us. Yes, Jesus was the Son of God the Father. But we are born into a relationship with the God who is both father and mother to us all.

Getting Back to the Middle of the River[16]

If you were paddling a canoe and paddled only on the left side, you would quickly find yourself crashing into the bank on your right. By consistently and exclusively using masculine language to talk about God, I believe we have (figuratively) crashed into the bank of God's supposed masculinity. We are stuck there in the shallows, entangled in branches, and find it difficult to move forward on the journey towards knowing God. Perhaps we cannot even see the other side of the river . . . rumor has it there may not be another side. How can we return to the middle of the river, where we can freely race along in the joy of knowing God as God truly is?

We can mentally acknowledge that just because we call God "he" does not mean that "he" is actually male. But that sentence, "He is not male," does not even make logical sense in our language. And no matter how many times we repeat it to ourselves, it still leaves us on that masculine riverbank. Even if we know in our heads that we ought to be in the middle of the river, our hearts will not automatically make that journey.

If I were actually in that canoe, trying to get back to the middle of the river, I would need to paddle exclusively on the right side *for awhile*. Not forever, or I would just end up stuck on the left bank. But for a season, to truly correct my error, I would need to keep my paddle mostly on the right, with perhaps an occasional left stroke here and there. In general, it would not be any more appropriate to consistently use feminine language

---

16. Based on content that first appeared in the Fall 2021 issue of CBE International's *Mutuality* magazine. https://www.cbeinternational.org/resource/article/mutuality-blog-magazine/rainflies-canoes-and-god-our-mum

to talk about God, because God is not a woman, any more than God is a man. But for a season, to help us move away from the masculine imagery for God that has been so deeply ingrained in our imaginations, it may be helpful to focus, for a season, on the feminine language and imagery that the Bible uses to describe God. These reflections are my attempt to help us disentangle our hearts from the masculine side of the river.

I'm not suggesting that masculine imagery for God should be permanently discarded or entirely replaced by feminine imagery. I believe there is a place for both. But if you (like me) have spent most of your life relating to God as a predominantly male figure, I invite you to come with me to the middle of the river and see what else Scripture has to say about God's nature and relationship with us.

2

BIRTHING IMAGERY

God Hovers

In the beginning God created the heavens and the earth. The earth was formless and empty, and darkness covered the deep waters. And the Spirit of God was hovering over the surface of the waters. (Gen 1:1–2, NLT)

In the beginning, God created. And God's first recorded action in this creative process was to *hover*, like the mother eagle described in Deut 32:10–11:

God found them in a desert land, in an empty, howling wasteland. He surrounded them and watched over them; he guarded them as he would guard his own eyes. Like an eagle that rouses her chicks and hovers over her young, so he spread his wings to take them up and carried them safely on his pinions. (NLT)

Some scholars suggest that Deut 32:11 may be a "deliberate echo" of Gen 1:2.[1] Like a mother bird hovering over her young, Mother God hovered over the newly born nation of Israel, swooping down to rescue them and carry them along each time they fell too far into thirst, hunger, despair, or sin. But long before that, while the earth was still formless and empty, Mother God hovered over and around the embryonic creation. Apart from God, Israel could never have survived in the "empty, howling

---

1. Mathews, *Genesis 1—11:26*, 131.

wasteland." Apart from God, no life could have existed in the formless, empty darkness. All life began in the womb of God.

God Makes Life

On each day of creation, God simply speaks and those words become reality.

> "Let there be light," and there was light.
>
> "Let there be a space between the waters," and that is what happened.
>
> "Let the waters flow together," and that is what happened.
>
> "Let lights appear in the sky," and that is what happened.
>
> "Let the waters swarm with fish. Let the skies be filled with birds."
>
> "Let the earth produce every sort of animal," and that is what happened. (Gen 1:3, 6–7, 9, 14–15, 20, 24, NLT)

Of course, it was God who created the light, water, and animals, but God is not the grammatical subject in this part of the narrative. The lights appear, the waters swarm with fish, and the earth produces animals. These things happen instantly, and things appear out of nothing.

But when it's time for the masterpiece, God's children, the language changes:

> "Let us make human beings in our image." So God created human beings. (Gen 1:26–27, NLT)
>
> Then the LORD God formed the man from the dust of the ground. He breathed the breath of life into the man's nostrils, and the man became a living person. (Gen 2:7, NLT)
>
> While the man slept, the LORD God took out one of the man's ribs and closed up the opening. Then the LORD God made a woman from the rib. (Gen 2:21–22, NLT)

God's children do not instantaneously appear. Their creation is a process, and God is described as being directly and intimately involved. We are told little details of the process, like closing up the opening in the man's chest. Furthermore, humans are not created out of nothing. God "formed" the man out of dust, "breathed" life into his nostrils, and (literally) "built" the woman out of a rib. As the original Artist, God takes raw materials and deliberately transforms them into the crown of creation.

Part of the wonder of that masterpiece is that God designed the woman's body to be able to repeat that creative process again and again. A woman's body takes the raw elements from the dust (consumed as plants and the animals that ate them) and the calcium from her bones and transforms those materials into a human being, literally sustaining that life through the breath of her nostrils. Yes, it is God who creates life in the womb, but God's daughters are allowed to participate in the process of "forming" and "building" the next generation, as God formed and built the first.

Eve recognized this miraculous partnership after the birth of her first child when she exclaimed, "I have created a man just as the LORD did!" (Gen 4:1, NET) Without the Lord's help, it would not have been possible and yet, in a very real sense, Eve "created" a man, just like her mother did. The word she uses is the same one used in Ps 139:13: "You *created* my inmost being" (NIV), and in Deut 32:6, to describe God, "your Creator, who *made* you and formed you" (NIV). The Creator of all life made God's daughters in God's image, to make life themselves.

God Labors and Gives Birth

You have forgotten the Rock who fathered you, and put out of mind the God who gave you birth. (Deut 32:18, NET)

One of the ways that we, as women, profoundly reflect the image of God is through our ability to give life to another person with our own bodies. As previously mentioned, it is difficult and inadvisable to try to nail down "feminine characteristics" as opposed to "masculine characteristics." But there is that one thing that indisputably qualifies as a feminine characteristic: the ability to give birth. Only a woman can give birth to a baby. And yet God is described as, "The God who gave you birth."

Now, let's pause for a moment and remember that God is not actually a woman, or in any way female, any more than God is male. In fact, God is not human at all, and does not even have a body (except for Jesus). However, God does not hesitate to use human imagery to speak as if God did have a body, to help us understand things beyond our understanding.

- Jesus is sitting "at the right *hand* of God." (Heb 10:12, NET)

- Jesus said, "People do not live by bread alone, but by every word that comes from the *mouth* of God." (Matt 4:4, NLT)
- The *eyes* of the LORD are toward the righteous and his *ears* are open to their cry. (Ps 34:15, NASB)

Does God literally have eyes, ears, hands, or a mouth? No, but God speaks to us as if God did, because those are things we can understand. *God also speaks to us as if God had a uterus and a birth canal,* both necessary prerequisites for giving birth. Of course, God does not actually have these body parts, but God is not afraid to metaphorically speak as if God had the two human body parts that (more than anything else) indisputably define a body as female rather than male. God self-identifies as our mother with the graphic imagery of being in labor and giving birth. The Hebrew word used in the second phrase of Deut 32:18 *(chayal)* carries the connotation of giving birth specifically *"through labor pains."*[2] There is another word that more generally means "give birth" without referencing the pain of labor. This word *(yalad)* can mean "beget" when the subject is a man, or "give birth" when the subject is a woman.[3] Interestingly, that is the word translated as "fathered" in the first phrase of Deut 32:18, which could also be accurately translated as: *You neglected the Rock who had given you birth; you forgot the God who birthed you through the pains of labor.*

The ESV takes this approach and translates it as, "You were unmindful of the Rock that bore you, and you forgot the God who gave you birth." Perhaps "fathered" is the most appropriate translation, because it allows the verse to refer to God as both Father and Mother in one sentence, making it clear that God cannot be tied to either human gender. Still, the flexibility for *yalad* to refer to either gender is noteworthy, as is the vividly feminine imagery required by *chayal*. If we ignore God's maternal self-descriptions, we will be just like the Israelites, forgetting the God who birthed us through the pains of labor!

---

2. *HALOT* 310.
3. *HALOT* 411.

The Rock Who Gives Birth

You neglected the Rock who had given you birth; you forgot the God who birthed you through the pains of labor. (Deut 32:18[4])

Let's look again at this beautiful verse, in which God is metaphorically described as the One who gave birth to God's children through the pains of labor. The one who gave birth to a child is, by definition, that child's mother, so if you have any lingering doubts about thinking of God as a mother, there it is. God said it first.

God is the Rock who gave birth. Does it seem odd that God is referred to as a rock in the context of giving birth? I tend to think of a rock as an uncomfortable place to sit, an annoyance in my shoe, or perhaps an obstacle in my path. But let's consider some of the ideas associated with rocks in the rest of the Old Testament.

One lexicon defines the Hebrew word *tsur* 'rock' as "a place of protection, safety and refuge."[5] God is often called a *tsur* 'rock' and a *mitsurah* 'fortress' in the same sentence,[6] and a *mitsurah* refers to a "mountain stronghold,"[7] a king's military stronghold. A *tsur* is a safe place, where your enemies cannot harm you.

- *Lead me to the towering rock of safety, for you are my safe refuge, a fortress where my enemies cannot reach me. (Ps 61:2–3, NLT)*
- *Be my rock of protection, a fortress where I will be safe. (Ps 31:2–3, NLT)*
- *[God] will place me out of reach on a high rock. (Ps 27:5, NLT)*

A rock is a safe place, not only because you are out of reach, but also because it is a place where you are hidden.

- *Be my rock of safety where I can always hide. (Ps 71:3, NLT)*
- *The* LORD *is my fortress; my God is the mighty rock where I hide. (Ps 94:22, NLT)*

A rock is so safe that even the most vulnerable can find safety there.

---

4. Author's translation
5. *HALOT* 1017.
6. e.g., Ps 31:2
7. *HALOT* 622.

- *There are four things on earth that are small but unusually wise: . . . Hyraxes—they aren't powerful but they make their homes among the rocks. (Prov 30:24, 26, NLT)*

A rock is a place where you cannot be shaken, regardless of what is going on around you.

- *So many enemies against one man—all of them trying to kill me. . . . [God] alone is my rock and my salvation, my fortress where I will not be shaken. (Ps 62:3, 6, NLT)*

God is our only Rock, and our Rock is our only hope.

- *You are my witnesses—is there any other God? No! There is no other Rock—not one! (Isa 44:8, NLT)*
- *I pray to you, O Lord, my rock. Do not turn a deaf ear to me. For if you are silent, I might as well give up and die. (Ps 28:1, NLT)*

Our Rock prepares us for what is ahead.

- *Praise the Lord, who is my rock. He trains my hands for war and gives my fingers skill for battle. (Ps 144:1-2, NLT)*

God is an eternal Rock. God existed before our collective human memories even began.

- *Trust in the Lord always, for the Lord God is the eternal Rock. (Isa 26:4, NLT)*

A rock, in the Old Testament, is also seen as a source of sustenance and nourishment. This is understandable since God literally made water flow out of a rock on two separate occasions![8] These miracles are mentioned again and again.

- *You gave them bread from heaven when they were hungry and water from the rock when they were thirsty. (Neh 9:15, NLT)*
- *[God] divided the rock, and water gushed out for them to drink. (Isa 48:21, NLT)*
- *All of [our ancestors] drank the same spiritual water. For they drank from the spiritual rock that traveled with them, and that rock was Christ. (1 Cor 10:4, NLT)*

---

8. Deut 17:6 and Num 20:8

- *Jesus stood and shouted, "Anyone who is thirsty may come . . . and drink! For the Scriptures declare, 'Rivers of living water will flow from his heart.'" (When he said "living water," he was speaking of the Spirit.) (John 7:37-39, NLT)*

God, as a rock, provides not only water but food as well.

- *But I [God] would feed you with the finest wheat. I would satisfy you with wild honey from the rock. (Ps 81:16, NLT)*
- *He nourished [breastfed] them with honey from the rock and olive oil from the stony ground. (Deut 32:13, NLT)*

To summarize, a rock is a place of protection and safety, a place where we are hidden and harmful things cannot reach us, a place where even the most vulnerable can be safe. A rock is a place where we will not be shaken, even if everything around us is shaking, and where we are prepared for what lies ahead. There is only one true Rock, which has existed long before we were conscious and is our only hope for future existence. This Rock is a place of abundant water and nourishment.

A rock is a unique place, but there is one other place that is remarkably similar, a place where every human on earth began their life. This is another place of protection and safety, where even the tiniest, most vulnerable human can be safe, hidden from anything that could harm her. It is a place where a new person is prepared for the life ahead of her, floating securely in abundant water so that she will not be shaken, regardless of what happens outside her rock. For each of us, there was only one possible place for us to begin our existence—it was there long before we were conscious and was literally our only hope for future survival. It was a place of constant nourishment.

Yes, a Rock is very much like a womb. Perhaps it's not so odd that our Rock gave birth to us.

Mother of the Earth

When I think about God creating the earth, I tend to visualize God as an artist, planning out a masterpiece and then carefully crafting each lovely detail. I don't think this is an inaccurate idea, but did you know that the Bible also describes God as the mother of the earth?! Psalm 90:2 says that God gave birth to the earth:

Before the mountains were born, before you gave birth to the earth and the world, from beginning to end, you are God. (NLT)

The word used for "birth" is *chayal*, the same word that is used in Deut 32:18, the one that emphasizes the pain and process of labor. God labored with the earth and the world!

Not only did God metaphorically give birth to creation as a whole, but God also birthed each individual part of creation. As Psalm 90 refers to the birth of the mountains, Job 38 refers to the birth of the dew, the ice, the frost, and the ocean. This chapter contains a series of God's questions for Job, and the implied answer to each question is: God and God alone.

Who gives birth to the dew? Who is the mother of the ice? Who gives birth to the frost from the heavens? (Job 38:28–29, NLT)

Who kept the sea inside its boundaries as it burst from the womb, and as I clothed it with clouds and wrapped [swaddled] it in thick darkness? I fixed limits for it and set its doors and bars in place. I said, "This far you may come and no farther; here is where your proud waves halt." (Job 38:8–9, NLT and 10–11, NIV)

"The ancient Semites thought that the sea or the waters of the deep were the original element of the world."[9] With a powerful image, God is proclaimed to be the mother even of the world's original element. Even the ocean, with all of its terrifying power, came from God's womb, was swaddled by God, and is still required to stay within the boundaries its mother has set for it.

Even the creation account in Genesis 2 uses a word (translated by the ESV as "generations") that is derived from the Hebrew word *yalad*, which can mean "to father" or "to give birth."

These are the generations of the heavens and the earth when they were created, in the day that the Lord God made the earth and the heavens. (Gen 2:4, ESV)

The fact that God is the mother of the earth is a compelling reason to care for the earth! As humans in God's image, we are God's children in a unique way, but if all of creation is also God's child in some sense, surely we must love the earth and treat it gently.

When God is referred to as our mother, many people become uncomfortable because the title "Mother" in a religious sense brings up connotations of "Mother Earth" as a goddess, and all the pagan ideas

---

9. Hartley, *The Book of Job*, 495.

associated with earth worship. Perhaps people throughout history have felt the need to worship the earth as a mother because we have forgotten our true mother, or been prohibited from calling God "Mother". We know we need a powerful mother, and it feels natural for many people to fill that gap with "Mother Earth." It's time to give the title back to the mother of the earth, who is our own mother as well.

The Warrior and the Birthing Mother

Sing a new song to the Lord*! Sing his praises from the ends of the earth! Let the whole world glorify the* Lord*; let it sing his praise. The* Lord *will march forth like a mighty hero; he will come out like a warrior, full of fury. He will shout his battle cry and crush all his enemies. He will say, "I have long been silent; yes, I have restrained myself. But now, like a woman in labor, I will cry and groan and pant." (Isa 42:10, 12–15, NLT)*

Isaiah 42 contains a song of praise to the God who promises to come with strength to save God's children from their enemies. The song is followed by two parallel images of strength and victory: a heroic warrior and a mother giving birth.

First, the author describes Yahweh as a "mighty hero," a warrior shouting a battle cry. Then Yahweh, the mighty warrior, speaks and self-describes as a laboring mother shouting as her child is born.

At first glance, these may seem like two very different images, but they actually have quite a bit in common. Both the warrior and the mother are doing something that takes an incredible amount of strength. They are both laboring for life—one to protect life and one to produce life—and they both labor with a shout of victory.[10]

As a mother myself, I love that God recognizes the strength and valor required to give birth, and chooses that image to describe the climax of God's salvation in this passage. It may not be an accident that the Hebrew word for "strength" shares the same root as the word that means "to give birth through the pains of labor."[11] Few things require the same degree of mental, physical, and emotional strength as giving birth, and God openly describes God's powerful salvation as the shout of a mother who is bringing a new life into the world.

10. Oswalt, *The Book of Isaiah, Chapters 40–66*, 124.
11. Clines, ed., *The Dictionary of Classical Hebrew*, 213.

Waiting in Labor

> *Don't worry about the wicked or envy those who do wrong. Trust in the Lord and do good. Then you will live safely in the land and prosper. Take delight in the Lord, and he will give you your heart's desires. Commit everything you do to the Lord. Trust him, and he will help you. He will make your innocence radiate like the dawn, and the justice of your cause will shine like the noonday sun. Be still in the presence of the Lord and wait patiently for him to act.* (Psalm 37:1, 3–7, NLT)

Being in labor is a unique, active kind of waiting. There's nothing you can do to make the process go much faster or slower, and you are waiting for your body to do something that is completely outside of your control. And yet your whole being—mind, body and emotions—is actively participating in every moment of the process. You can't change or control what's going on inside you, you can only control how you respond to it. But the most unique, intense part is that you can't stop waiting, not even for a second. In almost any other situation, you could potentially decide whether to actively sit there and wait, or go do something else for awhile. Many times in the middle of a long labor, I felt that I could endure anything if I could just stop and have a nap first, but that's not how it works. You can't stop waiting, not for a moment, until you're holding the person you've been waiting for.

"Wait patiently for God." The verb used in that phrase, in Ps 37:7, is our old friend *chayal* . . . to writhe in the pain of labor. Like being in labor, waiting for God is an active, expectant waiting. It's not an apathetic, disengaged attitude of, "Oh well, God will do whatever God wants anyway, I'll just wait and see what happens and go amuse myself in the meantime." We may not be in control of the outcome, but as we follow the Spirit and respond to each move God makes, we are actively waiting for God, sometimes writhing in the pain of labor through the process.

Labor is exhausting, but thankfully God does not ask us to labor constantly. Most of the time, it is best to leave our burdens in God's hands and move on, but occasionally God asks us to wait with God, laboring in prayer alongside our mother, eager to see what God will do next. When that happens, God will never leave us to labor alone.

> *For we know that all creation has been groaning as in the pains of childbirth right up to the present time. And we believers also groan. We, too, wait with eager hope. And the Holy Spirit prays*

for us with groanings that cannot be expressed in words. (Rom 8:22–23, 26, NLT)

As we labor with God, the Holy Spirit groans with us. The Greek word translated as "groan" refers to "an involuntary expression of great concern or stress."[12] As my mother watched me groan in labor with my first baby, she groaned with me and I know she would have given anything to take some of my pain on herself. As we groan through the pains of spiritual labor, the Holy Spirit groans and labors along with God's laboring children, and God *is* able to carry the pain along with us, and even carry some of the pain for us. Wait patiently for God to act. God is waiting patiently right there with you.

Yahweh the Midwife

"Before the birth pains even begin, Jerusalem gives birth to a son. Who has ever seen anything as strange as this? Who ever heard of such a thing? Has a nation ever been born in a single day? Has a country ever come forth in a mere moment? But by the time Jerusalem's birth pains begin, her children will be born. Would I ever bring this nation to the point of birth and then not deliver it?" asks the Lord. *"No! I would never keep this nation from being born," says your God. This is what the* Lord *says: "I will give Jerusalem a river of peace and prosperity. I will comfort you there in Jerusalem as a mother comforts her child." When you see these things, your heart will rejoice. (Isa 66:7–9, 12–14, NLT)*

Isaiah 65 and the rest of 66 suggest that these chapters are talking about the day when God's Kingdom will be fully realized and the new heavens and the new earth established. One of the ways this day is described is with this unique description of an unusual birth.

Yahweh (the Lord) is the midwife in this delivery.[13] When the Lord asks, "Would I ever bring this nation to the point of birth and then not deliver it?" the word translated as "bring to the point of birth" literally means to "cause to break through,"[14] possibly referring specifically to breaking the sac of amniotic fluid.[15] This is an extremely personal event,

---

12. BDAG 942.
13. Watts, *Isaiah 34–66*, 938.
14. Clines, ed., *The Dictionary of Classical Hebrew*, 252.
15. Oswalt, *The Book of Isaiah*, 676.

a procedure that only the woman most intimately involved in the process of labor would perform. God's involvement with this birth process is as personal, as gentle, and as involved as that of the midwife who breaks the water, or is standing by at the moment the water breaks.

The other striking feature of this analogy is that the birth process is painless.[16]

> *Before the birth pains even begin, Jerusalem gives birth to a son.*

This painless birth at the end of the story stands in stark contrast to the beginning of the story, when God said to Eve in Genesis 3:16:

> *I will sharpen the pain of your pregnancy, and in pain you will give birth. (NLT)*

Now, in the new heavens and the new earth, death is defeated, the curse is broken, and even the metaphoric birth that marks the beginning of this eternal Kingdom is painless.

> *Look! I am creating a new heavens and a new earth, . . . and the sound of weeping and crying will be heard in it no more. (Isa 65:17, 19, NLT)*

Once Yahweh the midwife has safely delivered her children into this new kingdom, the imagery shifts and we discover that Yahweh is also the mother.

> *I will comfort you there in Jerusalem as a mother comforts her child. When you see these things, your heart will rejoice.*

Our hearts rejoice in anticipation of that day, but it has not come yet and these days are still filled with the painful groans of childbirth, whether literal or figurative. But the mother and midwife who will deliver her children safely into God's eternal Kingdom is with us now, today in our pain, gently guiding, encouraging, and supporting us through each step of our birthing process.

> *"Would I ever bring to the point of birth and then not deliver?" asks the Lord. "No!"*

The day of the Lord is coming, but our Midwife is here now. Keep breathing.

---

16. Smith, *Isaiah 40–66*, 739 (footnote 44).

More on God as Midwife

> *For we know that all creation has been groaning as in the pains of childbirth right up to the present time. And we believers also groan, even though we have the Holy Spirit within us as a foretaste of future glory. But the Holy Spirit prays for us with groanings that cannot be expressed in words. (Rom 8:22–23, 26, NLT)*

> *Would I ever bring this nation to the point of birth and then not deliver it?" asks the Lord. "No! I would never keep this nation from being born," says your God. (Isa 66:9, NLT)*

There were moments as I groaned in the pains of childbirth, possibly the most intense moments of my life, when the person I needed more than any other human was my midwife. As much as I loved my husband and my mother, in those moments of greatest need it was the midwife that I needed even more than them.

These women who helped my babies leave my body saw me at my worst, in humiliating circumstances, but they treated me with dignity and respect. I entrusted them with my body in my most vulnerable moments, and entrusted them with the lives of my children. They were with me in my greatest pain. During the toughest part of my hardest labor, the midwife sat on the floor beside me for hours, and I found out later that she had been crying herself (I was too distracted to notice at the time). Later, after that little baby was safely born and had relieved herself all over this midwife, the midwife remarked cheerily, "Well, that makes four kinds of bodily fluids on my scrubs now!"

Nothing is too gross, or too personal, or too bloody, or too painful, or too messy for a midwife to handle. As she facilitates the entry of new life into the world, she fully engages with the messiest moments of humanity, and does so without a second thought. It's all in a day's work for her.

As it is for God, the midwife of our souls. As we are born into a full realization of the Kingdom of God, nothing is too messy, too painful, too gross, or too personal for God to engage with. And as we groan in the painful labor of spiritual birth and spiritual growth, the Holy Spirit groans with us, sitting right beside us in our pain, crying with and for us.

Becca De Souza expresses this truth beautifully, describing how she

> "met God as midwife and mother, absorbing our pain into her body, hands covered with the blood of new life. . . . God is not

distantly orchestrating all that happens on earth, waiting for the right time to whisk us off to our spiritual home. Instead, I see God as the great midwife: resourceful and wise, present with us in our pain, giving words of courage, and using counter-pressure to relieve our lower back. God is vulnerable, taking great risks to bring new life from all the world's grief and pain. She is with us in our suffering, carrying our trauma as her own."[17]

---

17. De Souza, "My Body Kept Score," para. 14.

3

BREASTFEEDING IMAGERY

El Shaddai as the God of the Breast

When Abram was ninety-nine years old, the Lord appeared to him and said, "I am El Shaddai. I will make a covenant with you, by which I will guarantee to give you countless descendants." (Gen 17:1–2, NLT)

You have probably heard the title *El Shaddai* translated as "God Almighty." *El* is the Hebrew word for God, but did you know that *Shaddai* does not actually mean "Almighty"? The truth is that nobody knows exactly what it means. Some have suggested that it is related to the Akkadian word *shadu*, which means mountain,[1] or the Hebrew word *shadad* 'to destroy.'[2] When the Old Testament was translated into Greek, *El Shaddai* was translated as *pantokrator*, which literally means "all-powerful," and the English tradition of "God Almighty" is based on this translation choice. The obvious problem with this translation is that "all-powerful" is not even one of the possible meanings of *Shaddai*.

Rather than relying entirely on etymology or linguistic similarity when considering the meaning of a name, it is more helpful to examine the contexts within which that name is used. There is a very specific context in which *El Shaddai* is consistently used, and the Hebrew word that is most linguistically similar to *Shaddai* is consistent with that context.

---

1. Albright, "The Names Shaddai and Abram," 182.
2. Hamilton, *The Book of Genesis, Chapters 1–17*, 462.

The Hebrew word *shad* means "breast."[3] Throughout the Old Testament it is almost always used to refer specifically to a woman's breast, usually within the context of breastfeeding or sexuality. Within the ancient Near-East worldview, breasts were associated with fertility, which in turn led to prosperity, and a thorough study of the use of *El Shaddai* in the Old Testament reveals that this is precisely the context in which the title is consistently used. Throughout the Old Testament, the name *El Shaddai* is almost always associated with the concept of children, the prosperity resulting from children, or the devastation resulting from lack of children. If we are willing to accept the fact that God could, in fact be associated with a feminine word like "breast," then the title *El Shaddai*—"God of the breast"—becomes consistently logical, both linguistically and contextually.

El Shaddai, as a name for God, was used early in Old Testament history, but appears to have largely fallen out of use after the time of Ruth. In Exodus 6:2–3, when Moses is commissioned to go before Pharaoh, God says to him, "I am the LORD. I appeared to Abraham, to Isaac, and to Jacob as God Almighty [*El Shaddai*] but by my name 'the LORD' I was not known to them" (NET). In Israel's infancy, immediately after Abram's birth into a covenant relationship with God, God self-revealed as *El Shaddai*, the God of the breast. Like a baby born into an instant nursing relationship with her mother, Israel was born into relationship with *El Shaddai* and gradually grew and matured into a broader relationship with Yahweh, *I Am*, the God who is who God is. Names, pronouns, and words all fail utterly to express who God truly is. God just *is*.

God of the Breast Gives Children

God is the first one to use the title *El Shaddai*. In Gen 17:1–2 God says to Abram, "I am *El Shaddai*. I will make a covenant with you, by which I will guarantee to give you countless descendants" (NLT). The introduction of a title often provides valuable insight into the meaning or concepts associated with that title. It is significant that it is God who introduces the title, and that God introduces *El Shaddai* as the one who would provide "countless descendants." *El Shaddai* appears six times in Genesis,[4] and children or descendants are specifically mentioned in every single one of

---

3. Clines, ed., *The Dictionary of Classical Hebrew*, 265.
4. 17:1, 28:3, 35:11, 43:14, 48:3–4, 49:25

these contexts. Five of these references refer to *El Shaddai* as the one who gives children. The sixth occurs in Gen 43:14 when Jacob finally agrees to let Benjamin go to Egypt with his brothers to buy food and bring Simeon back from prison. Jacob says, "May God Almighty [*El Shaddai*] give you mercy as you go before the man, so that he will release Simeon and let Benjamin return. But if I must lose my children, so be it" (NLT). Jacob recognizes that his children are a gift from *El Shaddai*, so it is to *El Shaddai* that he appeals for their protection.

When Balaam blesses Israel in Numbers 24, we are told that "the Spirit of God came upon him" (Num 24:2, NLT) and he gave "the message of one . . . who sees a vision from the Almighty [*El Shaddai*]" (Num 24:4, NLT). Balaam, under the direct influence of God's Spirit, proclaims *El Shaddai* as the one who is going to bless Israel with prosperity. As Balaam goes on to describe this prosperity, it is clear that it will come through the gift of children, or descendants: "How beautiful are your tents, O Jacob; how lovely are your homes, O Israel! Water will flow from their buckets; their offspring have all they need. A star will rise from Jacob; a scepter will emerge from Israel" (Num 24:5, 7, 17, NLT).

These initial references to *El Shaddai* in Genesis and Numbers consistently refer to *El Shaddai* as the one who gives children, a context that is consistent with the understanding of *El Shaddai* as the God of the breast.

El Shaddai Gives and El Shaddai Takes Away

> Job said, "The LORD gave and the LORD has taken away. Blessed be the name of the LORD." (Job 1:21, NASB)

The name *El Shaddai* is used forty-eight times in the Old Testament, and thirty-one of these uses are found in the book of Job. Its use in Job is therefore significant for understanding the use of *El Shaddai* as a name for God. Job is the story of a man who suddenly loses all of his children and prosperity in a series of events so bizarre that it seems unmistakably divine. Throughout the book, Job and all of his companions assume that it is *El Shaddai* who has brought this disaster upon Job. This is most clearly seen in Job 8:3–4, 22:17–18, 27:13–14, and 29:4–5. *El Shaddai* is the one who gives children and, Job assumes, also the one who takes them away. Nevertheless, at the end of the book Job is once again given children and prosperity even greater than he enjoyed at the beginning of the narrative.

Given the predominance of the title *El Shaddai* throughout the book, it seems clear that these blessings come from *El Shaddai*.

Similarly, when Naomi returns to Bethlehem after losing all of her children and all hope of future children or grandchildren she says that it is *El Shaddai* who has made her life bitter (Ruth 1:20). Naomi's use of the title reveals her assumption that it is *El Shaddai* who has taken her children away, but it also foreshadows the end of her story, in which *El Shaddai* will not only provide a grandchild for Naomi, but through that grandchild keep the promises made to Abraham.[5]

Even in the passages where *El Shaddai* is portrayed as a terrifying judge, the theme of fertility (or the lack thereof) remains consistent. Isaiah 13 proclaims the judgement that is coming on Babylon. Verse 6 declares that it is *El Shaddai* who will bring this judgement, and verses 15–16 and 18 specifically mention the death of their children, their hope for future prosperity. According to verse 20, "Babylon will remain empty for generation after generation" (NLT). *El Shaddai*, who made Abram into a great nation by giving him offspring, also has the right to remove a great nation by removing its offspring.

Similarly, Joel 1:15 predicts *El Shaddai's* coming judgement on Israel, judgement that will strip the land bare. Once again, *El Shaddai* brings fertility, to people and the land they inhabit, and *El Shaddai* has the right to make the land barren.

The loss of children is not always the result of any direct action on God's part. Sometimes it's just part of the pain of this broken world, but that pain can be exacerbated by the idea that God would ever take a child away. I won't pretend to understand why anyone walks through that pain, but there is hope when we keep our eyes on the end of the story. God always gives more than God takes away, and one day all that is good will be restored forever.

> *"Look around you and see, for all your children will come back to you. As surely as I live," says the Lord, "they will be like jewels or bridal ornaments for you to display. Though you were ruined and made desolate, now you will be too small for your people. The children of whom you were bereaved will yet say in your ears, 'The place is too cramped for me; make room for me that I may live here.' Then you will think to yourself, 'Who has given me all these descendants? For most of my children were killed, and the rest were carried away into exile., since I have been bereaved of my*

---

5. Wardlaw, "Shaddai, Providence, and the Narrative Structure of Ruth," 39–40.

children? I was left here all alone. Where did all these people come from? Who bore these children? Who raised them for me?' All the world will know that I, the Lord, am your Savior and your Redeemer, the Mighty One of Israel." Isaiah 49:18 (NLT), 19 (NIV), 20 (NASB), 21 and 26 (NLT)

The Warrior God of the Breast

O God, when you went forth before your people, when you marched through the wilderness . . . the heavens also dropped rain at the presence of God. You shed abroad a plentiful rain, O God; you confirmed your inheritance when it was parched. Your creatures settled in it; you provided in your goodness for the poor, O God. The Lord *gives the command; the women who proclaim the good tidings are a great host. Enemy kings and their armies flee, while the women of Israel divide the plunder. The Almighty [Shaddai] scattered the enemy kings like a blowing snowstorm on Mount Zalmon. Praise God our savior! For each day he carries us in his arms. Praise the* Lord, *the source of Israel's life. Sing to the One who rides across the ancient heavens, his mighty voice thundering from the sky. Psalm 68:7–11 (NASB), 12, 14, 19, 26, 33 (NLT)*

Psalm 68 offers a rich and complex image of God's nature and interaction with God's children. *Shaddai*, the God of the breast, is portrayed as a terrifyingly powerful being who scatters enemy kings and rides the clouds across the ancient heavens, God's mighty voice thundering from the sky. This same God is the one who carries, feeds, nourishes and provides for God's children. The presence of *Shaddai*, the source life itself, sustains life as rain drips and then pours in abundance, like milk from a full breast. The Psalm evokes the image of a strong mother, securely holding a nursing baby in her left arm while using a sword with her right arm to defend that baby.

Psalm 68 is a celebration of *Shaddai's* victory over the enemies of God's children, and the daughters of *Shaddai* played a key role in that victory. It was a great army of women who announced that the enemy kings and their armies had fled, and it was the women who divided the plunder. "The division of spoil was the privilege and work of victorious warriors."[6] The daughters of Shaddai are victorious warriors like their

---

6. Tate, *Psalms* 51–100, 178.

mother, who tenderly nurses God's children and then rises in fierce anger to send those children's enemies fleeing in fear.

God's Secret Place

> *Those who live in the secret place of the Most High will spend the night in the protection of Shaddai. (Ps 91:1[7])*

During her first six months of life, my first child literally spent almost all of her time (and my time) on my breast. I did not plan or choose this situation, but anytime I tried to remove her she would wake up (if she was asleep) and cry (if she was awake). I know, I probably could've done things differently, but I was a new mom, at home full time, and that's how it played out. I sat on the couch and read while she napped on me, and she spent the night either on me or attached to me, receiving continuous nourishment and comfort throughout the night. To leave the house, I would put her in a baby sling and wear a nursing cover so she could continue her feasting as I walked along. I got pretty good at pushing a shopping cart with one hand, so she could nurse (or sleep on my breast) while I shopped. I also learned to eat quite well with my left hand, because half the time I was eating she was nursing (or sleeping) on my right breast. People started asking me if I actually had a baby under that nursing cover, because few people got to see her. She lived there. In her secret place, nursing under the cover, she was utterly content, and didn't know or care where I went as long as she went too—on my breast. I'm not going to pretend that this was a fairytale life for me, but for her it was absolutely lovely.

"Those who live in the shelter of the Most High" (NLT) have the same privilege. The word translated as *shelter* is used to talk about a secret hiding place, a place of protection, a cover.[8] No matter where you are right now, regardless of what is going on around you, picture yourself under God's nursing cover, nestled against God's breast. Your soul is utterly safe there. Find rest in the shadow of *Shaddai*. To "find rest" here literally means "to be resident throughout the night."[9] It is no accident that God is referred to as *Shaddai*—the God of the breast—in this verse. Babies

---

7. Author's translation
8. *HALOT* 772.
9. *HALOT* 529.

love to be resident on a breast throughout the night! Fall asleep believing that you are in the care of the God who "can provide for those whom he loves even when they sleep" (Ps 127:2, NET). God can nourish and comfort your soul all through the night, even when you are not awake. And when you wake up, you are still with God (Ps 139:18). Some of the most heartbroken cries I have ever heard have come from babies who fell asleep on my breast and woke up alone, in a cold empty bed. My own mother pointed out to me that when a baby falls asleep with her mother and wakes up still with her mother, that is perhaps the baby's first experience of the faithful love of God so beautifully expressed in Psalm 139:18.

Let your soul dwell, day and night, in the secret place of your Most High mother. Even as you sleep, let *Shaddai*, the God of the breast, nourish and comfort your soul. You will never wake up alone.

The Pourer-Forth

The following words were written by Andrew Jukes, a curate in the Church of England who later became a Baptist minister in the late 1800s.

> The thought expressed in the name "Shaddai" describes power; but it is the power, not of violence, but of all-bountifulness. "Shaddai" primarily means "Breasted," being formed directly from the Hebrew word "Shad," that is, "the breast," or, more exactly, a "woman's breast." Our English word to "shed" is said by some to come from the same root, which can be traced also in Sanscrit.) Parkhurst thus explains the name:—"Shaddai, one of the Divine titles, meaning 'The Pourer or Shedder forth,' that is, of blessings, temporal and spiritual."
>
> "El Shaddai" is the true Giver of his own life. If this is seen, I need hardly explain how this title, the "Breasted," or the "Pourer-forth," came to mean "Almighty." Mothers at least will understand it. A babe is crying,—restless. Nothing can quiet it. Yes: the breast can. A babe is pining,—starving. Its life is going out. It cannot take man's proper food: it will die. No: the breast can give it fresh life, and nourish it. By her breast the mother has almost infinite power over the child. Some perhaps will remember the old Greek story, which has come down to us in different forms, of the babe laid down near some cliff by its mother, while she was busy with her herd of goats. The babe, unperceived, crawled to the edge. The mother, afraid to take a step, lest the child should move further and fall over the precipice,

only uncovered her breast, and so drew back the infant to her. It is this figure which God himself has chosen in this third name, by which to express to us the nature of his Almightiness.

The Almightiness which will make his creatures like him is not of the sword or of mere force. His Almightiness is of the breast, that is, of bountiful, self-sacrificing, love, giving and pouring itself out for others. Therefore he can quiet the restless, as the breast quiets the child: therefore he can nourish and strengthen, as the breast nourishes: therefore he can attract, as the breast attracts, when we are in peril of falling from him. This is the "Almighty." And so St. John, when he receives the vision of One who declares, "I am Alpha and Omega, the beginning and the ending, which is, and which was, and which is to come, the Almighty," marks that he, who says, "I am the Almighty," is "clothed with a garment down to the foot, and girt about the paps with a golden girdle" (Rev 1:8, 13). Here is the woman's dress and the woman's breast, while yet the speaker is "The Almighty." This is "El Shaddai," the "Pourer-forth," who pours himself out for his creatures; who gives them his lifeblood (Acts 20:28); who "sheds forth his Spirit" (Acts 2:17, 33), and says, "Come unto me and drink" (John 7:37): "Open thy mouth wide and I will fill it" (Ps 81:10): and who thus, by the sacrifice of himself, gives himself and his very nature to those who will receive him, that thus his perfect will may be accomplished in them. The blessed Sacrament of the body and blood of Christ is the ceaseless witness of this his giving himself to us. We may, and we must, "Eat his flesh and drink his blood," if he is to live and work his works in us. Only so, "if we eat his flesh and drink his blood," can we "abide in him and he in us" (John 6:53–57). Only so, in virtue of his indwelling, can he fulfil his purpose, and be Almighty in us.[10]

Isaiah offers several beautiful descriptions of this abundant, pouring out nature of *Shaddai*.

> *When the poor and needy search for water and there is none, and their tongues are parched from thirst, then I, the* Lord, *will answer them. I, the God of Israel, will never abandon them. I will open up rivers for them on the high plateaus. I will give them fountains of water in the valleys. I will fill the desert with pools of water. Rivers fed by springs will flow across the parched ground.* (Isa 41:17–18, NLT)

---

10. Jukes, *The Names of God in Holy Scripture*, 66–69.

> *For I am about to do something new. See, I have already begun! Do you not see it? I will make a pathway through the wilderness. I will create rivers in the dry wasteland. The wild animals in the fields will thank me, the jackals and owls, too, for giving them water in the desert. Yes, I will make rivers in the dry wasteland so my chosen people can be refreshed. (Isa 43:19-20, NLT)*

> *For I will pour out water to quench your thirst and to irrigate your parched fields. And I will pour out my Spirit on your descendants, and my blessing on your children. They will thrive like watered grass, like willows on a riverbank. (Isa 44:3-4, NLT)*

> *The Lord will guide you continually, giving you water when you are dry and restoring your strength. You will be like a well-watered garden, like an ever-flowing spring. (Isa 58:11, NLT)*

God's abundance can never be used up; no matter how much *Shaddai* pours out, there will always be more. And there is nothing good that God will not pour out for God's children—even God's own life.

> *After supper he took another cup of wine and said, "This cup is the new covenant between God and his people—an agreement confirmed with my blood, which is poured out as a sacrifice for you." (Luke 22:20, NLT)*

> *But when they came to Jesus, they saw that he was already dead, so they didn't break his legs. One of the soldiers, however, pierced his side with a spear, and immediately blood and water flowed out. (John 19:33-34, NLT)*

Jesus' blood, pouring out of his side at his death, opened the door for God's Spirit to be poured out!

> *Then I will pour out my Spirit upon all people. Your sons and daughters will prophesy. In those days I will pour out my Spirit even on servants—men and women alike. (Joel 2:28-29, NLT)*

In Joel 2:28-29, the word that describes the pouring out of God's Spirit is the word that is usually used to talk about the pouring out or the shedding of blood, or the pouring out of God's anger, fury and judgement. Because God's blood was poured out, God now pours out God's Spirit on God's children instead of God's judgement. And once God's Spirit has been poured out on us, we are enabled to pour out God's love ourselves. As Paul put it in Philippians 2:17:

> *I will rejoice even if I lose my life, pouring it out like a liquid offering to God, just like your faithful service is an offering to God. And I want all of you to share that joy. (NLT)*

El Shaddai, the God of never-ending abundance, pours out milk to nourish us, poured out God's own blood through Jesus, and now pours out God's Spirit to transform us into people who pour out God's love.

The One Like the Son of Man

> *And standing in the middle of the lampstands was someone like the Son of Man. He was wearing a long robe with a gold sash across his chest. (Rev 1:13, NLT)*

Here are some facts about Rev 1:13. The word translated as "chest" is the Greek word *mastos,* which usually refers to a woman's breasts. *Mastos* is only used in two other places in the New Testament, but in each of these cases it is undoubtedly referring to women's breasts (Luke 11:27, 23:29). In the Greek translation of the Old Testament, *mastos* is used thirty-four times. Twenty-seven of these occurrences refer specifically to a woman's breast, and it is used four times in Song of Solomon to refer to romantic love. The other three occurrences are figurative and have nothing to do with chests or breasts at all.

There is another Greek word, *stethos,* which means "chest" and is used generically to talk about the chest of a man or a woman. People beat their *stethos* when they were grieving (Luke 18:13), and the "disciple Jesus loved" reclined on Jesus' *stethos* (John 13:23). In Revelation 15:6, John saw seven angels wearing long robes with gold sashes across their *stethos*. But in Revelation 1:13, the "one like the Son of Man" had a gold sash across his *mastos*.

What does this mean? Why would John use a word that usually had feminine connotations when referring to the one member of the Trinity who was and is actually male? Especially when there was another, perfectly good word without these feminine connotations? The beloved disciple had reclined on that very *stethos,* and yet John now describes it as *mastos*. "Caird wisely cautions against overinterpretation, noting that to track down the source of each descriptive phrase and compile a catalogue would be 'to unweave the rainbow'. John uses his allusions 'for their evocative and emotive power.... His aim is to set the echoes of memory and association ringing . . . to call forth from his readers the same response of overwhelming and annihilating wonder which he experienced in his prophetic trance.'"[11]

God is vastly more complex than we could ever imagine, and our conceptualization of the Trinity is merely our feeble attempt to grasp what is ungraspable. The Son of Man and *El Shaddai* are one and the same God. John sees this God "wearing a long robe, with a gold sash around his breasts." Sit under that rainbow for awhile.

Nursing from the Rock

> *[God] made him ride on the high places of the land, and he ate the produce of the field, and he suckled him with honey out of the rock, and oil out of the flinty rock. Curds from the herd, and milk from the flock, with fat of lambs, rams of Bashan and goats, with the very finest of the wheat—and you drank foaming wine made from the blood of the grape. (Deut 32:13–14, ESV)*

What? You don't remember the verse about God breastfeeding? Well, that's because the NIV and NLT say that God "nourished them with honey," the NASB says that God "made them suck honey", and the ESV uses the accurate but archaic word "suckled." But the Hebrew word means "to breastfeed." It's not a complicated word, nor does it have any other meanings. It just means to breastfeed a baby.

These beautiful verses describe *El Shaddai's* motherly care for the Israelites during their journey through the desert. God "let them ride" (NLT) and God breastfed them. Imagine a baby riding along in a baby sling on her mother's breast, safely carried along with a constant food supply at her mouth. That's what the Bible says God did for God's people through their long, weary years in the wilderness. It is significant that they were breastfed from "the Rock" . . .

> *All of them ate the same spiritual food, and all of them drank the same spiritual water. For they drank from the spiritual Rock that traveled with them, and that Rock was Christ. (1 Cor 10:3–4, NLT)*

---

11. Mounce, *The Book of Revelation*, 58.

Jesus Christ, the One who revealed himself to John with a gold sash around his breasts, who was eternally One with *Shaddai* 'God of the breast,' was there as a Rock—the Rock they nursed from.

But as they grew older, they also grew ungrateful and forgot the Rock who kept them alive. If you have ever nursed an older, larger baby, the next verse will resonate with you. And notice that this verse explicitly identifies the Rock (the one they nursed from) as their Savior.

> *[They] grew fat and kicked; filled with food, they became heavy and sleek. They abandoned the God who made them and rejected the Rock their Savior. (Deut 32:15, NIV)*

That verse always seemed odd to me until I realized that the context was the image of breastfeeding. As babies grow fat and heavy, they also tend to be unruly while they nurse. They kick. They bite. They try to turn their head around to look out the window while they're still sucking. Eventually, they get bored and wander off to play, forgetting the mother whose own body made and nourished them.

> *You were unmindful of the Rock that bore you, and you forgot the God who gave you birth. (Deut 32:18, ESV)*

For a literal baby, forgetting the breast is a natural and healthy process. No human mother wants to nurse her baby forever! But we will always be God's babies, and we will always need God daily, even hourly, for our spiritual survival. I think this is one aspect of abiding and remaining in Christ.

> *Remain in me, and I will remain in you. For a branch cannot produce fruit if it is severed from the vine, and you cannot be fruitful unless you remain in me. Those who remain in me, and I in them, will produce much fruit. For apart from me you can do nothing. Anyone who does not remain in me is thrown away like a useless branch and withers. (John 15:4–6, NLT)*

A baby without her mother's breast would literally wither and die. (These words were written before bottles existed!) If we try to live apart from the constant nourishment of our Rock, we will spiritually wither and die. Even worse, if we try to satisfy our hunger and thirst elsewhere, we will only bring our own death upon ourselves. Anything besides breastmilk (or proper formula, but this was before formula!) is actually harmful to an infant. When Israel wandered away and forgot their mother, God says that they tried to find food elsewhere—food that turned out to be poison.

> *They offered sacrifices to demons, which are not God, to gods they had not known before, to new gods only recently arrived. Their wine is the venom of serpents, the deadly poison of cobras. (Deut 32:17, 33, NLT)*

A parallel passage in Job, describing the fate of those who abandon God, uses the same Hebrew word for "breastfeed" in the context of drinking poison:

> *They will suck [breastfeed] the poison of cobras. The viper will kill them. They will never again enjoy streams of olive oil or rivers of milk and honey. (Job 20:16, 17, NLT)*

God, as our mother, offers us a free, constant, limitless supply of the very best nourishment available. With God we can drink deeply from abundant streams of milk, honey, olive oil and the finest wine. Apart from God, we will find ourselves nursing on the poison of snakes. God invites you to come, just as you are, and allow yourself to be carried and nourished by your Heavenly Mother.

> *Is anyone thirsty? Come and drink—even if you have no money! Come, take your choice of wine or milk—it's all free! Why spend your money on food that does not give you strength? Why pay for food that does you no good? Listen to Me, and you will eat what is good. You will enjoy the finest food. (Isaiah 55:1-2, NLT)*

> *When the poor and needy search for water and there is none, and their tongues are parched from thirst, then I, the Lord, will answer them. I, the God of Israel, will never abandon them. For I will pour out water to quench your thirst and to irrigate your parched fields. And I will pour out my Spirit on your descendants, and my blessing on your children. (Isa 41:17, 44:3, NLT)*

> *Jesus stood and shouted to the crowds, "Anyone who is thirsty may come to me! Anyone who believes in me may come and drink! For the Scriptures declare, 'Rivers of living water will flow from his heart.'" (When he said, "living water," he was speaking of the Spirit, who would be given to everyone believing in him.) (John 7:37-39, NLT)*

Come nurse from the Rock, and you will never be thirsty again. Cry out to *El Shaddai*, and God will breastfeed you with the best food there is.

Flowing with Milk and Honey

> *Then the Lord told [Moses], "I have certainly seen the oppression of my people in Egypt. I have heard their cries of distress because of their harsh slave drivers. Yes, I am aware of their suffering. So I have come down to rescue them from the power of the Egyptians and lead them out of Egypt into their own fertile and spacious land. It is a land flowing with milk and honey." (Ex 3:7-8, NLT)*

As a child, I had a vivid mental image of walking through a knee-deep, flowing river of swirling honey and cream. It sounded delicious, if a bit sticky. I assumed the milk and honey was flowing the way a river flows through the land, but I have just discovered that it's even more intriguing than that.

Remember Deuteronomy 32:13–14? *God breastfed them with honey from the rock . . . and milk from the flock.* These verses suggest that, rather than flowing along as an impersonal river, the milk and honey is metaphorically flowing from God's breasts.

The Hebrew word translated as "flowing" in Ex 3:8 is never used to talk about a flowing river. It's actually the word used to describe a bodily discharge or secretion.[12] The only times it refers to water is in passages like Ps 105:41, describing the water that miraculously gushed out of the rock in the wilderness, the Rock who was Christ (1 Cor 10:4). Once again, this language suggests that the water, milk, and honey is not simply flowing along . . . it is flowing out of Someone.

God is the source of the milk and honey. It was not a magical land that was guaranteed to always flow with milk and honey; rather, the milk and honey flowed from God and God's children received it *when they were in relationship with God*. In Deuteronomy 29:23 we read about what would happen outside of relationship with God.

> *The whole land is devastated by sulfur and salt. It is a wasteland with nothing planted and nothing growing, not even a blade of grass. (NLT)*

A nursing baby cannot reject relationship with her mother and still find food to eat. Israel could not reject relationship with Yahweh and still partake of the milk and honey that flowed from the breasts of *Shaddai*. Outside of a deep, intimate relationship with our Mother, our souls cannot be nourished or fed.

---

12. Clines, ed., *The Dictionary of Classical Hebrew*, 95.

Our Holy Mother

Many times I have thoughtlessly used the expression, "Holy mother!" to express shock or amazement. Recently, however, I've grown reluctant to use the phrase flippantly as I've grown to realize that we do, indeed, have a Holy Mother. Holiness is one of God's most definitive characteristics and, fascinatingly, it's also one of God's most motherly characteristics. Let me explain.

You have probably heard holiness defined as moral purity and/or transcendence. According to this definition, God is holy because God is absolutely pure, and absolutely transcendent over all that is created; or totally "other." Recent scholarship,[13] however, suggests that this definition is inconsistent with the contextual use of the word "holy" throughout the Old Testament. Peter Gentry notes that God is described as holy not when God is most transcendent or unapproachable, but when God is most present and devoted.[14] In Exodus 3, God tells Moses to take off his shoes because the place where he is already standing is holy ground. While Moses is told not to come any closer, the holiness of the ground is the reason he is supposed to take off his shoes, not the reason he is told not to come closer to the bush where God's presence has come near. Moses is not told to stay away from the holy ground; he is already standing on the holy ground. The ground is holy because of the nearness of God's presence, not because of God's transcendence or otherness. "Rather than being marked as set apart, 'holy' ground is ground consecrated, devoted, or prepared for the meeting of God and man."[15]

Similarly, in Exodus 19 Moses is told to make the people holy, specifically because God is coming near to meet with them. "Israel as a *qadosh* 'holy' nation is a nation given access to the presence of Yahweh and devoted solely to the service and worship of the Lord. . . . So then, the greater the consecration, the greater is the distance noticeably diminished. Consecration appears correctly in Exodus 19 as the opposite of separation."[16]

Holiness, therefore, has less to do with transcendence and separation, and more to do with commitment and devotion.

---

13. Claude Bernard Costecalde in 1986 and Peter Gentry in 2013
14. Gentry, "The Meaning of 'Holy,'" 400–417.
15. Gentry, "The Meaning of 'Holy,'" 404.
16. Gentry, "The Meaning of 'Holy,'" 407.

> *But now you must be holy in everything you do, just as God who chose you is holy. For the Scriptures say, 'You must be holy because I am holy.'* (1 Pet 1:15–16, NLT)

We can only be holy, all in, fully devoted and committed to God, when we live with the unshakeable confidence that, like a mother fully devoted to the ultimate well-being of her children, our Holy Mother is fully committed to bringing us safely to our home in God's presence.

Holy, Holy, Holy

So what does it mean to say that God is holy? It does not mean that God is transcendent and unapproachable because of God's absolute moral purity, true as that may be. Rather, holiness means that God is absolutely devoted to keeping God's promises to God's people! In Num 20:12, after Moses hits the rock instead of following God's instructions and speaking to it, God says to him, "Because you did not trust me enough to demonstrate my holiness to the people of Israel, you will not lead them into the land I am giving them!" (NLT) As Gentry says, "Moses' and Aaron's act of disobedience did not treat Yahweh as holy—as completely devoted to the job of bringing the people out of Egypt and into the Promised Land. Even so, the actions of Yahweh *did* demonstrate precisely the fact that he was fully consecrated and devoted to his promise and task."[17]

> *But I will never stop loving him nor fail to keep my promise to him. No, I will not break my covenant; I will not take back a single word I said. I have sworn an oath to David, and in my holiness I cannot lie.* (Ps 89:33–35, NLT)

"The basic meaning of the word is 'consecrated' or 'devoted'. In Scripture it operates within the context of covenant relationships and expresses commitment. One day in the barnyard, the hen and the pig were discussing the difference in meaning between the words 'involvement' and 'commitment'. The pig told the hen, 'When the farmer comes for breakfast tomorrow, you're only involved, but I'm committed.' The cross is a revelation of divine holiness."[18]

Holiness is one of God's most definitive and frequently mentioned characteristics. And God's holiness, God's commitment and devotion to

---

17. Gentry, "The Meaning of 'Holy,'" 412.
18. Gentry, "The Meaning of 'Holy,'" 417.

God's people, devotion that was faithful even to the point of death, is perhaps God's most motherly characteristic. While there are certainly many fathers who are similarly devoted to their children (including mine!), devotion is more of a deliberate choice for a father. For a mother, on the other hand, this kind of holy devotion to the well-being of her children is almost a biological need. Especially when a child is newly born, mothers experience strong emotional and physiological devotion to their children, and it requires truly extraordinary circumstances for a mother to ignore the devotion, the holiness, that urges her to protect and care for her child at any cost—even the cost of her life. God, as our perfectly Holy Mother, will never change in God's holy devotion to God's children, and has already proven that no cost—not even death itself—is too great a price for our life and wholeness.

> *I saw a throne in heaven and someone sitting on it. Around the throne were four living beings. Day after day and night after night they keep on saying, "Holy, holy, holy is the Lord God, the Almighty." (Rev 4:2, 6, 8, NLT)*

When we encounter the unreserved and undeserved holiness of God—God's unchanging commitment and devotion—the only possible response is to worship our Holy Mother.

Nursing Mothers Never Forget

> *Can a mother forget her nursing child? Can she feel no love for the child she has borne? But even if that were possible, I would not forget you! See, I have written your name on the palms of my hands! (Isa 49:15–16, NLT)*

Being away from your nursing baby feels a little bit like leaving a part of your body somewhere else. The first time I left my five-week-old baby, she was peacefully asleep in the arms of my kind and capable mother-in-law, and my husband and I walked a couple blocks to a nearby coffee shop. We were only gone for forty-five minutes, and I had been longing to leave the house, but once I was away I literally spent every minute wondering how my baby was doing. What if she woke up and was sad? What if she got hungry and I wasn't there? I honestly don't remember what the report was when we got back, but I vividly remember my emotional angst while I was away. Even after the umbilical cord is cut, there seems to be an invisible cord linking a mother's heart to the hearts of her children. Thankfully for us human mothers, the pull of that emotional umbilical cord does diminish to some degree as our children grow older and less dependent on us, but for me it has always been quite strong while a baby is at the nursing stage, totally dependent on my body for her food.

This is the way *El Shaddai* feels about her children. It is significant that the Bible describes God as a *nursing* mother, in particular. As one commentator observed, "After all, the child has never drawn its life from the father's body either in the womb or after. But the attachment of the mother and child is direct, and thus almost mystical."[19] Any nursing mother who has gone for more than a few hours without nursing can tell you that this attachment is much more than mystical.

When I was ready to night-wean my daughter, I took advantage of the opportunity to spend my first night without nursing away from home at a women's retreat. I drove home to nurse her at bedtime and then drove away for the night, leaving my courageous husband to deal with the consequences. It was a glorious night of unbroken sleep, but the second I woke up I was keenly aware that I was a nursing mother who had not nursed for twelve hours. It was not a mystical experience. Grateful for my baggy flannel shirt, I gingerly made my way to my car, dripping and wincing with every step. It was only a ten-minute drive home but it was on an unpaved, bumpy dirt road . . . it was agonizing. Even if I could have somehow mentally and emotionally forgotten my daughter, I had an intense physical reminder, impossible to ignore, that there was a baby that wanted some milk. I had never been so grateful to feel my daughter latch on and start to drink. In that moment, I needed her as much as she needed me.

In our day, it is so easy to use bottles and breast pumps that we can miss the intensity of the imagery God uses in this passage. When Isaiah was written, nobody could buy baby formula, and a mother did not have the option of pumping when she was away from her baby. Without a mother's breast, the baby would certainly die. Without her baby, a mother was guaranteed to be very, very uncomfortable, and eventually experience intense pain. This is the image God chooses to describe God's relationship with God's children. Not only an intense emotional connection, but also a physical need to be together. Of course, God does not intrinsically need us in any way. But God has chosen to have a nursing mother's deep and

---

19. Oswalt, *The Book of Isaiah, Chapters 40–66*, 305.

steadfast love for us—a love that brings actual pain when there is separation. God voluntarily entered into a relationship with us that would bring God genuine pain when we turned our backs on God—which God knew would happen. God has no loopholes or escape hatches in this relationship. God is all in, completely devoted—holy as only a mother can be. A nursing mother's relationship with her baby is holy in the sense that no other human relationship involves a level of commitment with such inescapable physical consequences (for both people!) if it is broken. As our Holy Mother, God has chosen to be completely devoted—even more devoted than a nursing mother—in relationship with us.

The theme of God's holy devotion to God's children, God's committed love that is even stronger than the love or commitment of a nursing mother, continues in Isaiah 49:16, "See, I have written your name on the palms of my hands!" This is not like jotting a quick reminder about tomorrow's shopping list on your hand with washable ink. The Hebrew phrase literally reads "I have inscribed you on my palms." There was a "custom of branding or tattooing on the forehead, arm or wrist of a slave the name of his master, of a soldier the name of his general, of an idolater the name of his divinity."[20] The "son" in Proverbs 7:3 was told, "Tie [my instructions] on your fingers as a reminder. Write them deep within your heart." Notice that in all these cases, it is the ones who owe allegiance who are inscribed with the names of the ones to whom they owe allegiance. The ones who are committed write on themselves the names of the ones to whom they are committed. For God to inscribe Godself with the names of God's children is remarkable. God owes us nothing, and yet God has chosen to enter into a relationship of unbreakable commitment. As a child of God, you are permanently branded on the palms of your Holy Mother, who is wholly devoted to maintaining relationship with you. God's love for you is literally scarred into the palms of Jesus, who demonstrated just how far God was willing to go to be with you.

Like Newborn Babies

> *Like newborn babies, you must crave pure spiritual milk so that you will grow into a full experience of salvation. Cry out for this nourishment, now that you have had a taste of the Lord's kindness. (1 Peter 2:2–3, NLT)*

20. Lange, *Commentary on the Holy Scriptures*, 538.

My baby has been breathing the air of this world for all of five minutes. Still kind of purple, slightly alien looking, and very slimy, she is squirming helplessly on my chest, unable even to lift her own head, screaming at the top of her fresh little lungs for . . . well, she doesn't know what, but she knows she needs something. I know what she needs, so I tuck the warmed blanket around her bare shoulders and gently place her crying lips on my breast. Instinct kicks in, the screaming suddenly stops, and she snuggles down contentedly to enjoy her very first meal. Not all newborn babies are so easily convinced that a meal is what they need. Many engage the experience of eating with a lot more struggle. But once they taste the milk of their mother, that is all they want.

My little girl is no exception. A week later, she is an avid eater. In fact, it's all she wants to do! But when she is hungry, all she can do is cry. She has no ability whatsoever to get food for herself, to get herself to the food, or even to articulate the fact that she needs food. Most of the time she doesn't even have the energy to open her eyes. So she cries out, opens her little mouth, and starts blindly moving her head around, waiting for the beloved milk to appear in her mouth. She knows it will, because it always does, though she sometimes has to cry through the eternity of three minutes while I get a drink or finish wolfing down my own food. She never stops crying until I respond, but as she gets older, she occasionally quiets down once she knows that I've heard her. When she hears my voice, starts to get swaddled, or finds herself moved to the bed where she nurses, the open mouth continues searching but the crying stops because she knows help is on the way.

This is the image Peter uses to describe our relationship with God. We crave and long for what only God can give us, and cry out to God to meet our spiritual needs. When we cry out to God for spiritual nourishment, God *always* hears us, and God *always* responds with exactly what our souls need in each moment. We may not immediately perceive God's response, and it may not be exactly what we had in mind, but as we grow in our relationship with God, we will grow more aware of God's response, and perceive more quickly the way in which God is answering our cries. And when we truly taste the kindness of the Lord, we will want more and more, and we will naturally cry out for more. All we have to do is ask—cry out for God's pure spiritual milk!

Cry Out!

So get rid of all evil behavior. Be done with all deceit, hypocrisy, jealousy, and all unkind speech. Instead, make every effort to be righteous: full of truth, sincerity, contentment and kindness. 1 Pe—Oh wait, sorry, that's not how it goes. Here, let me try again.

So get rid of all evil behavior. Be done with all deceit, hypocrisy, jealousy, and all unkind speech. Like newborn babies, you must crave pure spiritual milk so that you will grow into a full experience of salvation. Cry out for this nourishment, now that you have had a taste of the Lord's kindness. You are coming to Christ, who is the living cornerstone. (1 Pet 2:1-4, NLT)

Last night my three-year-old woke up because she had thrown her blanket off and gotten cold. She could have easily reached down and pulled the blanket back up, but instead she chose to lay there crying out, waiting until I managed to sleepily stumble up the stairs to do it for her. For her, it was not the most efficient road to getting warm again—it would have been much faster for her to do it herself. But in the spiritual realm, she had the right idea. It's tempting to feel like if we try hard enough, reach far enough, we can pull up our own blanket, fix our own problems, and leave God out of it.

Peter tells us to get rid of all evil behavior and then, instead of telling us to try really hard to do the right thing, he tells us to become like newborn babies at God's breast, longing and crying out for something only God can provide.[21] We cannot do for ourselves what needs to be done for us. Our only hope for spiritual maturity is (like Jesus said in Matt 18:3) to get littler—so little that we stop trying to fix ourselves and instead cry out for our Mother to meet our spiritual needs. And when God does, once we taste God's kindness, we will want more and more.

Instead of trying harder to act in a way that seems spiritually mature, cry out louder for your Mother to come and do what only God can do. It is only by becoming younger in God's presence that we will "grow into a full experience of salvation," and true spiritual maturity flows out of an attitude of utter dependence on the presence and love of God. When we experience the comfort and connection of a deep relationship with God, receiving the love of our Mother, love and kindness for the people around us will flow out of that experience.

---

21. Davids, *The First Epistle of Peter*, 81.

When we cry out for pure spiritual milk, we are coming to Christ, the living Stone, the Rock who nurses us, who gave his life so that we could be born into relationship with God (1 Pet 1:3, 23). It is the full experience of that relationship that we desperately crave and cry out for.

When the Righteous Cry Out for Milk

The eyes of the Lord are toward the righteous and his ears are open to their cry. (Ps 34:15, NLT)

Taste and see that the Lord is good. Oh, the joys of those who take refuge in him! (Ps 34:8, NLT)

So put away all malice, and all deceit and hypocrisy and envy and all slander. Like newborn infants, long for the pure spiritual milk, that by it you may grow up into salvation—if indeed you have tasted that the Lord is good. (1 Pet 2:1–3, ESV)

Psalm 34 offers a delightful promise to "the righteous": God will watch over them, and God's ears will always be open to their cries for help. It's a wonderful promise, but I tend to need it most on the days when I am feeling least righteous. However, Psalm 34 offers a detailed description of this righteous living, and the beautiful thing about it is that it has nothing to do with keeping rules or being good, and everything to do with recognizing my deep need for God's goodness towards me.[22]

According to Psalm 34, the righteous are those who boast only in the Lord, are helpless, pray to the Lord in desperation, look to God for help, fear God, take refuge in God, trust in God, and cry out for help. Righteousness, in this Psalm, is all about dependence on the goodness of God. And all of us, regardless of how we have or have not behaved, are invited to taste this goodness that, through Jesus, defines us as righteous.

Taste and see that the Lord is good.

Cry out for pure spiritual milk, now that you have tasted that the Lord is good.

Peter probably had Psalm 34 in mind, since 1 Peter 2:3 is a direct quote from the Greek version of Psalm 34:8, and 1 Peter 3:10–12 is a quote from Psalm 34:12–16.[23] So it should not be surprising that Peter has the same

---

22. Jacobson and Tanner, "Book One of the Psalter," 328.
23. Davids, *The First Epistle of Peter*, 84.

definition of righteousness. Peter tells us that the way to get rid of all evil behavior (1 Pet 2:1), is not to work hard at following the rules, but to cry out for pure spiritual milk like a newborn baby. Once again, righteousness has nothing to do with being good, and everything to do with being dependent—as dependent as a tiny baby who can do nothing but cry.

The good news is that even (and especially) on those days when you are feeling particularly unrighteous, if you recognize that feeling as a need for God's love, and cry out for God to feed you, that recognition and cry define you as righteous, and so God promises to hear your cries. If you are crying out for pure spiritual milk, those cries of dependence on Jesus make you righteous, and you are guaranteed to be fed. It is not those who feel righteous who will taste God's goodness and be satisfied, but those whose desperate hunger and thirst drive them to cry out to Christ, the living Stone who is our source of spiritual milk and living water.

> *Blessed are those who hunger and thirst for righteousness, for they will be satisfied. God blesses those who are poor and realize their need for him, for the Kingdom of Heaven is theirs. (Matt 5:6, NET; and 5:3, NLT)*

Open Your Mouth Wide

Open your mouth wide, and I will fill it with good things. (Ps 81:10, NLT)

[When latching on your baby,] "encourage him to open his mouth wide." —La Leche League International[24]

Taste and see that the Lord is good. Oh, the joys of those who take refuge in him! (Ps 34:8, NLT)

When my first baby was born, I naively assumed that I would just hold her up to my breast and she would start drinking. It was not that simple. It took me quite awhile to figure out how to get her to latch properly, and there were some hungry and frustrating hours and days during the process.

Breastfeeding can be challenging for all kinds of reasons, but most difficulties are somehow related to the way the baby is latched on to the breast. It's a tricky business. Especially in the beginning, you have to sit just right, hold the baby at just the right angle with her head in just the

---

24. La Leche League International, "Positioning," para. 12.

right place, and support her neck in just the right way. A newborn baby is no help at all in this process. She cannot move herself into the right position, or even keep her own head in the right place. But the baby does have one very important job, a job that only the baby can do, without which the whole process will fail. The baby must open her mouth wide before she can latch correctly. It has to be wide. Dainty nibbling at the breast leads to sore mommies and skinny babies, but good nourishment can happen when the baby opens her mouth as wide as she can and sinks her gums into a substantial mouthful of flesh. It's impossible to pry a baby's mouth open wide enough for this kind of solid latch to take place; the baby has to open voluntarily. But the mother can coax and tempt the baby, putting the baby's lips near her breast and even putting a drop of milk on the baby's tongue. "Taste and see how good it is! Open your mouth wide and I will fill it!" The milk is there, and the milk is good, and all the baby needs to do is open her mouth. Wide.

As a newborn, my tiny twin had a lot of trouble getting latched, staying latched, and getting enough milk to grow. I spent a lot of time trying to coax that miniscule mouth open, poised and ready to shove myself in the instant it opened wide enough. God is ready and waiting to fill your soul with good things! The milk is there, and the milk is good, and all you have to do is open your mouth to receive it. Taste and see that the Lord is good, then open your mouth wide and let your Mother fill it! A dainty sip here and there will not give enough nourishment for your soul to grow. Be still with God, open your heart wide, and drink deeply of all that God offers you.

Nourishment through God's Word

> *But the word of the Lord remains forever. And that word is the Good News that was preached to you. Like newborn babies, you must crave pure spiritual milk so that you will grow into a full experience of salvation. Cry out for this nourishment, now that you have had a taste of the Lord's kindness.* (1 Pet 1:25, 2:2-3, NLT)

So what exactly is this "pure spiritual milk", the "nourishment" that we cry out for and open our mouths wide for? Given Peter's mention of God's word in the previous verse, it's tempting to assume that Scripture, the word of God, *is* the spiritual milk Peter is talking about.

But have you ever had one of those days where you read the Bible, desperately craving some kind of encouragement or connection with God, and yet you felt just as dry and empty when you finished as you did when you started? True story, I had one of those years. Several of them, actually. I was diligently and faithfully reading the Bible, "drinking my milk" every day, and yet I was starving inside. Why wasn't it "working"?

I slowly began to realize that Scripture itself is not the milk. It is certainly one of God's primary means of getting the milk to us, but it is not the milk—God is.

It is significant that Peter uses the imagery of nursing like a newborn baby, not just eating or drinking in general. For an adult, food and drink can come from many sources, but a newborn baby has only one source—her mother. And nursing, for a baby, is not just about the food. A baby's need for food drives the longing to nurse, but nursing also meets a baby's emotional and relational needs for comfort and connection with her mother. When we "crave pure spiritual milk," we are longing for spiritual nourishment from God that can come in many different forms, but it is only meaningful if we experience it in the presence of God. The word of God is a significant source of pure spiritual milk, but Scripture itself is not the milk. God is. And unless we consume Scripture in the presence of God, in communion and relationship with our Mother, allowing the Spirit of God to digest it for us, it will not nourish us as God intends.

The "bad news" is that reading the words on the page of your Bible will not automatically cause you to "grow into a full experience of salvation." It's not that simple. But the good news is that it's even simpler. It's not our job to nourish ourselves; our only job is to cry out. Cry out for God's nourishment, but don't just yell once and then rush on with life. Keep crying out and then stop and listen for God's answer, look for God's milk. Very often it comes to us through God's written words, but be ready to notice God's nourishing presence however God chooses to give it to you.

So How Do I Open My Mouth?

Of course it sounds great, in theory, to drink deeply of the good nourishment that God offers your soul, but how does one do that? What does it actually look like to open your heart wide to receive the good things that God has for you?

As in breastfeeding, there is no one-size-fits-all right answer for everybody. Each mother/baby pair is unique, and each mom has to find the breastfeeding positions and techniques that work best for her. The same mom might even find that different approaches work better for different babies. So it is with you and God. You have an utterly unique relationship with your Heavenly Mother, and I cannot tell you the perfect way for you to receive nourishment from God. Experiment, try different approaches, and see what makes you most eager to open your mouth wide.

I have found Centering Prayer to be a tool that helps me to open my heart wide in practice, not just in theory. Basically, Centering Prayer is the discipline of being still and quiet in God's presence and allowing God to work in your heart however God chooses. God knows what we need in each moment, and practicing Centering Prayer helps me to be still long enough to notice the nourishment God is offering me each day. You can find out more about Centering Prayer at *www.contemplativeoutreach.com* or in the book *Open Mind, Open Heart* by Thomas Keating.

Other people find that they are better able to open their hearts wide to God when they are talking out loud to God, or walking outside in nature, or listening to music, or making music, or dancing, or reading Scripture, or journaling, or painting, or practicing yoga. You may even find different ways of connecting to God to be more helpful on different days, or in different seasons of your life. If the way you are relating to God right now is not genuinely refreshing to your soul, try something else! And keep trying different things until you find something that allows you to truly connect with God.

Once you discover what allows you to open your heart wide, make that a priority above all else. It's your food! Even when you don't feel eager to do it, do it anyway. Every time you make the choice to come to God and open your mouth wide, God will nourish your soul, and God is still working even when you don't feel noticeably refreshed. Don't plod on indefinitely in a practice that never leaves your soul feeling nourished, but once you find ways to genuinely connect with God, have the discipline to do those things even on the days when they don't feel nourishing. God gives to God's beloved even in their sleep (Ps 127:2), and God is nourishing your soul even when you are not aware of it. But for deep growth to take place, you must choose to open your mouth wide on a regular basis. God will fill you with good things!

Cleansing Milk

It was very late on Christmas Eve—after ten o'clock. The presents were all wrapped but I was still up nursing my two-week-old twins, trying to reach that elusive moment when both tummies were full enough for all four eyes to close. I was surprised to hear a knock on our front door, but even more surprised when my husband came and said,

"It's the neighbor . . . she's wondering if you have any extra breast milk."

"What? She doesn't have a baby! What does she want breast milk for?"

It turned out that her young son had a nasty infection in his eye, and all the pharmacies were closed that late on Christmas Eve. She didn't want to wait another night without treating it somehow, and she knew that breast milk has antibacterial properties,[25] so she came over to ask if I could spare a few tablespoons. I could.

Mothers not only nourish our babies with our milk, we also use it to cleanse them. My twins were born with overly attached tongues and upper lips, and the surgeon who revised them recommended that we put frozen breast milk on the sore spots, both to soothe the soreness and to fight infection. When a baby had a goopy eye, a sore, or a wound, our pediatrician recommended that I routinely wash it with breast milk before every feeding. My milk fed my babies, but it also washed and healed them.

> So get rid of all evil behavior. Be done with all deceit, hypocrisy, jealousy, and all unkind speech. Like newborn babies, you must crave pure spiritual milk so that you will grow into a full experience of salvation. (1 Pet 2:1–2, NLT)

As Kristin Wright-Bettner said, "God's milk is pure, and it also purifies."[26] God's pure spiritual milk nourishes our souls, but it also washes away our deceit, hypocrisy, jealousy and unkind speech. As bacteria cannot survive prolonged exposure to breast milk, neither will our sins survive a regular exposure to the purifying milk of our Mother. It heals our inner wounds, cleanses our souls, and washes the sin and sadness from our hearts.

---

25. Wambach and Spencer, *Breastfeeding and Human Lactation*, 110.
26. Wright-Bettner, personal communication, 2021.

Psalm Sixty-Three[27]

O God, you are my God; I earnestly search for you.
I hear her calling out for me. Her squinty eyes are mostly closed, but her tiny mouth is wide open, searching earnestly for me.
My soul thirsts for you; my whole body longs for you in this parched and weary land where there is no water.
She thirsts for me; her whole body longs for my milk in her parched and weary bed where there is nothing she can eat or drink.
I have seen you in your sanctuary and gazed upon your power and glory.
I peek over the edge of her crib and now the squinty eyes have seen me. She goes cross-eyed trying to focus and for a few seconds gazes upon my face.
Your unfailing love is better than life itself; how I praise you!
My unfailing love is all she knows of life, and I am all she wants.
I will praise you as long as I live, lifting up my hands to you in prayer.
She babbles in delight, lifting up her tiny hands to me.
You satisfy me more than the richest feast. I will praise you with songs of joy.
She latches, gulps, and my milk satisfies her more than the richest feast. More delighted gurgles.
I lie awake thinking of you, meditating on you through the night.
She lies awake in my arms thinking of me, meditating on me through the night until she finally drifts back to sleep.
Because you are my helper, I sing for joy in the shadow of your wings.
Because I am the one able to help her, she is filled with joy in the comfort of my arms.
I cling to you; your strong right hand holds me securely.
Her sleeping fingers cling to mine; my strong right arm holds her securely.
But those plotting to destroy me will come to ruin. They will go down into the depths of the earth.
She sleeps without fear, sensing that I would do anything to keep her safe.

---

27. Psalm 63:1–10 (NLT) in italics

Like a Weaned Child

> *O Lord, my heart is not proud, nor my eyes haughty; nor do I involve myself in great matters, or in things too difficult for me. Surely I have composed and quieted my soul; like a weaned child rests against his mother, my soul is like a weaned child within me. O Israel, put your hope in the Lord—now and always.* (Psalm 131, NASB)

My first baby, as you may recall, did little besides nurse during her first few months of life. There were many days when I felt more like a milk machine than a mother, and I wondered if she even knew that I was a person with other body parts that did other things besides make milk. But there eventually came a moment when she stopped nursing, found my face, and looked into my eyes with love. It was only for a second, and she immediately started nursing again, but I treasured that moment, and thought of it often during the rest of my career as a milk machine. It was precious to me because it let me know that, to the best of her tiny baby ability, she did love me for who I was and not only for the milk I produced.

In the mind of a nursing baby, Mommy and milk are almost synonymous. Where Mommy is, there is milk; and if there's milk, Mommy is there. A nursing baby's love for her mother is inextricably tied to her love for her mother's milk, and there's nothing wrong with that. She needs that milk to live and grow, and it is good and right for a baby to adore her mother for the milk she produces. But when a baby is weaned and her mother is no longer a source of food, the relationship changes. When a weaned child wants to rest in her mother's arms, it is purely because she delights in her mother as a person. There are no ulterior motives or secret plans to snatch a mouthful of milk in the process. She just loves to be held by her mom.

The Hebrew word used in Psalm 131 could refer to a weaned child or to a nursing baby who is full, whose hunger has already been satisfied by her mother's breast.[28] Some of my very sweetest mothering moments have involved cuddling a sleeping, sated baby. When her stomach is full, she stops sucking but leaves her mouth on my breast, wanting to stay in that place she loves even when it's no longer a biological need. The

---

28. deClaissé-Walford et al., "The Songs of the Ascents," 931.

corners of her tiny lips pull up in a smile as a bit of extra milk dribbles out of her mouth, and I hold her closer and let her stay.

It's not wrong for us to want and ask for the things God can give us and do for us, any more than it's wrong for a baby to love her mother's milk. God loves to give us good things. But I think God also treasures the moments when, like a weaned or sated child, we come to God simply for who God is, just to be with God. The moments when we can truly say, "The one thing I ask of the Lord—the thing I seek most—is to live in the house of the Lord all the days of my life, delighting in the Lord's perfections" (Ps 27:4, NLT). Not only does God delight in these moments, but they delight and satisfy us as nothing else can.

4

JESUS, MOTHERHOOD, AND THE KINGDOM OF GOD

The Fullness of God . . . in a Man?

For in Christ lives all the fullness of God in a human body. (Col 2:9, NLT)

I have been saying that God is neither male nor female, and this is completely true about two out of the three Persons of the Godhead. But what about Jesus? Jesus, the Son, became a human man and was therefore undeniably male. According to Philippians 3:20–21, he still exists in his resurrected body and therefore still is male. Furthermore, Colossians 2:9 tells us that "in Christ lives *all the fullness of God* in a human body." If "all the fullness of God" can exist in a male body, does that mean that men, alone, actually can be an adequate reflection of God's image? What does that mean for women? As we all strive to be more like Jesus, do men have a better shot at that?

According to John (1:1–2), God the Son has eternally existed, and presumably before the Incarnation took place this Person of the Godhead was neither male nor female. Then, at the moment that Mary "became pregnant through the power of the Holy Spirit" (Matt 1:18, NLT), humanity was welded to deity and God the Son became a human being. By doing so, he voluntarily took upon himself all of the characteristics inherent to humanity, thereby consenting to live within the limiting parameters of those human characteristics. An eternal being stepped into our timeline and consented to live within our progression of time. An omnipresent being chose to exist as a physical body, occupying only one particular space at a time. A being beyond gender condescended to exist as a creature that must, by nature, have one and only one gender.

One Person of the Godhead chose to live within human parameters, but the Trinity as a whole is not defined by those parameters. Jesus had other physical characteristics besides his gender, but we would never conclude that those characteristics in any way define Yahweh, the Triune God. Jesus had a particular color of eyes and hair, a specific height, and a certain shade of skin. Do any of these physical traits tell us anything about God? Are people who more closely resemble Jesus' physical appearance somehow more like God, or a more accurate reflection of God's image? Of course not!

Even if we assume that gender differences exist at a deeper level than the physical, the Godhead as a whole is still not entirely defined by Jesus' nonphysical characteristics. Every human has a distinct personality, a unique set of nonphysical traits that make him or her completely different from any other human. Jesus also had a human personality, and though his was perfect in the sense of being unmarred by sin, it was still not inherently better than any other type of human personality. Even if we knew Jesus' enneagram numbers, we would not say that people with those numbers more accurately reflected the image of God than people with different numbers. In the same way, even though Jesus was male, it does not follow that people who are not male are in any way a lesser reflection of God.

When Paul says in Colossians 2:9 that "all the fullness of God" lives in Jesus, "the fullness of deity was Paul's way of stating that Jesus is every bit God. The fullness refers to the completeness of the divine nature, but it does not mean that Christ is all there is of God. Jesus is every bit God, but does not exhaust the dimensions of deity. Father and Spirit are equally divine."[1]

Jesus, therefore, existed in a state of fully being God. He wasn't part God and part man, he was fully God in a human body. But he was still not the complete representation of all that makes up all three Persons of the Godhead. Jesus told his disciples in John 16:7, "It is best for you that I go away, because if I don't, the Advocate won't come" (NLT). This implies that our relationship with the Holy Spirit is, in some way, different than our relationship with Jesus. If it were not, it would not matter whether the

---

1. Melick, *Philippians, Colossians, Philemon*, 255.

disciples had Jesus or the Holy Spirit there. Jesus is all God, but he is not "all there is of God."[2]

My skin may be a different color than Jesus' was. My personality may be very different from his. My gender is completely different. These characteristics are irrelevant to my calling to be like Jesus by loving God and others. One Person of the Godhead chose to live within the parameters of one specific human body and nature. This does not prevent the image of the triune God from being effectively reflected in billions of different ways by billions of different human bodies and natures. Even female ones.

Jesus Gives His Body for Our Spiritual Birth[3]

> "Our Saviour is our Very Mother in whom we be endlessly borne, and never shall come out of Him."[4]—Julian of Norwich

Although Jesus came to earth as a man, he refused to be defined by the gender expectations of the patriarchal culture in which he lived, and he was not afraid to do things that were more culturally appropriate for a mother than a rabbi. Like a mother, he invited his daughters to freely participate alongside his sons (Luke 8:1–3, 10:38–42), and he talked to women as equals when it would have been more culturally appropriate for him to ignore or rebuke them (John 4:4–26).

Jesus consistently and repeatedly did things that would have been unusual for first-century Palestinian men, things that were considered "women's work." He cooked food and fed people (John 21:9, 6:26). He held small children (Mark 10:13–16). He washed people with his own spit (Mark 7:33, John 9:6). He stopped in the road to publicly talk to a woman about her never-ending period (Luke 8:43–48), and he praised her for stepping out in faith to touch him (an event that made him ceremonially unclean according to Leviticus 15:19, 25–27). These are not things that a male Jew (or Roman) was supposed to do! They were things that your mother would do, but certainly not a rabbi, let alone the long-awaited Messiah.

2. Melick, *Philippians, Colossians, Philemon*, 255.

3. This article first appeared in the Spring 2022 issue of CBE International's *Mutuality* magazine. https://www.cbeinternational.org/resource/article/mutuality-blog-magazine/my-body-broken-you-motherhood-jesus-and-julian-norwich

4. Julian of Norwich, *Revelations of Divine Love*, 68.

Yes, Jesus was very comfortable going around doing motherly things, and he even used motherly language to talk about himself!

> *Jerusalem, Jerusalem, you who kill the prophets and stone those sent to you, how often I have longed to gather your children together, as a hen gathers her chicks under her wings, and you were not willing. (Matt 23:37, NIV)*

Of course, many of the gender expectations that Jesus defied were merely cultural stereotypes—there's nothing inherently motherly or womanly about holding children, cooking, or washing people. But God has designed unique differences between men and women, and one of the most concrete, striking differences is women's ability to provide nourishment and to protect and sustain life with their own bodies. Perhaps the most motherly thing that God did through the person of Jesus, something that transcends cultural stereotypes, was to give his body for our life and nourishment.

During a silent retreat, my friend Kristin was meditating on the depth of the love Jesus expressed for her when he literally gave his own body to bring her into relationship with God. Filled with awe she prayed, "Thank you, Jesus. Nobody else has loved me that way." Instantly God replied, "Except your mother."

And it's true. For most of us, our mother is the only human who has literally sacrificed her own body so that we could live. The only human except Jesus. While most men never have the opportunity to literally sacrifice any part of their body so that somebody else can live, mothers around the world do so every single day. So did Jesus. And not only did Jesus give up his body in the sense of enduring pain and gaining scars but, like a mother who died in childbirth, he gave his very life so that we could live.

Jesus Gives His Body for Our Spiritual Nourishment[5]

Not only did Jesus endure pain and give up his body and even his life so that we could live, like a mother he also continually offers us his body for our spiritual nourishment. In John 6:51, 54 he says:

---

5. This article first appeared in the Spring 2022 issue of CBE International's *Mutuality* magazine. https://www.cbeinternational.org/resource/article/mutuality-blog-magazine/my-body-broken-you-motherhood-jesus-and-julian-norwich

> *I am the living bread that came down from heaven. Whoever eats this bread will live forever. This bread is my flesh, which I will give for the life of the world. . . . Whoever eats my flesh and drinks my blood has eternal life, and I will raise them up at the last day.* (NIV)

Assuming that Jesus was not referring to cannibalism, there is only one context in which a person is nourished by the flesh and blood of another human: motherhood. A baby in the womb draws her life from the flesh and blood of her mother, at times literally consuming the mother's flesh if the mother does not take in enough calories. There is no other food babies can eat before birth.

Perhaps this is one reason that Jesus compares being in relationship with him to being born again (John 3:3–8). When we recognize who Jesus is and enter a relationship with him, we find ourselves depending on him as completely as an unborn child on her mother. Julian of Norwich described it as "fall[ing] into our Lord's breast . . . knowing our feebleness and great need."[6] Apart from Jesus' flesh and blood, there is no other food that can keep our souls alive.

When we allow our souls to be held and nurtured within the womb of God, we become connected to the source of life itself. When we come to drink the living water that Jesus offers, we will never be thirsty again (John 4:10–14), not because we will never need to drink again, but because we will never stop drinking! We will be permanently connected to the source of the spring, like a branch connected to a vine (John 15:5), like an unborn child connected to her mother. As only a mother can, Jesus offers us the chance to drink and be nourished from his body. As a baby in the womb is never thirsty because a constant supply of fresh water is continually flowing from the mother's body, we will never be thirsty when we remain in Jesus, because a constant supply of living water flows from his body.

What Jesus' Motherhood Means for Mothers (and Fathers!)[7]

As a human man, Jesus forged a path for other men to follow, showing by example that men can and should be successfully involved in things

---

6. Julian, *Revelations of Divine Love*, 86.

7. This article first appeared in the Spring 2022 issue of CBE International's *Mutuality* magazine. https://www.cbeinternational.org/resource/article/mutuality-blog-magazine/my-body-broken-you-motherhood-jesus-and-julian-norwich

that his (and our) patriarchal cultures often define as "women's work." Men, do you want to be like Jesus? Then pick up a little child (Mark 9:36) and cook somebody breakfast (John 21:9). Give someone a bath (John 13:4–9) and do some laundry (Eph. 5:26–27).

But cultural stereotypes aside, Jesus did something even more significant for women. Jesus, "the unique One, who is himself God, is near to the Father's heart. He has revealed God to us" (John 1:18, NLT). And he has revealed God as not only a father, but a mother as well. Only a mother can conceive, sustain, and nourish new life within her body, as Jesus did and continues to do for us. Women are created in the image of God, and as mothers (whether biological, adoptive, or spiritual) we reflect God's motherly nature to the world around us. As egalitarian mothers, we don't need to downplay or minimize our motherly role in order to take our full and equal place in the kingdom of God. As we mother, we are being like God in a uniquely beautiful way.

Throughout much of world history, women have been treated as second to men, and motherhood has been viewed as a menial and insignificant task relegated to the "less capable" members of society. Western first-wave feminists exposed the lie that women are "less capable," and offered women equality with men. Second-wave feminism continued to make progress, but at a price: they felt that to be equal with men, they needed to become more like men and leave their femininity behind. Even today, as we are immersed in what many term the fourth wave, women who choose motherhood as a full-time career are viewed with suspicion, and we often feel that we have to justify or explain ourselves even to our Christian friends.

But women do not have to become more like men in order to accurately represent God. God's motherhood can be clearly seen through the life and death of Jesus, who came "to do the service and the office of Motherhood in all things."[8] When we pour ourselves into motherhood, we are pouring out the love of our heavenly Mother, living out the image of the God who is both Father and Mother to us all. As we give our bodies and souls for the life and nourishment of our biological, adoptive, and spiritual children, we are showing the world who Jesus is and what Jesus has to offer. What a beautiful and powerful gift!

---

8. Julian, *Revelations of Divine Love*, 71.

Flowing from His Body

> *Jesus replied, "Anyone who drinks this water will soon become thirsty again. But those who drink the water I give them will never be thirsty again. It becomes a fresh, bubbling spring within them, giving them eternal life."*
>
> *"Please, sir," the woman said, "give me this water! Then I'll never be thirsty again, and I won't have to come here to get water." (John 4:13–15, NLT)*

If someone offered you a drink and said that after one sip you would never be thirsty again, you would be wise to read the ingredient label very carefully. Come to think of it, you would be even wiser if you ran away very fast without looking back. A lot of people insult the Samaritan woman's intelligence by assuming that she was so drawn to the idea of not having to come to the well every day that her interest in physical water blinded her to the spiritual meaning of Jesus' words. I doubt she was that stupid. While she did initially think he was talking about physical water, and offering a one-time fix, I think she was subtly mocking him for making such a ludicrous offer. "Oh, sure, give me a magic cup of water and then I'll never have to drink water again. That would be handy."

But Jesus is not a one-time fix, nor does he offer one-time fixes. What he does offer is a chance to be connected to the source of life itself. When we come to drink the living water that Jesus offers, we will never be thirsty again, not because we will never need to drink again, but because we will never stop drinking! We will be permanently connected to the source of the spring, like a branch connected to a vine, like an unborn child connected to her mother.

> *Anyone who is thirsty may come to me! Anyone who believes in me may come and drink! For the Scriptures declare, "Rivers of living water will flow from his heart." (John 7:38, NLT)*

The Greek phrase "living water" refers to flowing water, like a spring or a river, rather than standing water like a pond or a cistern.[9] Living water is constantly being renewed and replenished, and thus can never be used up.

The Scriptures, according to Jesus, say that this spring of life flows from Jesus' *koilia*. Most English versions translate this as "heart," because

---

9. BDAG 426.

it is occasionally used to refer to the seat of emotions like the word "heart" does in English. But most often *koilia* is used to talk about an actual, physical part of the human body: the abdomen in general, or the stomach or womb in particular. As only a mother can, Jesus offers us the chance to drink and be nourished from his body. As a baby in the womb is never thirsty because a constant supply of fresh water is continually flowing from the mother's body, we will never be thirsty when we remain in Jesus, because a constant supply of living water flows from his body.

Jesus made this astounding offer during the Festival of Shelters, a time when the Israelites remembered God's provision of water from the Rock in the desert, and asked God to continue to provide water throughout the coming year. One of the passages that was read during the festival was Zechariah 14, which describes "the day of the Lord" (v.1). The "Scripture" that Jesus was quoting in John 7:38 may have been Zechariah 14:8:

> *On that day life-giving waters will flow out from Jerusalem, . . . flowing continuously in both summer and winter. (NLT)*

Jesus was claiming that "the day of the Lord" had arrived, in his person, and that he was the Rock who had given them water in the desert (1 Cor 10:4). The Rock that gave birth to them (Deut 32:18) and breastfed them (Deut 32:13) was now living among them as a human man, offering them the chance to be spiritually born, offering to feed them with his own body.

The Joy Awaiting Him

> *Yet when his life is made an offering for sin, he will have many descendants. When he sees all that is accomplished by his anguish, he will be satisfied. (Isa 53:10–11, NLT)*

> *Let us strip off every weight that slows us down, and let us run with endurance the race God has set before us. We do this by keeping our eyes fixed on Jesus, the champion who initiates and perfects our faith. Because of the joy awaiting him, he endured the cross, disregarding its shame. (Heb 12:1–2, NLT)*

When I was expecting my first baby, I knew everything I needed to know about the birth process. I had read all the books, and I was so ready to do everything right. After my water broke early in the morning, I had very mild pre-labor contractions throughout the day, and I felt like I was pretty awesome at this natural labor thing. Then the real contractions started.

Holy crap! Why didn't the books tell me it would hurt this much!? My baby was eventually born, but there was a lot of shouting involved and I was not the example of strong endurance that I had imagined myself to be.

When I was expecting my second baby, I was terrified because now I *truly* knew everything I needed to know—mostly how much it would actually hurt. But early on in the labor process I discovered that mentally handling the pain of labor was not very different from mentally handling the pain of competitive running, which I'd done for years. With every contraction, I would visualize myself running around a track. *Breathe in (start around the first curve), breath out, breathe in (finishing the first curve), breathe out, breathe in (start down the far side), etc.* One time around my mental track would usually get me through the contraction, and then I could "walk" for a few minutes until the next one. Of course, there was still lots of shouting involved. It was hard labor, "work, travail, suffering"—all connotations of the Hebrew word meaning "anguish" in Isaiah 53:11.[10] Avoiding emotional collapse required all of my concentration, and I had to strip off every mental weight (and occasionally articles of clothing) that kept me from fully focusing on getting around that track one more time.

There was only one other thought allowed in my mind, only one thought that could energize and encourage me rather than slow me down. Occasionally, when it seemed impossible to make it around the track again, I would remember the joy awaiting me, the prize at the end of the race. Few joys are deeper than the joy of holding a new life in your arms, a life whose existence has literally been accomplished by your own anguish.

You were the joy awaiting Jesus when he endured the cross. When he saw what had been accomplished by his anguish—the restoration of your life and relationship with him—he was satisfied. You are worth it.

> *Yet when his life is made an offering for sin, he will have many descendants. When he sees all that is accomplished by his anguish, he will be satisfied. (Isa 53:10–11, NLT)*

---

10. Smith, *Isaiah 40–66*, 461.

Disregarding the Shame

Because of the joy awaiting him, he endured the cross, disregarding its shame. (Heb 12:2, NLT)

I will never understand people who want a video record of their labor and delivery. I mean, I suppose if you were bored on a Friday night you might want to go back and relive that process, but personally I would rather walk a mile barefoot in a blizzard. That would be over sooner, and less painful.

But it's not just that I don't want a reminder of the pain. More than that, I wouldn't want a record of the shame. Birth is not a dignified event. In a natural birth, there tends to be a lot of shouting, weird groaning, and walking around without nearly enough clothes on, but at least there's usually only one or two midwives there to see it all. You might act less crazy with an epidural or a C-section, but a dozen people have seen you naked before all is said and done. In the moment, the pain usually blocks out the shame, but the shame can linger in the memory.

Jesus gets this. Crucifixion was the most shameful way you could possibly die. If you were hanging on a cross, everyone knew that you were the lowest of the low, the most despicable human in existence. Not only that, but you hung there naked, for hours, and anyone who walked by was free to spit on you, mock you, or torment you however they pleased.

But Jesus *disregarded the shame*. Why? Because of the joy awaiting him. You. He even inspired a public written record of his shame, allowing us to read all the details of our undignified spiritual birth.

I'm still glad my shame is not recorded, but it was worth every last weird groan to have my children here with me. Jesus feels the same way about you.

My Body, Broken for You[11]

Jesus took some bread and gave thanks to God for it. Then he broke it in pieces and gave it to the disciples, saying, "This is my body, which is given for you." Do this to remember me. (Luke 22:19, NLT)

---

11. This article first appeared in the Spring 2022 issue of CBE International's *Mutuality* magazine. https://www.cbeinternational.org/resource/article/mutuality-blog-magazine/my-body-broken-you-motherhood-jesus-and-julian-norwich

> *And he took a cup of wine and gave thanks to God for it. He gave it to them and said, "Each of you drink from it, for this is my blood, which confirms the covenant between God and his people. It is poured out as a sacrifice to forgive the sins of many." (Matt 26:27–28, NLT)*

My third daughter came quickly. Not many hours ago I had been at the zoo with my older girls, and suddenly here I was with this tiny, new girl nestled in my arms. My body still ached from the fast and furious labor, but the pain was swallowed up by joy as she snuggled into me for her first meal. I kissed her slimy, unwashed head and whispered, "My body broken for you, my blood poured out for you. Drink, my darling girl."

A few weeks later, I was sitting in the back row at church. The hardness of the pew reminded me of my recently broken body and the scars I would always have. My baby was drinking again, and I held the broken cracker and the tiny cup of juice in one hand. I had just yelled at my older girls on the way to church, and I didn't feel very clean inside. But suddenly Jesus was there with the scars he would always have, holding me, kissing my slimy head, and whispering, "This is my body, broken for you, my blood poured out for you. You are the joy that swallowed up my pain. Drink, my darling girl."

Operation Creep Up and Disappear

> *As Jesus went with Jairus, the leader of the local synagogue, all the people followed, crowding around him. A woman in the crowd had suffered for twelve years with constant bleeding. She had suffered a great deal from many doctors, and over the years she had spent everything she had to pay them, but she had gotten no better. In fact, she had gotten worse. She had heard about Jesus, so she came up behind him through the crowd and touched the fringe of his robe. For she thought to herself, "If I can just touch his robe, I will be healed." Immediately the bleeding stopped, and she could feel in her body that she had been healed of her terrible condition. Jesus realized at once that healing power had gone out from him, so he turned around in the crowd and asked, "Who touched my robe?" Everyone denied it, and his disciples said to him, "Master, this whole crowd is pressing up against you. How can you ask, 'Who touched me?'" But Jesus said, "Someone deliberately touched me, for I felt healing power go out from me." And he kept on looking around to see who had done it. Then the*

> *frightened woman realized that she could not stay hidden. Trembling, she came and fell to her knees in front of him. The whole crowd heard her explain why she had touched him and that she had been immediately healed. And he said to her, "Daughter, take courage. Your faith has made you well. Go in peace. Your suffering is over." (From Matt 9:18–22, Mark 5:22–34, Luke 8:41–48, NLT)*

Do you remember when you first started having periods, how embarrassing and awkward it felt? I can remember thinking how eternally mortified I would feel if any human besides my mother ever knew when I was having a period. It gets easier to talk about with other women, but in our culture it's not usually a comfortable topic of conversation in most social settings.

And it's not just our culture. Many cultures have social rules and taboos about menstruation. Where I used to work in Papua New Guinea, there are all kinds of cultural taboos for menstruating women . . . where you can't wash, who you can't cook for, what you can't step over, where you can't sleep, or sit, or walk. Jesus' culture was no exception. According to Jewish ceremonial law[12] any bleeding woman (whether or not it was a normal period) was considered ceremonially unclean. Anyone who touched her or anything she sat on would also be unclean for the rest of the day, and had to bathe and wash their clothes.

Imagine, for a moment, if your church had the same rules. You would have to stay home from church when you had your period, and if you tried to sneak in anyway and somebody found out, your chair would have to be sanitized and anybody who touched you would have to go home immediately, shower and wash their clothes, and isolate themselves for the rest of the day. Can you imagine the weight of shame that would be added to something that is a normal part of every woman's existence?

Now, imagine that you do sneak into this imaginary church with your period because there is a guest speaker that you really want to hear. It's a multi-church service, and people have driven in from all the surrounding cities to meet the preacher that everyone's been talking about. He shakes your hand as you walk in the door (oh, if he knew!) and you quietly sit in the back and try to act normal. But then, as soon as he gets up to speak, he looks around the giant auditorium. "There's someone here I need to talk to," he says. Your guilty conscience makes you blush, but of course he's not talking about you. There's no way he could know. There's a

---

12. Lev 15:19, 25–27

long, uncomfortable silence, and people start to shuffle uneasily. Then his eyes meet yours. "You," he says. You desperately look around you, hoping it's actually the guy next to you. But no. Your name echoes out of the microphone, and he asks you to come to the front. Everyone is looking at you now, as you slowly walk down the eternally long aisle and up the stairs to the podium, hoping that this will be the part where you wake up from the worst dream of your life. He hands you the microphone and asks you to please explain to everyone what you've done. Your own pastor is sitting in the front row, staring at you with puzzled eyes. You take a deep breath and, trembling, say those awful words, "I came to church with my period." The crowd rustles, and mutters, and the people who shook your hand get up and walk out. You know they are going home to shower and wash their clothes and hate you forever for making them miss this event. One of the deacons is already putting gloves on so he doesn't become unclean himself when he sprays your chair with bleach. You hand the microphone back, expecting the speaker to announce that the gathering is now over because he has to go back to his hotel room to shower, and he'll also miss his afternoon flight because he'll still be unclean. But no! He smiles at you, shakes your hand again, and says, "Way to be brave! Would you please open our time in prayer before you sit back down?"

Aren't you glad you don't live in that world? But the woman Jesus healed very much did live in that world, and if that story made you squirm, perhaps you'll have an inkling of how she felt. She was unclean according to Jewish law, and she was not supposed to be in that crowd. Each person she pushed past on her way to Jesus became unclean also, and if she'd been to every doctor in town, her problem was likely not a secret. Maybe she didn't even have to push past some people, as they saw her coming and fled in terror of her impurity, hurling insults as they tried to avoid touching her. As she got closer to Jesus, she saw that the leader of the synagogue was right next to him. Oh no! If he saw her touching a teacher! But she kept going anyway. "I'll just creep up and touch the hem of his robe, and then disappear forever." And the first part of her plan worked. As soon as she touched his robe, she was instantly healed! But as she began to execute the disappearing part, Jesus stopped. "Who touched me?" The woman froze. Everyone denied it. (I love that, by the way. The whole crowd is pressing up against him and everyone says, "Not me! Not me!")

This is where the woman's story diverges from our fantasy horror church service. Jesus didn't call her out by name. She was already healed, and she still could have disappeared. I can see the woman hesitate, torn between the desire to escape the impending shame and disgrace, and the irresistible urge to go talk to the One who had healed her. Jesus didn't give up. He "kept on looking around for the one who had touched him" (Mark 5:32, NLT). And Luke tells us that she "realized that she could not stay hidden" (8:47, NLT). Perhaps she could have stayed hidden from everyone else, but she understood that she could not stay hidden from Jesus. Trembling, she turned around and walked towards him, and the crowd probably edged away as she went by. She told the whole story. Luke tells us that "the whole crowd heard her explain why she had touched him and that she had been immediately healed" (8:47, NLT). Any visitors who hadn't known her shameful secret before knew it now. No wonder she was trembling. She was probably waiting for a rebuke from Jesus, or from Jairus, or from both!

This is one of those times when it's terribly important to notice what Jesus does *not* say next. After hearing the woman's story, everyone in that crowd would have known that even though she had been healed, *she was still unclean*. A woman was still considered unclean for seven days after she stopped bleeding, and then on the eighth day she needed to bring an offering to the temple before she could be ceremonially clean (Lev 15:28–30). Jairus, the leader of the synagogue who was standing there next to Jesus, certainly would have known this, and he was probably waiting to hear Jesus say it.

But Jesus does not say, "Take courage! In seven days you will be clean after you bring your offering to the temple. Sorry, Jairus, I can't help your daughter today, I have to go wash and be unclean until evening." Instead of relating to her as a rabbi, and telling her she's broken the law, Jesus gets all motherly again, calls her "daughter," and seems perfectly comfortable stopping in the road (in front of a huge crowd!) to have a heart to heart about periods.

Why did Jesus ignore the law? He said in Matthew 5:17 that he "did not come to abolish the law of Moses or the writings of the prophets, . . . [but] to accomplish their purpose" (NLT). Jesus wasn't ignoring the law, he was proclaiming that he had come to do what, according to Romans 8:3, "the law could not do"—make us truly clean.

The moment that woman touched Jesus, she was not only healed, she was also cleansed. You see, the old laws could never truly make anyone clean; they were there to remind everyone that they needed cleansing. Jesus fulfilled those laws, and offers the deep true cleansing that the laws could never offer. Jesus was publicly telling the whole crowd (including the leader of the synagogue) that he is bigger and better than the ritual laws, and that simply touching him is enough to make you clean. Now that Jesus is here, we don't need to wait until a certain time of the month or bring a dead bird to church to be clean. Reaching out for Jesus is enough.

After Jesus failed to say the "right" thing, the crowd probably looked at Jairus, the leader of the synagogue, to see what he would say. Would he speak up, and demand that Jesus follow the law and go cleanse himself? No. As the whole crowd watched, Jairus took the ritually unclean Jesus into his house, and allowed him to take his dead daughter by the hand (which would also have made Jesus unclean according to Levitical law.)[13] Jairus essentially condoned Jesus' astounding claim that he was the One who defined what or who was clean, and that connection to him was enough to bring cleansing, healing, and even life itself.

Still, why did Jesus sabotage the disappearing part of Operation Creep Up and Disappear? Even though it ended well, the encounter must have been terribly embarrassing for that woman. Why didn't Jesus just let her sneak off and enjoy her healing and wholeness in privacy?

Remember that Jesus didn't force her to reveal herself. He let her choose whether to sneak away and remain anonymous or come forward and tell her story. Had she chosen to disappear, she would no longer have had to live in pain and discomfort, but she would likely have remained an outcast. The shame of her condition would likely have followed her for the rest of her life, because who was going to believe that she had suddenly and inexplicably been cured? By giving her the opportunity to tell her story in front of the whole crowd, Jesus was not shaming her; he was publicly removing her disgrace and restoring her to community.

Not only that, but Jesus also offered her a platform, a voice where she had previously had none. By allowing her to tell her story publicly Jesus not only removed her personal shame, he also gave her a part in the removal of shame for all women everywhere. Jesus announced, through this courageous woman's story, that women can now participate fully in his kingdom, with or without their periods. A woman's participation in the community of God is no longer defined or constrained by her gender, or by any of the natural functions of her female body. This was a bold public precedent, and probably gave many Jewish Christian women the

---

13. Numbers 19:11

courage to participate fully in the life of the church at all times of the month.

One bankrupt, disgraced woman believed that contact with Jesus could change her life. Jesus gave her the chance to tell her story publicly and used her courage to change the lives of women everywhere. Zephaniah's words came true that day!

> Rejoice and exult with all your heart, O daughter of Jerusalem! The LORD your God is in your midst. I will save the lame and gather the outcast, and I will change their shame into praise and renown in all the earth. (Zeph 3:14, 17, 19, NASB)

The Fellowship of Suffering

> *Through suffering, our bodies continue to share in the death of Jesus so that the life of Jesus may also be seen in our bodies. (2 Cor 4:10, NLT)*

> *Together with Christ we are heirs of God's glory. But if we are to share his glory, we must also share his suffering. (Rom 8:17, NLT)*

> *For you have been given not only the privilege of trusting in Christ but also the privilege of suffering for him. (Phil 1:29, NLT)*

> *That I may know [Christ] and the power of his resurrection and the fellowship of his sufferings, being conformed to his death; in order that I may attain to the resurrection from the dead! (Phil 3:10–11, NASB)*

When I first arrived in Papua New Guinea, I spent three months in a cultural orientation course, along with people of all ages from five different countries. We were a diverse group, and many of us had very little in common, but together we lived through culture shock, dealt with new and terrifying wildlife (okay, just spiders but they were *really* big!), muddled through confusing social situations, hiked through thick jungles, and swam a mile in the ocean. By the end of the course we felt like family. The fellowship of suffering together, along with the joy of experiencing the beauty of a new culture and country together, had bonded us together in a uniquely powerful way.

The culmination (and most intense part) of the course was the time we spent living in a village. For four weeks, my friend Hannah and I lived together in a tiny bamboo hut without the conveniences of plumbing or electricity, alone in a community of people we had never met, who spoke a language we could barely understand, in a culture that still made very little sense to us. We struggled, and at times we suffered, but we struggled and suffered *together*, and that suffering fused our hearts together in a friendship that will last forever.

There is a depth of relationship that only comes through suffering together, and that is the kind of relationship with Jesus that Paul longed for. Nothing else knits your heart with someone else's in quite the same way as enduring hardship together, and there is a level of intimacy with Jesus that we will never experience until we suffer with him in some way. And this is one more way in which motherhood, and all the suffering it entails, is a precious (if heavy) gift.

Pregnancy and childbirth require you to give up your body completely for another person. Your back hurts, your stomach hurts, your breasts hurt, your teeth hurt and are more prone to cavities, your eyesight changes, exercise is more difficult and you gain weight, you feel nauseous and eating is no longer fun but you still have to eat and it matters what you eat. You get stretch marks, tears, incisions and scars, not to mention the pain of labor and sometimes pain during breastfeeding. Yet I can honestly say that it was worth it all to have my children here with me.

Jesus gave up his body even more completely, and he did it so that you and I could be here with him, born into his Kingdom! And yet that spiritual birth would never have been possible without the mothers who birthed us physically. Mothers have a special partnership in God's business of adding children to the Kingdom of Heaven, and in a physical way we "fill up what is lacking in Christ's afflictions" (Col 1:24, ESV). It's like God saved some suffering for us to share, not because God needed us, not because anyone's salvation is incomplete without us, but to give us the chance to experience the intimacy with God that only comes from shared suffering. When we give up our bodies so that someone else can live, we participate in Christ's suffering in a way that most men never have the chance to.

Being a mom has brought me joy in a way that nothing else has, and that joy comes with a cost of suffering, but when the suffering ushers us into intimacy with Jesus it comes full circle back to joy. As a mother I can say, with Paul:

> *I am glad when I suffer for you in my body, for I am participating in the sufferings of Christ that continue for his body, the church.* (Col 1:24, NLT)

Christ's suffering at his death was fully sufficient for our salvation, but as people everywhere enter and grow in Christ's Kingdom, "the sufferings of Christ continue for his body, the church." Since we are his body, Jesus feels the pain that we feel (Acts 9:4). And as Christ's sufferings continue for his body, we are invited to carry some of his suffering in our own bodies. It is through suffering that we enter the Kingdom of God (Acts 14:22)—sometimes our own suffering draws us deeper into the heart of God, and sometimes we are drawn further into God's Kingdom when others suffer on our behalf.

Mothers, who literally suffer in their bodies to bring new life into the Kingdom of God, have a unique opportunity to participate in the suffering of Christ, suffering that can lead to a deep, sweet fellowship and intimacy with Christ.

> *For the more we suffer for Christ, the more God will shower us with his comfort through Christ. (2 Cor 1:5, NLT)*

It is comforting, as a mother, to know that Jesus understands and has experienced our suffering so thoroughly. As you mother, whether you are experiencing the physical suffering of growing a tiny body for a brand new member of God's Kingdom, the emotional suffering of pouring out more than you have for young members of God's Kingdom, or the suffering of laboring through the birth of spiritual children, let your own Mother shower you with comfort, and let your heart be knit together with God's as you share in the fellowship of Christ's suffering for God's children.

All Alone

> *Early the next morning Jesus went out to an isolated place. The crowds searched everywhere for him, and when they finally found him, they begged him not to leave them. (Luke 4:42, NLT)*

> *Jesus went away privately in a boat to an isolated place. But when the crowd heard about it, they followed him on foot from the towns. As he got out he saw the large crowd, and he had compassion on them. He welcomed them, spoke to them about the kingdom of God, and cured those who needed healing. When evening arrived, his disciples came to him saying, "Send the crowds away so that they can go and buy food for themselves." But Jesus replied, "They don't need to go. You give them something to eat."*

> *He took the five loaves and two fish, and looking up to heaven he gave thanks and broke the loaves. They all ate and were satisfied, and they picked up the broken pieces left over, twelve baskets full. (From Matt 14:13–21 and Luke 9:10–17, NET)*

> *All alone! Whether you like it or not, alone will be something you'll be quite a lot!* —Dr. Seuss[14]

I'd like to have a little chat with Dr. Seuss. As brilliant as the guy is, I'm pretty sure he got that alone part wrong. As a mom of small kids, whether I like it or not, all alone may be something I wish for, dream about, and pretend that I have to pee in order to achieve, but it is most certainly not something that I am quite a lot. I can remember as a child looking all through the house for my own mom, who was probably just trying to have a quiet moment alone herself. Now that I am a mom, I know how precious even a few solitary moments can be.

Young children need so much of our time. When my first baby was born I loved to be with her, but I struggled with suddenly having so very little time to do anything besides care for her. I wonder if Jesus felt a similar frustration as an eternal being, outside of time, who consented to be born into the confining limits of time. Not only was he suddenly limited by time, but in a human body it was necessary for him to use time for things like eating and sleeping. And his children asked for so much of his time. When he went off to be alone they would search for him and follow him, just like my children do! When Jesus stepped off the boat that he'd gone off in to be alone and saw that a huge crowd was waiting for him, did his heart sink like mine does when I get up extra early to be alone and discover a welcoming committee waiting for me in the living room? Whether it did or not, his response was not irritation or resentment (like mine often is) but compassion. Instead of being annoyed, ignoring them, or telling them to go away, he feels compassion and out of that compassion he teaches them, heals them, and feeds them. Which is what mothers do. No matter how tired, hungry, frustrated, or upset I am, no matter how many other things I would love to do but know I will now not do for days, when my little baby wakes up crying because she's hungry, I have compassion on her. I feel compassion because I love her, and I know I am the only one who can meet her need. If I don't give her food, what else will she do? Where else can she go? And, though I do feel moments of

---

14. Geisel, *Oh, the Places You'll Go!*, 34.

frustration, I don't begrudge her those hours of nursing because she is my little daughter and I love her.

Jesus felt that way about each person in the crowd that followed him around the sea, and he feels that way now about you and me! God knows that I am hungry, that I need God, that God is the only one who can help me, and that if God does not answer my cries in the night, I have nowhere else to go. My soul will waste away. And so God has compassion on me, and on you, and on each person who cries out to God in the darkness, because God loves us and we are God's little children.

If you, like me, are dreaming about a far off day when Dr. Seuss's words will come true and you will find yourself all alone for just a few minutes, let me leave you with an encouragement and a caution. Be encouraged that Jesus knows exactly how you feel—he experienced exactly what you are experiencing as a mother surrounded by needy, adoring, demanding children. Take your frustration to God, and let that fellowship of motherly suffering draw you into a close relationship with your heavenly mother. But (and here is the caution) don't stop chasing time alone with God! So many times, as mothers, we have to give up our own desires for solitude and keep pouring ourselves out for our children instead. But your children need you to be whole and healthy, and for that you do need time to be filled back up yourself. There are no rules about when to come out and have compassion and when to keep hiding in the bathroom—it's a tricky dance of following the Spirit. Whatever season you're in, I pray that our Mother will provide abundant compassion when you're in the middle of the crowds, and also the time you need alone for God's Spirit to refill you.

Born from Above

> *For you have been born again, but not to a life that will quickly end. Your new life will last forever because it comes from the eternal, living Word of God. (1 Pet 1:23, NLT)*

> *But to all who believed [Jesus] and accepted him, he gave the right to become children of God. They are reborn—not with a physical birth resulting from human passion or plan, but a birth that comes from God. (John 1:13, NLT)*

> *I tell you the truth, unless you are born again [from above], you cannot see the Kingdom of God. I assure you, no one can enter*

> *the Kingdom of God without being born of water and the Spirit. Humans can reproduce only human life, but the Holy Spirit gives birth to spiritual life. (John 3:3, 5–6, NLT)*

If you have spent much time at all around American Christians, I'm sure you've heard the phrase "born again." "Have you been born again?" It's a common phrase in many of our churches, and has become synonymous with the idea of "becoming a Christian" or identifying yourself with Jesus. It's also a biblical phrase, and for the most part it is meant to be used the way people typically use it—to talk about becoming part of God's Kingdom through Jesus.

However, this phrase has become such a common part of "Christianese" language that we fail to grasp its significance. John tells us (logically enough) that to be God's children, we have to be born again, from above (the Greek word means both "again" and "from above").[15] You cannot be born unless somebody gives birth to you! And it is the Holy Spirit who "gives birth to spiritual life."

If you are part of God's family, the Holy Spirit gave birth to you! Identifying yourself with Jesus means identifying God's Spirit as your mother. Being a part of God's Kingdom means being like a little baby in God's arms (like the baby Jesus held in Luke 18:16), and even like an unborn baby in God's womb. We cannot even "see" the Kingdom of God without this relationship of complete and utter dependence on God.

In John 3, Nicodemus calls Jesus, "Teacher," comments on the miracles he's performed, and says that he must be sent from God, but Jesus (in his typical style) gets right to the point. Admiring the miracles done by a teacher sent from God is not enough. It's all or nothing in the Kingdom of God, and if you want to be in you have to be all in—all the way in God. "If you want to see God's Kingdom, you have to be born. From above this time." Coming to God as our Teacher, our King, or our Father is good and right, but Jesus doesn't use any of those metaphors because those are all relationships that we could potentially walk away from and stay alive. Instead, Jesus says that being part of God's Kingdom means relating to God as an unborn baby relates to her mother, entirely dependent on God for our very spiritual existence. We cannot leave that relationship and live.

Being a part of God's Kingdom is not a day job, where we go do a bunch of useful things for God and then take some time off. It is a state of being in a constant, connected relationship of dependence on God.

---

15. BDAG 92.

God's Kingdom was ushered in by God's own birth into a relationship of connection, trust and dependence on a human mother. It is only fitting that we enter God's Kingdom in the same way, through birth into a relationship of complete and continual connection, trust, and dependence on our eternal mother.

Living in God

> *Jesus replied, "I tell you the truth, unless you are born again, you cannot see the Kingdom of God." "What do you mean?" exclaimed Nicodemus. "How can an old man go back into his mother's womb and be born again?" Jesus replied, "I assure you, no one can enter the Kingdom of God without being born of water and the Spirit. . . . The Holy Spirit gives birth to spiritual life." (John 3:3–6, NLT)*

> *All who confess that Jesus is the Son of God have God living in them, and they live in God. We know how much God loves us, and we have put our trust in his love. God is love, and all who live in love live in God, and God lives in them. And as we live in God, our love grows more perfect. Such love has no fear, because perfect love expels all fear. (1 John 4:15–18, NLT)*

We cannot enter God's Kingdom unless the Holy Spirit gives birth to us. As Nicodemus so perceptively pointed out, we cannot climb back into our human mother's womb to be born again. But we can metaphorically be brought into God's womb, and that is the imagery Jesus uses to describe entering the Kingdom of God. It's also consistent with the imagery John uses to describe life in the Kingdom of God. When we recognize and accept who Jesus is, the Holy Spirit lives in us, and we start a new life inside of God.

What does it mean to live in God? If I were literally a baby living inside of God's womb, God would always be there, I would always be safe, I would never be hungry, I would never be thirsty, I would always be perfectly warm, and all of my needs would be met before I was even aware of them.

This is the invitation Jesus extends to our souls, and it becomes a spiritual reality when we enter into relationship with Jesus. We get inside of God by receiving God inside of us.

> *All who confess that Jesus is the Son of God have God living in them, and they live in God. We know how much God loves us . . .*
> *(1 John 4: 15–16, NLT)*

As we live inside of God, as we notice God inside of us, we will *know* how much God loves us. This is an experiential kind of knowing; it is the word used as a euphemism for marital intimacy, a word that can also mean "to be aware of, perceive, notice, realize."[16]

As we live in God, experiencing and noticing God's love for us, *our love grows more perfect. Such love has no fear, because perfect love expels all fear.*

When we come into God's Kingdom, into God's womb, we are utterly safe and there is no space left for fear. It is all full of warmth, abundant satisfaction, and perfect love.

Getting Littler

> *The disciples came to Jesus and asked, "Who, then, is greatest in the Kingdom of Heaven?" He called a little child to him and placed the child among them. And he said, "Truly I tell you, unless you change and become like little children, you will never enter the Kingdom of Heaven. Therefore, whoever takes the lowly position of this child is the greatest in the Kingdom of Heaven. (Matt 18:1–4, NIV)*

> *One day some parents brought their little children to Jesus so he could touch and bless them. But when the disciples saw this, they scolded the parents for bothering him. When Jesus saw what was happening, he was angry with his disciples. He said to them, "Let the children come to me. Don't stop them! For the Kingdom of God belongs to those who are like these children. I tell you the truth, anyone who doesn't receive the Kingdom of God like a child will never enter it." Then he took the children in his arms and placed his hands on their heads and blessed them. (Luke 18:15, Mark 10:14–16, NLT)*

When my children really want to insult each other, they start calling each other "little." Everyone obviously wants to be "big," and whoever is the biggest must also be the best, so to be called "little" is pretty much the worst thing ever. It sounds like Jesus' disciples might have fit right in at

---

16. BDAG 200.

my house. "No way, Matthew, you're not the biggest. Peter, you're just little. You know what, let's go ask Jesus who's the biggest." So they did. And Jesus told them all to get littler.

But later on, when some even littler people showed up, the disciples tried to send them away. "You're too little to be here! You'll just bother Jesus, go away!" Actually, it was the little people's parents they were scolding, because the little people themselves were so very little that they didn't even have the ability to voluntarily go or stay. Luke refers to them with a word that means "infants."[17]

This made Jesus angry! He didn't just allow the parents to bring him their babies, he got mad at the people trying to stop them! And he said something shocking: "The Kingdom of Heaven *belongs* to those who are like these little babies. Anyone who doesn't *receive* the Kingdom of Heaven like a child will never enter it."

Children are good at receiving. When my kids are hungry, they don't present me with a list of the good things they have done or the reasons why they deserve to be fed. They say, "Mom, I'm hungry!" and happily receive the food I give them. Even if they have been downright horrid all day (calling everyone around them "little"), when dinner time comes around they assume I'm going to feed them and they come to the table to receive.

A little baby, like the one Jesus was likely holding when he made that statement, can do little besides receive. When my tiny baby is hungry, all she can do is cry. She has no ability whatsoever to get food for herself, to get herself to the food, or even to articulate the fact that she needs food. Most of the time she doesn't even have the energy to open her eyes. So she cries out, opens her little mouth, and starts blindly moving her head around, waiting for the beloved milk to appear in her mouth. Waiting to receive.

Jesus says that the only way to be a part of God's Kingdom is to *receive* it like that little baby. We don't need to come to God with a list of the ways we have contributed to the Kingdom of Heaven or the reasons why we should be a part of it. We just have to open our little mouth, open our hands and heart, and receive it.

> *Open your mouth wide, and I will fill it with good things. (Ps 81:10, NLT)*

---

17. BDAG 183.

When you are hungry, you never need to bring God a list of reasons why you should be allowed to sit at God's table and eat God's food, or why you should be nursed by the Rock who is *Shaddai*. Even when you don't have the strength to ask, just open your mouth and *receive* like the little baby Jesus held as he said, "The Kingdom of Heaven belongs to such as these."

Receiving from Our Mother

Truly I tell you, unless you change and become like little children, you will never enter the Kingdom of Heaven. (Matt 18:3, NIV)

I tell you the truth, anyone who doesn't receive the Kingdom of God like a child will never enter it." (Mark 10:15, NLT)

Jesus made it clear that to be part of God's Kingdom, we have to come to God like children, *little* children. We have to allow ourselves to be born from the Holy Spirit, recognize that we are as dependent on God as an unborn baby on her mother, and be willing to simply receive.

It's much harder to receive the Kingdom of God this way if we don't allow ourselves to think of God as our mother. Thinking of God only as a father makes us more likely to think of ourselves as God's adult children, or teenage children, or at least older children, because our relationship with our father tends to grow deeper as we grow older. We are not born with an automatic relationship with our father; it's something that has to grow and develop. With our mother, on the other hand, we are born into an instant physical relationship of dependence, of *receiving*. This is why little babies often show a preference for their mother, even when their father is perfectly loving and present. They have a constant need to *receive* the nourishment that only their mother can provide. To be sure, our relationship with our mother also grows, develops, and matures but a baby's relationship with her mother begins even before birth.

It certainly is vitally important to put time and effort into developing a mature relationship with God as our Father. But God's Kingdom already *belongs* to you the moment you are born into God's family (and even before!—Eph 1:5-6). Receive God's Kingdom like a little child!

Becoming Little

—written by Kristin Wright-Bettner

Truly I tell you, unless you change and become like little children, you will never enter the kingdom of heaven. (Matt 18:3, NIV)

"I hadn't realized that I had come to the lake and said feed me, *but my empty heart was fed. I had a good mother. She gives what we need without being asked."*[18] *—Robin Kimmerer*

When I was little, my mom gave me food before I knew how to ask for it. In the cold and snowy winters of upstate New York, she put warm clothes on me before I knew I would need them. And in the hot and humid summers, as I was about to run outside to play in the sprinklers, she'd stop me mid-stride to rub sunscreen on my skin, though I didn't know I needed it. But she knew I did, and so she gave it to me.

I am in a season of remembering how to be little again, spiritually little. Not little as in "insignificant"; little as in "young." God is not letting me get away with being old; Mother God is giving me what I need, without me asking for it, as mothers do.

In this season, I haven't been able to pray much—"pray" in the sense of asking for things. Even good things, things that I know are in line with God's will. Oftentimes, asking for things feels too hard. A couple weeks ago I tried to pray for a loved one who is going through a hard season. As I tried to summon up the strength to ask on their behalf, Mother God said gently, "No. Just be."

One might say, "Well, pull yourself up by your bootstraps and pray anyway. It doesn't matter that it feels too hard!" But that's something an old person would say.

Jesus said that in order to enter the Kingdom of Heaven, we have to *change*. We need to do something differently than we've been doing. And that something different involves us becoming little again. I used to think, subconsciously, that Jesus was prescribing a law. If we don't obey and become like little children, then God is going to actively prevent us from entering the Kingdom. But now I think perhaps Jesus was simply stating a fact—describing, not prescribing. Not becoming little, in itself, is the thing that keeps us from entering the Kingdom. We just won't fit.

---

18. Kimmerer, *Braiding Sweetgrass*, 2013.

The birth canal is a narrow passage, after all. Small is the gate, narrow is the path that leads to life.[19] To fit through, you have to be little.

There is a time for everything, a season for every activity under the heavens.[20] There is a time to ask for things, and that time will come again. Once we've entered the Kingdom, then we can grow again, grow big in the ways of the Kingdom.

But first things first. First we need to be little, so we can enter the Kingdom. And little ones just receive. There is a time to receive, and it is okay to be in that time. Not just okay—it is *necessary* to be in that time. Before I can get bigger again, I need to receive all the nourishment Mother God has for me. I need to be grounded in the truth that God is a good Mother, and so gives me what I need without me asking.

I have a good Mother. You give me what I need without being asked. We have a good Mother. You give us what we need without being asked.

The Small Ones

God blesses those who are poor and realize their need for him, for the Kingdom of Heaven is theirs. (Matt 5:3, NLT)

Both my twins were small, but one of them was two pounds smaller than the other, and had a lot of trouble gaining weight after birth. In fact, they were delivered early because the smaller one had stopped growing in the womb. I didn't love the little guy any more or less than his bigger, squishier brother, but I did feel a greater weight of concern for him. The bigger baby was every bit as important to me as the smaller one, but his need for me was not as great. I knew that as long as I offered him plenty of food at appropriate times, he would get what he needed and do okay for himself. The smaller guy required a more complex feeding strategy, because in the beginning he did not even have the energy to stay awake long enough to get enough food.

Spiritually, we are all God's tiny twins. When life is going well we might imagine that, like the plumper brother, we can do okay for ourselves as long as we check in with God from time to time. But whether we realize it or not, we all need God just as desperately as my sleepy,

---

19. Matt 7:14
20. Eccl 3:1

malnourished baby needed my constant care and attention. And it is when we recognize that need that the Kingdom of Heaven becomes ours.

In a very physical and practical way, there are people in the world who, for a variety of reasons, have less power, are more vulnerable, or need extra care from those around them. Throughout Scripture we see that God, as our mother, feels a special care and concern for these tiniest and most vulnerable ones. I have often felt like one of those tinies, especially during the times when I was pregnant or nursing. While my body was so profoundly given to sustain another body, I had very little physical or emotional margin, and spent many days feeling rather needy and vulnerable. During those months of vulnerability, it was so sweet to know that God was offering me extra care and gentleness.

> *[God] will feed his flock like a shepherd. He will carry the lambs in his arms, holding them close to his heart. He will gently lead the mother sheep with their young. (Isa 40:11, NLT)*

Since he is God, Jesus shares this motherly heart of compassion for mothers. While Jesus was telling his disciples about the difficult days ahead, he thought particularly about how hard it would be for mothers, and felt sad for them.

> *How terrible it will be for pregnant women and for nursing mothers in those days. (Matt 24:19, NLT)*

There were so many categories of people who would experience extra hardship, who surely needed Jesus' compassion just as much—the elderly, the sick, the lame. But it was the mothers he mentioned. The women who would be struggling not just for their own lives but also for the tiny lives dependent on theirs. Perhaps he mentioned them because their struggle was so representative of his own motherly heart and the struggle that lay ahead of him—to lay down his life for the trillions of lives dependent on his sacrifice.

Pregnant and nursing women reflect Jesus' motherly sacrifice in a graphic, almost literal way, but there are many others who lay down their lives and struggle just as powerfully for the life of a small one. Whenever you pour yourself out for the vulnerable, whether through prayer, conversation, advocacy, or practical care, you are raising up Jesus' precious children as a spiritual mother.

As spiritual and biological mothers, especially during intense seasons like pregnancy and nursing, we have the privilege of living out God's

Mother heart of care for the tiniest and most vulnerable in a vividly profound way. This often leaves us feeling tiny and vulnerable ourselves, which becomes a blessing when we receive our smallness and realize that the Kingdom of Heaven is ours.

> *Be comforted, small one, in your smallness. He lays no merit on you. Receive and be glad.*[21] —C. S. Lewis

A Simple Request

> *Now Naaman, the commander of the king of Syria's army, . . . had a skin disease. So Naaman came with his horses and chariots and stood in the doorway of Elisha's house. Elisha sent out a messenger who told him, "Go and wash seven times in the Jordan; your skin will be restored and you will be healed." Naaman went away angry. He said, "Look, I thought for sure he would come out, stand there, invoke the name of the Lord his God, wave his hand over the area, and cure the skin disease. The rivers of Damascus, the Abana and Pharpar, are better than any of the waters of Israel! Could I not wash in them and be healed?" So he turned around and went away angry. His servants approached and said to him, "O master, if the prophet had told you to do some difficult task, you would have been willing to do it. It seems you should be happy that he simply said, "Wash and you will be healed." So he went down and dipped in the Jordan seven times, as the prophet had instructed. His skin became as smooth as a young child's and he was healed. (2 Kgs 1, 9–14, NET)*

If Jesus came today and asked me to preach in front of thousands of people, I would gladly obey.

If Jesus came today and asked me to host an angel, I would start cooking.

If Jesus came today and asked me to lead a protest, free a slave, start a church, or build houses for homeless people, I would say, "I'm on it."

Jesus did come today, and he looked like a dirty, hungry two-year-old, and his request was very simple. He asked me to wash his muddy feet and make him a peanut butter sandwich. If he had told me to do something very difficult, wouldn't I have done it? So I should certainly obey him when he says simply, "Feed my lambs."

---

21. Lewis, *Perelandra*, 197.

If I listen to this simple request, if I turn from my pride and gladly feed "the least of these,"[22] humbly showering them with love, will I, like Naaman, find my healing there? Will my heart become as healthy as the heart of a young child, young enough to receive the Kingdom of God?

> *I tell you the truth, just as you did it for one of the least of these brothers or sisters of mine, you did it for me. (Matt 25:40, NET)*

At Home on the Way Home

Lord, through all the generations you have been our home! (Ps 90:1, NLT)

The first home that I remember was a tiny gray apartment near downtown Denver. We moved away when I was very young, but I have a vague memory of splashing in a wading pool on a sunny day, snacking on crackers and juice, and getting stung by a bee. That was where my parents brought me home from the hospital, and yet it was not my first home. My first home was my mother. For nine months I lived in her, sleeping and waking, playing and resting, drinking and being fed. In her I lived and moved and had my being (Acts 17:28). There was no other home where I could live.

For a while after birth, a baby's mother is still effectively her home. Many times I have carried a nursing or sleeping baby through a mall, an airport, or some other strange noisy place and the baby felt perfectly at home as long as she was with me. My presence provided food, comfort, and a place to rest, and in my arms she was always at home, even on an airplane between homes.

As children grow older, and more affected by their surroundings, home is still defined to some degree by the presence of their mother (and father!). As a child, I moved to many new homes, but each new home always felt like home right away because my parents were there. Had I stayed in the old home without them, it would no longer have been home. Home was always where my mom and dad were.

Even now, as an adult, going to visit my mom and dad feels like going home. They are living in a place I never lived in as a child, so there are no childhood memories or nostalgia to make it feel like home. But the presence of my mother and my father transforms that house into a home.

---

22. Matt 25:40

Coming into God's presence is coming home. When you come home you let down your guard, you get comfortable, and you can be your true self (for better or for worse!). When you come home you can take off whatever uniform or business casual outfit you were required to wear away from home, be cleansed of whatever germs and grime you picked up along the way, and receive rest and refreshment. Home is where your needs can be met, where you eat and sleep and bathe and relax. Being at home restores us and renews our strength to engage with those outside our home.

Wherever we are, regardless of what is going on around us, we are at home when we are with God, like a nursing baby in a crowded mall. And as our relationship with God grows deeper, as we journey farther into the Kingdom of Heaven and grow littler, we will grow more and more at home in God, until we are as safe and satisfied in God's presence as an unborn baby in her mother's womb. This is why the Psalmist can say:

> *Because you have made the* LORD *your dwelling place, no evil will conquer you, no plague will come near your home. (Ps 91:9, ESV; 91:10, NLT)*

Evil will always surround us and threaten to overwhelm us, but it cannot touch our soul when we are at home in the womb of God. And yet, on the days when we encounter evil and pain at its most horrible depths, our soul can ache to be born into the full realization of the home God is preparing for us, and preparing us for.

> *Then I saw a new heaven and a new earth, for the old heaven and the old earth had disappeared. I heard a loud shout from the throne, saying, "Look, God's home is now among his people! He will live with them, and they will be his people. God himself will be with them. He will wipe every tear from their eyes, and there will be no more death or sorrow or crying or pain. All these things are gone forever. (Rev 21:1, 3–4, NLT)*

As Henri Nouwen put it, "Going home is a lifelong journey. . . . As we walk home we often realize how long the way is. But let us not be discouraged. Jesus walks with us and speaks to us on the road. When we listen carefully we discover that we are already home while on the way."[23] This is the good news of Jesus, Emmanuel, God who made a home among us, who has come to bring us Home and be our Home on the way.

---

23. Nouwen, *The Only Necessary Thing*, 105.

5

MOTHERHOOD IN THE OLD TESTAMENT

On the Importance of Clothing

Then God said, "Look! I have given you every seed-bearing plant throughout the earth and all the fruit trees for your food." (Gen 1:29, NLT)

And the Lord God made clothing from animal skins for Adam and his wife. (Gen 3:21, NLT)

Since I became a mother, I have spent a ridiculous amount of time dealing with clothing (not my own). I don't make clothing, but I have spent countless hours shopping for clothing, buying clothing, washing clothing, packing clothing, unpacking clothing, dressing people, undressing people, redressing people, and reundressing people (yes, that's a thing). If I had kept track of it all, it would probably add up to literally months of my life. Add food to that equation (buying food, cooking food, feeding food to people, cleaning up food) and that pretty much is my life right now. And I know I am not alone. Throughout history, the vast majority of mothers have spent the vast majority of their lives making sure that their children had food to eat and clothes to wear.

Now, let me be clear. There is no good reason on earth why women need to be or ought to be the ones in charge of food and clothes. There is nothing inherently feminine or womanly about feeding and clothing people, and these tasks could be (and often are) performed just as effectively by men as they are by women. Nevertheless, if you (like me) find yourself (for whatever reason) spending a significant portion of your time feeding and clothing people, be encouraged. *You are being like God!*

When God made people, the first thing God did was to bless them and tell them what their job was going to be. The very next thing God said (that we're told) was, "Look! I made you some food!" Like a new mother immediately holding her baby to her breast, God immediately presented food to God's newborn children.[1] And the very last thing God did before sending Adam and Eve out of the garden was to make them some clothes.

They had already made themselves clothes. Why did God make them new clothes? It reminds me of when a small child comes out of her room "dressed" in a way that is completely inappropriate for either the weather or the cultural sense of decency. "I'm ready to go play in the snow, Mom, I put on my kitty T-shirt and my transparent tights!"

Adam and Eve knew they had broken relationship with their mother, and they figured now they would be on their own, meeting their own needs, so they dressed themselves as well as they could. But, though they had forsaken God, God did not forsake them. Even while disciplining them severely God said, "Before you go, come here. Let me dress you. You're going to need these." Those clothes, made by their mother, would remind them of God's love and grace through the long, sorrowful years ahead of them. They would remind them that their sin had caused death, not just the death of the animals that used to own the clothes, and not just the eventual death of their bodies, but the death of the relationship they used to freely enjoy with God. But, as they snuggled deeper into those clothes the first time they felt cold, they would also be reminded that their mother had not abandoned them completely. God had still dressed them. And, though they could never have imagined how it would all play out, God always would dress them. Hope was on the way, in the form of new clothes.

> *I am overwhelmed with joy in the LORD my God! For he has dressed me with the clothing of salvation and draped me in a robe of righteousness. (Isa 61:10, NLT)*
>
> *We grow weary in our present bodies, and we long to put on our heavenly bodies like new clothing. (2 Cor 5:2, NLT)*

---

1. Acknowledgement to Siobahnne Duhe

Ezer

> *Then the* LORD *God said, "It is not good for the man to be alone. I will make a helper who is just right for him." So the* LORD *God caused the man to fall into a deep sleep. While the man slept, the* LORD *God took out one of the man's ribs and closed up the opening. Then the* LORD *God made a woman from the rib, and brought her to the man. (Gen 2:18, 21–22, NLT)*

It was not good for the man to be alone. It was not good for creation as a whole for the man to be alone, because Genesis 1:27 tells us that God chose to display his image in both male and female humans. Alone, the man was not the full reflection of God's image, and creation was not complete. God designed creation to be cared for by the man *and* the woman together (Gen 1:28), so creation's care would not be complete without the woman either.

Neither was it good for the man personally to be alone. So God made him a helper—the Hebrew word is *ezer*. In English, the word "helper" is rather vague. What kind of help, exactly, did God intend the woman to give the man? The Hebrew word *ezer* is much more specific, and gives us a clear picture of who God created us, as women, to be.

Ezer, in the Old Testament, almost always refers to God as a helper, rather than a human helper. An *ezer* is God's agent of help on earth to those around her, and as a being bearing the image of God she offers the kind of help that God offers.

God, as our *ezer*, is a rescuer.

> *The God of my ancestors was my helper [ezer]; he rescued me from the sword of Pharaoh. (Ex 18:4, NLT)*

God, as our *ezer*, is a savior for the poor and needy.

> *But as for me, I am poor and needy; please hurry to my aid, O God. You are my helper [ezer] and my savior. (Ps 70:5, NLT)*

God, as our *ezer*, is a strong, empowering protector.

> *God is your shield and helper [ezer] and your glorious sword. Your enemies will cower before you. (Deut 33:29, NIV)*

God our *ezer* is strong, but God also strengthens others. When God is your *ezer*, "your enemies will cower before *you*," not just before God!

According to the Theological Wordbook of the Old Testament, the root of *ezer* "generally indicates military assistance."[2] God, as our *ezer*, is a warrior.

> Hear, Lord, the cry of Judah; bring him to his people. With his own hands he defends his cause. Oh, be his help [ezer] against his foes! (Deut 33:7, NIV)

To be a woman in the image of God is to be an *ezer*—a rescuer, a savior, a warrior, and a strong protector who empowers others to be victorious themselves. Men need us (as we need them[3]), creation needs us, and the enemy of our souls will do everything in his power to keep us from fulfilling the role God designed us to fill. We are an essential part of Christ's church, and as the *ezers* in the church are released to rescue, protect, empower, and fight for God's people, the gates of hell will crumble.[4]

Our Enemy's Dreaded Foe

> And I will put enmity between you and the woman, and between your offspring and hers; he will crush your head, and you will strike his heel. (Gen 3:15, NIV)

My daughters studied ancient Greek and Roman history last year and a lot of ugly things came to light. Girls couldn't go to school? Women weren't citizens? Women couldn't participate in the original Olympics? Women were completely under their husband's control? Women couldn't vote? What!?! Then we watched Mary Poppins and they discovered that these problems were not limited to ancient history. Women *still* couldn't vote by then? One of my girls asked, "Mom, why have there always been so many bad things for women?"

Why indeed? Why, since the beginning of recorded history until today, across cultures that are in other ways wildly divergent, have women so consistently been marginalized, excluded, oppressed, and abused? The answer, I believe, lies in Genesis 3:15, but not in the way you might think.

When God pronounced the curses in Genesis 3, God said to Satan, "I will put enmity between you and the woman." First of all, the fact that God specifically said "you and the woman" rules out the possibility that

2. Harris, *Theological Wordbook of the Old Testament*, 1598.
3. 1 Cor 11:11
4. Matt 16:18

God is talking about a generic enmity between Satan and all of humankind. That enmity does exist, but it's not what God was referring to with the words "you and the woman." If God had said, "you and the man," it would have been possible to interpret it as enmity between Satan and males in particular, or enmity between Satan and humans in general, because masculine is the unmarked (less specific) gender in Hebrew. The feminine, on the other hand, is marked, and "woman" always refers specifically to a female, never to a human in general. God was, therefore, announcing enmity between Satan and *women*, in particular. This certainly explains the relentless oppression of women that has been a common thread through nearly every time, place, and culture.

It may seem like this enmity is part of Eve's punishment, but remember that *God is not talking to Eve at this point.* This is part of the curse on Satan! Also, notice that the phrase "enmity between" indicates enmity *in both directions*. This is not a one-way street of Satan oppressing women. God is telling Satan that part of his punishment for rebelling and leading humanity into rebellion is having women as his enemies. "'Enmity' has the intensity of hostility experienced among nations in warfare (e.g. Ezek 25:15, 35:5) and the level of animosity that results in murder (e.g. Numbers 35:21). The language of the passage indicates a life-and-death struggle between combatants."[5] "Both this context and other passages suggest that long lasting enmity is meant."[6] God is effectively putting Eve and her daughters on the front lines of a world-wide spiritual war that will last until Jesus (who had no human father but was the son of a human woman) crushes Satan forever. Eve and her descendants are appointed to execute part of God's judgment on Satan and his dominion.

The fact that Satan has relentlessly attacked women, in particular, ever since God uttered these words suggests that he finds this a terrifying prospect. Genesis 3:1 indicates that Satan is cunning and clever. A smart adversary strikes his enemy in the place that he perceives as the greatest threat to himself, and in the place that he thinks will most greatly incapacitate his opponent. Satan apparently thinks that women pose a great threat to his plans and/or that incapacitating women would greatly incapacitate human resistance to his plans. Satan probably thinks this because God said it: "The woman is now your enemy."

---

5. Mathews, *Genesis 1–11:26*, 245.
6. Wenham, *Genesis 1–50*, 79.

Whatever battle you're in, whatever oppression you're facing, take courage. Satan fears you greatly. You are our enemy's dreaded foe!

Training for the Battle

Immediately after assigning Eve the job of taking point on the spiritual war that she and her husband had just caused, God told Eve how she was going to be trained for this job.

> *Then God said to the woman, "I will sharpen the pain of your pregnancy, and in pain you will give birth." (Gen 3:16, NLT)*

"I will put enmity between you and the woman" and "I will greatly increase your pain" are the only two phrases in the entire curse oracle where God is the subject. Everything else sounds more like a description of how things will be now, and leaves open the possibility that God is not directly causing this state of affairs, simply informing everyone of the natural consequences of their actions. "You will crawl . . . You will desire to control your husband . . . He will rule over you . . . The ground is cursed . . . You will struggle . . . It will grow thorns . . . You will sweat . . . You will return to dust."[7] But God clearly states that God is the one putting enmity between Satan and the woman, and that God is the one increasing the woman's pain. This is hard to hear, especially since the rest of the curse affects both women and men, but painful childbirth most definitely only affects women. Did God give women an extra punishment?

> *The Lord disciplines those he loves . . . No discipline is enjoyable while it is happening—it's painful! (Heb 12:6, 11, NLT)*

Rather than being a punishment, I believe that pain in childbirth is discipline in the sense of *training* for a difficult task. Think of discipline in the military context. When my brother went through Marine boot camp, he had to hike for three days without sleeping, carrying ninety pounds with only two meals to eat. This did not happen to him because his superior officers were angry with him or didn't like him, or because he'd done anything wrong. It happened because he had agreed to do a very important, very difficult job, and to survive that job he needed training—discipline. There would likely be situations in which he would need to be able to do that kind of thing in order to stay alive, and so he consented to that

---

7. See Gen 3:14-19

painful discipline so that he could serve his fellow Americans to the best of his abilities, with the best chance of survival.

In the same way, God had just commissioned Eve to lead the impending war with Satan and all of his forces. She would need discipline—training. God, in a mysteriously beautiful way, did not provide this training through pointless exercises, but through something that brought life, and deep joy along with the pain. The physical pain of childbirth itself (which is significant!) is only the tip of the iceberg here. The entire process of pregnancy, labor, birth, breastfeeding and motherhood (not to mention periods!) is an all-consuming, demanding, exhausting, painful experience. Nobody can come through it unchanged. Neither does it magically change you for the better. *But it can.*

While my husband was earning his Master of Theology, I had a baby, breastfed the baby for a year, and then had twins. He was the one with the degree at the end (they should really give degrees for having babies!), but I am fully convinced that I experienced just as much spiritual growth as he did during that season, and quite possibly more. It was an intense time of spiritual training for me, and a lot of it was quite painful, in so many ways. But I would not give it up for anything. Now I am enjoying the "peaceful harvest" promised in Hebrews 12:11, a harvest of intimacy with God and strength for the spiritual war at hand that is more than worth every bit of the pain. Not to mention my darling children who bring me so much joy and who are already joining me in the battle.

But this didn't happen to me automatically. Motherhood is a constant, continual sacrifice of your own comforts, desires, and freedom, and once that baby is inside you, you don't really get to choose whether to make that sacrifice or not. It can feel like your comforts, desires, and freedom are simply being ripped out of your hands and you get no say in the matter. But you do get a choice. You get to choose whether you resent the sacrifices you are forced to make in every moment, or whether you embrace the opportunity to lay down your life for another person. It's a constant struggle, but each time you choose the latter, you are choosing to allow God's training to prepare you for battle.

> *When troubles come your way, consider it an opportunity for great joy. For you know that when your faith is tested, your endurance has a chance to grow. So let it grow, for when your endurance is fully developed, you will be perfect and complete, needing nothing.* (Jas 1:2–4, NLT)

Notice that the difficulties don't automatically give you joy. They're painful, and often sad! But they are an *opportunity* for the joyful harvest that discipline brings. These trials don't automatically give you endurance, either. They give endurance *a chance to grow*. You get to choose whether it grows or not. You have to choose to *let it grow*, so that God's training has its intended effect and you can be *perfect and complete, lacking nothing* for the spiritual war we are in.

Of course, I am not suggesting that men are less important or less involved in this spiritual war than women are. Some men are much more involved than some women! But if there is such a thing as "gender roles," it seems that one of the roles God has given women is being the dread foe of Satan. Perhaps this offers some explanation for why there are more women than men involved in missions, and even in the church in general.

I am also *not* suggesting that women should decline pain relief during childbirth (just as there is no reason to avoid labor-saving technology that decreases the pain and difficulty of work). There's nothing wrong with dishwashers or epidurals, and thanks to the wisdom God has given us, childbirth itself does not need to be excruciatingly painful for everyone. Neither am I suggesting that women must physically give birth to children in order to be prepared for their unique role as Satan's dreaded foe. God has a unique training program for each of us, and for some women (and all men) physical childbirth is not a part of their training. Birthing our spiritual children into their own relationships with God can be even more excruciating (and last longer) than the physical pain of birthing our biological children. Paul acknowledged this pain in Galatians 4:19:

> *Oh, my dear children! I feel as if I'm going through labor pains for you again, and they will continue until Christ is fully developed in your lives.* (NLT)

Whatever your training program looks like, embrace it, and choose to let endurance grow so that you will become a mighty adversary in the war against the spiritual forces of evil. We are the daughters of *Shaddai*, the warrior God of the breast, and in God's strength we will scatter the enemy forces and send them shrieking in terror.[8]

---

8. Isa 13:6

Falling Down and Lifting Up

> *The LORD had regard for Abel and his offering, but for Cain and his offering he had no regard. So Cain was very angry, and his face fell. (Gen 4:4–5, ESV)*

> *It was by faith that Abel brought a more acceptable offering to God than Cain did. Abel's offering gave evidence that he was a righteous man, and God showed his approval of his gifts. (Heb 11:4, NLT)*

We don't know exactly why Abel's offering was acceptable and Cain's was not, but Hebrews 11:4 suggests that the root of the problem was in Cain's heart, rather than the offering itself. Abel's heart was lifted up in worship, but Cain's was not. When our heart is not lifted up to God, the only place for it to go is down into despair, often dragging our face with it. When Cain grew angry and his face fell, God could have just ignored him. God certainly didn't owe him anything. But his Mother came looking for him, pursuing relationship with him even while he was still off sulking. God reached out to Cain, and instead of judging, criticizing, or condemning him (which would have been well within God's rights), God addressed his heart directly, asked him about how he felt, and invited him into conversation.

> *Then the LORD said to Cain, "Why are you angry? And why has your countenance fallen? If you do well, will not your countenance be lifted up? And if you do not do well, sin is crouching at the door; and its desire is for you, but you must master it. (Gen 4:6–7, NASB)*

"Let me pick you up," says God. "Sin wants to pounce on you and drag you down permanently. Choose what is good and let me lift you up." Tragically, Cain did not accept this offer.

Few things make me angrier than seeing one of my children hurt by another person. And when that person is one of my other children, the situation feels unbearable. I am flaming mad at the one who did the hurting, and yet that one is still my beloved child. I think God shares this pain. The grief of a bereaved mother echoes in God's cry:

> *"What have you done? Listen! Your brother's blood cries out to me from the ground! (Gen 4:10, NLT)*

And yet, that was not where God started with Cain this time either. Again, God began that conversation with a question, giving him yet another opportunity to come back into conversation and relationship.

> *Where is your brother? (Gen 4:9, NLT)*

I can't help but wonder whether things might have turned out differently for Cain if, even then, he had lifted his heart back up to God. But he rejects this offer of relationship as well. Still, he remains God's beloved child. Even when he is banished from God's presence, he is not completely abandoned. He leaves with his Mother's mark on him. Whatever the heck that means.

A Mother's Sorrow

> *The Lord observed the extent of human wickedness on the earth, and he saw that everything they thought or imagined was consistently and totally evil. So the Lord was sorry he had ever made them and put them on the earth. It broke his heart. (Gen 6:5–6, NLT)*

I've always kind of had the idea that God sent the flood out of anger, and that it was God's judgement on the sins of humanity. But it is noteworthy that anger is never mentioned once in the entire flood narrative. Instead, we are told that God was sorry and grieved. Like the English word "sorry," the Hebrew word used here can have the connotation of either regret, sorrow, or pity.[9] It's the word used in Judges 2:18 to tell us that God "took pity on his people, who were burdened by oppression and suffering" (NLT).

I won't presume to know whether or not God felt regret over having created humanity, but the next phrase makes it clear that God felt both regret and sorrow about humanity's current state. "It broke God's heart" (NLT) and "grieved God to his heart" (ESV). The verb there shares a root with the word that is used in Genesis 3:16–17 to talk about the pain that sin brought into the world: both the painful labor of childbirth and the painful toil of finding food.[10]

When God told Eve that motherhood would now involve painful labor, God entered into that pain too, and God's own mothering in Genesis

---

9. *HALOT* 688.
10. Smith, *Holy Labor*, 17.

6 now involved painful grief and toil. Sin broke God's creation and our relationship with God, but it also broke God's own heart.

As a mother, I don't know of anything more painful than seeing my children suffer. Even after the umbilical cord is cut, there seems to be an invisible cord linking a mother's heart to the hearts of her children, and their pain quite literally becomes her own. One of my babies had to have three painful medical procedures within his first two months of life, and seeing him in pain felt like having my heart torn out, even though I knew all of it was ultimately in his best interest. I pray that I will never experience the pain of seeing my children suffer needlessly, or as a result of their own rebellion, but I imagine that pain would make life feel unbearable. Sin always brings pain, both to those who sin and to those around them, and as our mother God is deeply pained by the pain that our rebellion brings to us.

At the time of the flood, sin was filling God's heart with pity and grief. And so, in a sweeping act of mercy, God ended the pain as only God has the right to do. Yes, the flood did judge humanity. But "mercy triumphs over judgement" (Jas 2:13, ESV) and it was mercy, not judgement—pity, not anger—that motivated God's decision to send the flood. And the flood was not the end of the story for all of those people who broke God's heart.

> *After being made alive, [Jesus] went and made proclamation to the imprisoned spirits—those who were disobedient long ago when God waited patiently in the days of Noah while the ark was being built. (1 Pet 3:18-19, NIV)*

God waited patiently. God waits patiently for me when I get caught in a cycle of sin, snapping under pressure and snapping at my children, then getting angry at myself for snapping and taking that anger out on my children, which makes me hate myself even more and makes it even harder to turn my heart back to Jesus. God is not angry at me, even when I'm angry at myself and everybody else. God is full of pity, not anger, and God is grieving with me and my children for the grief that sin brings to our lives. God is toiling right beside me in the painful labor of mothering, and God is waiting patiently, just like God did in the days of Noah, for me to run into my Mother's arms and let God comfort my sadness, and love the anger out of my heart.

Too High for Our Own Good

> *"Come, let's build a great city for ourselves with a tower that reaches into the sky." But the Lord came down to look at the tower the people were building. "Look!" he said. "The people are united, and they all speak the same language. After this, nothing they set out to do will be impossible for them!"* (Gen 11:4–6, NLT)

The distance across my living room had never seemed so long. Full of terror, I vaulted over a baby gate and sprinted the twenty feet between me and the one-year-old standing on top of the piano. It took a long time for my heart to stop pounding, and the adrenaline rush left me exhausted for the rest of the afternoon. The next day I performed a similar act of athletic heroism to save my child from jumping off the dining room table.

There is a terrifying stage of toddlerhood when a child is physically able to do many very dangerous things, but she hasn't yet developed the wisdom to decide which of those life-threatening activities should be avoided. Small people seem to have an irresistible urge to get *higher*, and they cannot grasp the fact that life at such altitudes threatens their very existence. Every time they find a creative way to reach a new height, mean old boring old mom comes along to stop all the fun.

I'm not sure small people are the only ones with this problem. Humanity as a whole tends to develop the ability to achieve new things before we develop the wisdom or self-control to figure out how (or even if) those achievements are ethical or beneficial. In Genesis 11, we read about a time when humanity (in its toddlerhood) found a creative way to get very, very high. God knew that they did not have the wisdom or maturity they needed to make it spiritually safe for them to live at such a height. United as they were, they were capable of far more than was good for them. So their mother came and took them down. However, instead of unceremoniously depositing them on the ground (like I do to my small people), God forced them down with a gift—the gift of language. That's the kind of mother we have: One who adds beauty and creativity to our lives even while protecting us from ourselves.

There are times when physical limitations can not only protect us, but also create the space we need for spiritual growth. There was a season in my life when I felt formidably strong. Like the people building the tower at Babel, I felt that nothing would be impossible for me if I truly put my mind to it and exerted myself. It was only after I went through burnout and experienced severe limitations on my physical and emotional strength that I had spaces where I was dependent enough on God to grow where I needed to grow spiritually.

Sometimes motherhood provides those same kinds of physical limitations that create space for spiritual growth. It's easy to feel like you're doing well, and like you're a pretty decent human when you're free to go where you want, eat when you want, have long uninterrupted times with God, and finish every cup of coffee you start. You're on top of the tower! But when those things are removed, when you're taken off the tower and limited by your children's needs, that's when you're given space to lean on God, and that's when you grow.

Don't Be Afraid

Do not be afraid, Abram, for I will protect you, and your reward will be great. (Gen 15:1, NLT)

The moment that I held my first tiny new baby in my arms was like no other moment in my life. There was an entirely new person, with her whole life in front of her, and I got to be there with her through so many firsts. Not only that, but she was entirely dependent on me for her very survival. It's a weighty, joy-filled responsibility. As I looked into those tiny blue eyes staring back at me, I had two overwhelming desires: to keep her safe at all costs, and to fill her life with all that is good. Moreover, I wanted her to know that. I wanted her to know that she is safe with me and that I will do everything in my power to give her all that is good so that she will never be afraid of danger or scarcity.

God comes to Abram with the same mother's heart. *Abram, my child! I will keep you safe at all costs, and I have very good things in store for you. You don't need to be afraid!*

What would Abram have been afraid of? He had just defeated an alliance of four kings with his own personal army.[11] Perhaps it was God he was afraid of. Or perhaps his reply gives us a clue about the source of his fear, "O Sovereign Lord, what good are all your blessings when I don't even have a son?" (Gen 15:2, NLT). Three times already God had promised Abram that he would have numerous descendants, and yet he still didn't have a single child. Perhaps he was afraid that God would

---

11. Gen 14:1-16

not actually end up doing what God had promised to do. Without condemnation, with a mother's tender assurance, God initiates this fourth conversation with Abram. Abram didn't ask for this reassurance, but God knew he needed it so God came to him:

Abram! Don't be afraid! I am for you, and I will give you what is good.

Yes, God was going to do world-changing things through Abram and his descendants. But Abram was more than just an instrument in God's eternal plans. He was also his Mother's precious child and God wanted him to know that God was there to keep him safe and give him all that was good. The NIV's translation of Genesis 15:1 suggests that Abram's great reward was God:

Do not be afraid, Abram. I am your shield, your very great reward.

Don't be afraid. God is your shield. God will always give you what is good, and even better than that God will give you what is best—relationship with your FatherMother God.

Believing God

"Look up into the sky and count the stars if you can. That's how many descendants you will have!" And Abram believed the LORD, *and the* LORD *counted him as righteous because of his faith. The* LORD *kept his word and did for Sarah exactly what God had promised. She became pregnant, and she gave birth to a son for Abraham in his old age. (Gen 15:5-6, 21:1-2, NLT)*

It was by faith that even Sarah was able to have a child, though she was barren and was too old. She believed that God would keep his promise. And so a whole nation came from this one man who was as good as dead—a nation with so many people that, like the stars in the sky and the sand on the seashore, there is no way to count them. (Heb 11:11-12, NLT)

Very young children have a limitless faith in their parents' abilities. After a glass shattered into a thousand pieces and scattered across the floor my young daughter assured me, "Daddy will be able to fix it." If I announce that we are out of raisins she asks why I don't just make some real quick. In her mind, making raisins is no more miraculous than making bread, which I do all the time. Daddy can fix anything, and Mommy can make anything.

One summer day when my brother was very young, he longingly remarked that he wished he had a cup of ice-cold Coke. My mom suggested that if he closed his eyes and thought about Coke, maybe even water would taste like Coke. Full of child-like faith, he closed his eyes and took a sip from the cup she held out to him. "It worked!" he shouted, as he opened his eyes and saw that he was holding a cup of Coke. We all had a good laugh then, as my mom passed Coke out to everyone, and we still love the memory now.

If my brother hadn't confidently believed that my mom could do anything, even make water taste like Coke, he wouldn't have taken a sip from that cup, and he wouldn't have had his Coke. God actually can do anything, but if we don't believe that, we won't always take the step of faith that will allow us to experience the full extent of what God wants to do in our lives. With child-like faith, Abraham and Sarah believed that God could give them a child, and even give them countless descendants. God was able to do that whether they believed or not, but Hebrews 11 tells us that it was "through faith" that they received God's promise. Their belief that their MotherFather God could do anything was what allowed them to experience just how much God wanted to do for them.

Maybe that's why Jesus said that "anyone who doesn't receive the Kingdom of God like a child will never enter it" (Luke 18:17). Without a little child's limitless faith in our Mother's abilities, we'll never take that first sip, never step through that tiny Kingdom door, to receive the wonders God has for us there.

Asking Again

Abram replied, "O Sovereign Lord, how can I be sure that I will actually possess it?" (Gen 15:8, NLT)

True confessions—I get a little grumpy when my kids ask me the same thing again, and again, and again. Especially if the questions come less than two minutes apart. This is one of the (many) areas where my own mothering is a very poor reflection of God's. Jesus told us to *keep on asking* (Luke 18:1–4). And a look at Abram's conversations with God reveals that God is okay with saying the same thing again. And again. And again. And even, as we shall see, again.

By the time Abram asks the question recorded in Genesis 15:8, God has already told him not once, but *four times* (in four separate

MOTHERHOOD IN THE OLD TESTAMENT

conversations) that he will have many descendants, and that they will possess all the land around him.

1. *Go to the land that I will show you. I will make you into a great nation. (Gen 12:1-2, NLT)*

2. *And again . . . I will give this land to your descendants. (Gen 12:7, NLT)*

3. *And again . . . I am giving all this land, as far as you can see, to you and your descendants. And I will give you so many descendants that, like the dust of the earth, they cannot be counted! (Gen 13:15-16, NLT)*

The fourth time God comes to Abram, the conversation doesn't immediately start on the topic of descendants. It's Abram who brings that up, somewhat indirectly. My kids are also masters of the indirect questions that aren't technically questions. If I've already told them three times that it's not snack time yet, and they can sense that a fourth question might not go over so well, they wander by and make a general comment, to nobody in particular, "Wow, my stomach is grumbling. That banana bread sure smells delicious!" Abram's comment in Genesis 15:2 is just as thinly veiled, "O Sovereign Lord, what good are all your blessings when I don't even have a son?" God doesn't get annoyed like I would. No, God takes him stargazing and kindly makes the promise a fourth time.

> *Count the stars if you can. That's how many descendants you will have! And Abram believed the Lord, and the Lord counted him as righteous because of his faith. (Gen 15:5-6, NLT)*

Here's where it gets interesting, though. Even *after* "Abram believed God," he still had big questions. Or rather, he still had the same big question . . . again.

> *O Sovereign Lord, how can I be sure that I will actually possess it? (Gen 15:8, NLT)*

Abram, hero of the Hebrews hall of faith, the one who (according to Paul in Romans 4) kept hoping "even when there was no reason for hope," whose "faith did not weaken," who "never wavered in believing God's promise," and who "was fully convinced that God is able to do whatever he promises"[12]—this Abram wanted to ask the question, and hear God's answer, just one more time.

Really, God? Will you really do that?

Not only that, but a few chapters later, in Genesis 17:17, Abraham actually "laughed to himself in disbelief" (NLT) when God promised him a son again. I try not to disagree with Paul, but this just doesn't sound like unwavering faith to me. In fact, it sounds downright wavery. What's going on here?

It turns out that the author of Hebrews has the answer. "Abraham was confidently looking forward to a city with eternal foundations, a city designed and built by God" (Heb 11:10, NLT). You see, Abraham was playing the long game, which is good because he himself "did not receive what was promised, but saw it all from a distance and welcomed it" (Heb 11:13, NLT). The things we see from a distance can be fuzzy. And so Abraham lived with unwavering faith that he would someday, somehow, arrive in that eternal city, but he had lots of questions about the *how* part. His faith in God's ultimate power and goodness was unwavering, but he freely expressed his questions and his doubts along the way. And that is exactly the kind of relationship our Mother wants with us. Never doubt God's goodness or ability to bring you safely to the real Home your heart longs for. But on your way there, never hesitate to ask your questions and express your doubts—all of them, as many times as you need to. Your Heavenly Mother is much nicer than me, and God won't get grumpy even if you ask the same question again, and again, and again. Yes, and even again.

God Carries Our Pain

> *Abram cut each animal down the middle and laid the halves side by side. After the sun went down and darkness fell, Abram saw a smoking firepot and a flaming torch pass between the halves of the carcasses. So the Lord made a covenant with Abram that day. (Gen 15:10, 17-18, NLT)*

Why did God make the world as God did, knowing that there would be so much pain and grief for so many people? Couldn't an omnipotent God have found a way to avoid such massive suffering for so many people? I

---

12. From Rom 4:18-21 (NLT)

do not have answers to those questions. But there is one thing I know: when God decided to create humanity in spite of all the grief that lay ahead, God did so with the full knowledge that the greatest weight of that grief would fall upon Godself. God does not stand by coldly observing our grief, detached from our suffering. No, God shares our pain and participates in our grief, and this is one of the aspects of God's nature that mothers most brilliantly display.

I've already mentioned that emotional umbilical cord that connects a mother's heart to the hearts of her children—the one that can never truly be cut. God's mother heart is connected to ours in a similar way, and God suffers with us, and often for us, even when our suffering is a direct result of turning our backs on God.

> *Oh, how often they rebelled against [God] in the wilderness and grieved his heart in that dry wasteland. (Ps 78:40, NLT)*

> *But they rebelled against [God] and grieved his Holy Spirit. (Isa 63:10, NLT)*

It helps me to know that God feels my pain, even if it doesn't actually lessen the pain. But the even better news is that God carries some of the pain *instead of me*. Watching your children suffer is far worse than suffering yourself, and most mothers would gladly take their children's pain upon themselves if it were possible. All things are possible for God, and God takes our pain upon Godself in many ways, most significantly through the incarnation of Jesus Christ.

> *He was despised and rejected—a man of sorrows, acquainted with deepest grief. It was our weaknesses he carried; it was our sorrows that weighed him down. He was pierced for our rebellion, crushed for our sins. He was beaten so we could be whole. He was whipped so we could be healed. (Isa 53:3–5, NLT)*

When Abram asked God *again*, "How can I be sure?" after already hearing the promise four times, God does not immediately reply with words. Instead, God walks between the bloody halves of animals that have been cut down the middle. At the time, this was a way to make a binding covenant, to say, "If I break my promise, may I become as these animals." Normally *both* people involved would walk between the carcasses, placing themselves under the obligations of the covenant.[13] Abram, however,

---

13. Hamilton, *The Book of Genesis, Chapters 1–17*, 430.

stayed where he was, and God walked through alone. God's response to Abram's questions was a graphic act of love.

> *Do you still wonder if I will really keep my promise? Watch how far I'm willing to go—even to the point of bloody death. Not only that, but I will go there for both of us. When you fail, as you will, I will take the pain for you, and for all the descendants I'm going to give you.*

This is exactly what God did thousands of years later through the death of Jesus Christ.

> *But when they came to Jesus, they saw that he was already dead. One of the soldiers pierced his side with a spear, and immediately blood and water flowed out. (John 19:33–34, NLT)*

God, our eternal MotherFather, became a human, physically carried our pain for us, and when we broke the covenant, allowed his body to be broken so we could be whole.

Seen by God

> *The angel of the Lord found Hagar beside a spring of water in the wilderness, along the road to Shur. The angel said to her, "Hagar, Sarai's servant, where have you come from, and where are you going?" Thereafter, Hagar used another name to refer to the LORD, who had spoken to her. She said, "You are the God who sees me." She also said, "Have I truly seen the One who sees me?" So that well was named Beer-lahai-roi (which means, "well of the Living One who sees me"). (Genesis 16:7–8, 13–14, NLT)*

As a kid, I was convinced that my mom had magical knowledge superpowers, because she *knew* things that should have been impossible for any human to know. Like the time I very discreetly dropped some unwanted scrambled eggs on the floor during dinner. While sweeping the floor that night, my mom told me that I must never drop my food on the floor again. *How did she know?!* My kids often ask me the same question, "Mom! How did you know?" I smile mysteriously and reply, "Moms just know things. You can't hide anything from your mom!" We'll see how long I can maintain that reputation.

As I grew older, I eventually solved the mystery of my own mom's magical egg knowledge, but I also discovered that she truly did know things that should have been impossible for her to know. Like the time in high school when, out of the blue, she suggested that I consider studying linguistics. I immediately dismissed the idea, probably with a snarky reply. Guess who has a degree in linguistics now? Yep. That would be me. Even now, as an adult, I have a deep respect for my mom's advice because she still *knows* things. It can be a little creepy. She has a way of seeing through appearances to the reality behind them, and her perceptions of people or situations turn out to be accurate with an uncanny regularity.

I realize that not everyone's mom has the gift of discernment, so you may not have had the same experience with your own mother. Or perhaps you've had similar experiences with your father. But this ability to *know* things, to see them as they truly are, is one of the gifts God has given my mom, and it's one of the ways that I have seen the character of our heavenly mother clearly reflected by my own earthly mother. Because even when my mom magically knew all about my worst failings and indiscretions, she still loved me. Just like God, who knows even my most secret thoughts, is not fooled by the way I present myself to the world but sees me as I truly am, and still loves me deeply, constantly, perfectly.

In many ways, Hagar was unseen and unknown by everyone around her. Neither Abram nor Sarai ever used her name in this narrative, she was just "my servant," or "your servant." The baby in her womb was more valuable to them than she was, and she was little more than a tool, a pawn in their plan to become parents. Even within the framework of the biblical narrative, she is disturbingly referred to as just "the slave woman" who "will never share in the inheritance."[14]

But God has no pawns. God has only children, and Hagar, unseen by everyone else, was seen by the Mother who sees and knows each one of us. God looked for Hagar, and found her in the wilderness. When God is the one finding a human, the Hebrew verb "carries a technical meaning going well beyond the connotations of the English verb. The nuance is to find by search, rather than find by stumbling upon one."[15] It's the verb used to describe God finding Israel in Deuteronomy 32:10–11.

> *[God] found them in a desert land, in an empty, howling wasteland. He surrounded them and watched over them . . . like an eagle that rouses her chicks and hovers over her young.* (NLT)

---

14. See Gal 4:21–31, NIV
15. Hamilton, *The Book of Genesis, Chapters 1–17*, 451.

God searched for Hagar, and God's Spirit hovered protectively around her in that empty, howling wasteland. God already knew her name, her story, and everything about her, but still engaged her with a question, inviting her into conversation and relationship. And in that conversation, the unseen servant became the precious daughter. Unlike Abraham and Sarah, God addressed Hagar by name. Hagar was the first woman since Eve to receive a promise directly from God.[16] She is the only person in the entire Bible who has named God,[17] and one of the very few in the Old Testament to have had a direct conversation with God, and perhaps even seen God. And yet even this was not as wonderful to her as being seen by God. She didn't name God, "The God I got to see," but "God who sees me." Hagar was invited into a relationship with the living God that was so unique and deeply personal that she needed a new, personal name for God to describe it. But the name didn't stay between her and God. The author of Genesis knew what Hagar named God, and what Hagar named the well, which means that Hagar told her story to others. Not only was she seen by God, not only did she get to converse with and even name the God who saw her, she also got to teach others to know that God as well. Through Hagar, and God's love for her, even you and I get to know the God who sees us too.

God Knows

O Lord, you . . . know everything about me. You know my thoughts even when I'm far away. You see me. (Ps 139:1–3, NLT)

"Where is Sarah your wife?" the visitors asked. "She's inside the tent," Abraham replied. Then one of them said, "I will return to you about this time next year, and your wife, Sarah, will have a son!" Sarah was listening to this conversation from the tent, and Sarah was long past the age of having children. So she laughed silently to herself. Then the LORD said to Abraham, "Why did Sarah laugh?" Sarah was afraid, so she denied it, saying, "I didn't laugh." But the Lord said, "No, you did laugh." (from Gen 18:9–15, NLT)

Thirteen years have passed since Hagar met *God Who Sees Me*. Her son is now a young man, and Sarah is still childless. Has she told Sarah about

---

16. Mathews, *Genesis 11:27–50:26*, 189.
17. Hamilton, *The Book of Genesis, Chapters 1–17*, 451.

her experience with God? Does Sarah ever wonder whether God sees or knows her?

When three mysterious visitors arrive at Abraham's tent, Sarah is sitting inside. I can see her sitting behind the thin wall of the tent, invisible to those outside (so she thought) but able to hear every word. She knew that they could hear her as well as she could hear them, so of course she didn't laugh out loud. She laughed "silently, to herself." Imagine her shock when God asked her husband, "Why did Sarah laugh?" *How did God know?* Although we are told that the Lord directed the question to Abraham, Sarah must have known that it was truly meant for her, because she answers from inside the tent, "I didn't laugh!" True, in a way, since she didn't actually laugh out loud. But God looks beyond appearances, hears beyond audible sounds, and *knows* what is in Sarah's heart. "No, you did laugh." (I wonder if there was laughter in God's eyes at that moment.)

The conversation ends there. Sarah is not reprimanded for her lack of faith, or for laughing at God, or told that if she was going to laugh about it maybe she didn't deserve to have a son after all. She was *known*, seen behind the tent wall, heard even in her silent laughter, and still loved and blessed.

From the outside, it may appear that Sarah was eavesdropping on a men's conversation, but God had already specifically promised Abraham in a previous conversation that Sarah would give birth to a son (Gen 17:19). I believe the conversation in Genesis 18 was for Sarah—God paid her a visit to give her the promise personally. The experience was a memorable one for her, because a year later she named her son "Laughter," in honor of the God who *knew* what should have been impossible to know, the God who transformed her cynical laughter into laughter full of joy. Moms just know things, and even if your earthly mom didn't have the same superpowers as mine, you definitely can't hide *anything* from your heavenly mother. And why would you want to?! God already knows it all, and loves you anyway.

God Sees Our Pain

So Abraham got up early the next morning, prepared food and a container of water, and strapped them on Hagar's shoulders. Then he sent her away with their son, and she wandered aimlessly in the wilderness of Beersheba. When the water was gone, she put the

> boy in the shade of a bush. Then she went and sat down by herself about a hundred yards away. "I don't want to watch the boy die," she said, as she burst into tears. But God heard the boy crying, and the angel of God called to Hagar from heaven, "Hager, what's wrong? Do not be afraid! God has heard the boy crying as he lies there. Go to him and comfort him, for I will make a great nation from his descendants." Then God opened Hagar's eyes, and she saw a well full of water. She quickly filled her water container and gave the boy a drink. (Gen 21:14–19, NLT)

I didn't watch my sons' circumcisions. Their daddy was with them, but I was in the waiting room watching *The Jungle Book* with my daughters, trying not to think about what was happening behind that door. There are times when the pain of others, especially my children's pain, is more than I can handle. I want to close my eyes, disengage my heart, and turn away.

That's what Hagar did when her son was about to die. *She put the boy in the shade of a bush.* "When used with a human being as its object the verb [put] almost always refers to lowering a dead body into its grave, or the lowering of a person into what will presumably be his grave."[18] From Hagar's perspective, her son's life was over, but his pain was not over yet and she couldn't bear to watch. So *she went and sat down by herself about a hundred yards away.* A hundred yards away she would still have been able to see him, and perhaps even hear him, but she wouldn't have to watch the details of his death. *"I don't want to watch the boy die," she said, as she burst into tears.* Maybe her own crying drowned out the sound of her son's crying,[19] and her tears blurred her vision of the dying boy a hundred yards away.

Hagar thought she was sitting "by herself," but she wasn't. And even when Hagar couldn't bear to watch Ishmael's pain, the eyes of God-Who-Saw-Her were never turned away from her son's pain or her own. Human mothers cannot always bear to look, but our Holy Mother's eyes are never closed, even in our moments of deepest agony. And it's not because our pain doesn't hurt God. As we saw in Genesis 6:6, God has chosen to feel the painful effects of this broken creation along with us, and our pain grieves God deeply. But God's eyes are still "towards us" (Ps 34:15), even when it hurts to look.

---

18. Victor P. Hamilton, *The Book of Genesis, Chapters 18–50*, 83.
19. Mathews, *Genesis 11:27—50:26*, 273.

Neither Hagar nor Ishmael asked God for help. They had given up on life, and they just cried. Just grieved. But God saw their grief, and heard their cries, and came to Hagar with the tender words that mothers use to comfort a crying child: *Hagar, what's wrong? Don't be afraid!* Hagar wasn't there to comfort her son, but her Mother still came to comfort her, and to save her. *Then God opened Hagar's eyes, and she saw a well full of water.* It doesn't say that God opened a well that had not been there previously. It says that God opened Hagar's eyes, and she saw a well that she had not seen before.

> *Jesus replied, "If you only knew the gift God has for you, you would ask me, and I would give you living water. Those who drink the water I give them will never be thirsty again. It becomes a fresh, bubbling spring within them, giving them eternal life. When he said, "living water," he was speaking of the Spirit, who would be given to everyone believing in him. (John 4:10, 14, 7:39, NLT)*

God sees our pain. Like a mother, God feels our pain too, but God never turns away, not for a minute. May our eyes be opened to see our Holy Mother seeing us, to notice our Living Well, the Comforter who lives within us and grieves along with us through every moment of our pain.

Rebekah

> *Rebekah became pregnant with twins. But the two children struggled with each other in her womb. So she went to ask the Lord about it. "Why is this happening to me?" she asked. And the Lord told her, "The sons in your womb will become two nations. . . . And your older son will serve your younger son." (Gen 25:21–23, NLT)*

Based on personal experience, I can tell you that being pregnant with twins is no joke. Halfway through the pregnancy it feels like you already have a full-grown baby in there, and naturally there's twice as much kicking and punching. And they tend to sleep at the same time and then wake up to kick and punch at the same time. Rebekah's babies were apparently champion kickers and punchers, because "the verb used here for the fetal movements is a strong one and means 'to abuse, crush.'"[20]

---

20. Hamilton, *The Book of Genesis, Chapters 18–50*, 176.

The distress of motherhood and a difficult pregnancy—the pain, discomfort, and fear caused by the two fighting boys inside her—drove Rebekah towards God. *She went to ask the Lord about it.* It was the suffering of motherhood that pushed her into a deeper relationship with God, and the Lord honored her by speaking directly to her and giving her (not her husband) a glimpse into God's plans for her sons.

Throughout the Old Testament, this kind of direct access to God was extremely rare, especially for someone who was not a designated prophet or priest. Even Joshua, who had spent hours lingering in God's presence in the Tent of Meeting (Ex 33:11), ultimately had to go through a priest if he wanted to hear from God (Num 27:21). In the days of Samuel, "if people wanted a message from God, they would say, 'Let's go and ask the seer,' for prophets used to be called seers" (1 Sam 9:9, NLT). Ordinary lay people did occasionally have direct conversations with God, but almost all of these were initiated by God. Rebekah is one of the very few people who approached God herself and received an answer directly from God.

It was a great honor for Rebekah to be the one God told about her sons' future. But it was also a sweet personal gift for her to know in advance that she was going to have two babies. In those days without ultrasounds, you found out you were having twins when you pushed out a baby and there was still a baby inside you. It took me quite awhile to wrap my head and heart around the fact that I was going to have two babies on the same day, and I'm grateful that I had the opportunity to do that while they were still inside, before I was trying to figure out how to nurse two babies at the same time. Rebekah received that same gift, from Mother to mother—the chance to process and prepare for what lay ahead of her. I love that one of the few recorded conversations between God and a "regular person" was a conversation with a woman about her difficult pregnancy. May the trials and challenges of motherhood continually push us into conversation with God, into an always deepening relationship with the God who "will not forget the expectant mothers and women in labor" (Jer 31:8, NLT), and who is gentle with mothers and their babies (Is 40:11).

Although Rebekah was one of the very few humans in the Old Testament to initiate a personal conversation with God, that's not what she's usually remembered for. Instead, she tends to be remembered as an eavesdropping schemer who deceived her husband in order to advance the interests of her favorite child (and therefore her own interests). One commentator describes her as a "Machiavellian matriarch manipulating

Jacob to defeat the purpose of her blind and dying husband."[21] Now, I am by no means advocating deceit or parental favoritism, but I do think that Rebekah's actions and motives deserve a closer look, particularly in light of the promise God gave her.

God had told *her*, not her husband, that her older son would serve her younger son. Why did God say this to her, and not to Isaac who was the one responsible for blessing the oldest son? Did she tell Isaac what God had said? Did he believe her? Since we don't have answers to these questions, we can't assume that what happened in Genesis 27 was Rebekah's Plan A. For all we know, she may have tried (unsuccessfully) for years to convince Isaac to give the blessing to Jacob in obedience to God. Since God's words to her ended up in the biblical narrative, we know she shared them with someone at some point. Perhaps what she ended up doing was a last resort. After all, she was the one God had revealed the plan to—did she feel that she had been entrusted with a responsibility to carry it out?

She had been told that "one nation [would] be stronger than the other" (Gen 25:23, NLT), but she was not told which one was which. Esau, the accomplished hunter, probably had a lot more strength than Jacob, who preferred to stay at home, and Rebekah may have felt that God had revealed the future to her so that she could advocate for the younger, weaker son and fulfill the plans God had for him. She was not just advancing the interests of her favorite child (or her own interests), she was actively participating in fulfilling the will of God.

We don't know whether Rebekah ever asked for her husband's support in giving Jacob the blessing, but we do know that she did not have it. In fact, Isaac may have been intentionally working against the plan God had revealed to Rebekah. Word Biblical Commentary points out that "elsewhere in the OT, it is normal for a dying man to summon all his close male relatives and to bless them publicly and in this way to organize the succession (cf. Gen 49; 50:24–25). It is, to say the least, irregular for Isaac to summon merely one of his sons, especially since Jacob and Esau were twins."[22] Was Isaac trying to deceive Rebekah by summoning Esau to receive the blessing alone, without witnesses?

Regardless of the motives involved in this story, the result was that Jacob had to leave home. Many commentators interpret this as the

---

21. Wenham, *Genesis 16–50*, 208.
22. Wenham, *Genesis 16–50*, 205.

natural consequence that Rebekah received for her wicked actions. However, interestingly, it was Rebekah herself who initiated and engineered Jacob's departure (Gen 27:42—28:5). The plan she devised not only saved Jacob's life, it also led him directly to the women who would become the mothers of the nation of Israel. Once again, Rebekah was an active agent in fulfilling the plans of God.

Rebekah takes a lot of initiative in the life of her family. She approaches God with direct questions. She carries out a plan to bring about the future God revealed to her. She tells her husband to send Jacob away and he listens to her. And God uses her actions, and her initiative, to accomplish God's own plan—the birth of the nation of Israel through Rebekah's younger son.

We may condemn Rebekah for the way she carried out God's plans, but Scripture never does. Esau is condemned in both Genesis 25:34 and Hebrews 12:16-17, but Rebekah is never judged in either the Old or New Testament for anything that she did or said. I wonder, if Rebekah were here telling the story from her perspective, how would it go? Was she a Machiavellian manipulator, or was she a mother who went to ingenious lengths to lead her family towards God's plan for them?

Lifted in Worship

I didn't always lift my hands to worship God. There was a time when I thought it was a bit silly or over dramatic (at best) and pretentious (at worst). I believed that my heart and soul could worship just as well regardless of what my body was doing. And there is some truth to that—our bodies don't have to be in a certain position in order for our hearts to genuinely worship God. But on the day that, as my heart was genuinely engaged in worship, I finally dared to lift my hands a few inches above their customary place at my sides, I discovered something that surprised me. I discovered that my body and soul are not two discrete entities, operating independently of each other. I discovered that they are deeply connected, and that the posture of my body can actually influence the posture of my soul.

I wonder if Moses made the same discovery on the day the Israelites were attacked by Amalekite warriors, and Moses lifted his hands in prayer for God to rescue them.

> *As long as Moses held up the staff in his hand, the Israelites had the advantage. But whenever he dropped his hand, the Amalekites gained the advantage. Moses' arms soon became so tired he could no longer hold them up. So Aaron and Hur found a stone for him to sit on. Then they stood on each side of Moses, holding up his hands. So his hands held steady until sunset. (Ex 17:11–12, NLT)*

Why should it matter whether Moses' hands were raised or not? Couldn't he ask for God's help just as well with his hands down? I wonder if the real difficulty was that his heart grew weary and discouraged, and the physical movement of lifting his hands helped to lift his heart as well. Just like smiling when you're sad can cheer you up, and speaking true words that you don't feel can help you feel them, putting our bodies in a posture of worship can help to bring our hearts into a posture of worship. Or could the physical and spiritual worlds be so deeply tied together that a physical action had a tangible effect within the spiritual realm? But it also works the other way round. When our hearts are deeply engaged in worship, there are times when words are not enough to express it, and it is expressed by our bodies as well. If we do not allow our bodies to express what is in our hearts, the growth of our hearts in worship will be limited.

As I began to experience the way my body and soul influence each other, I shared another discovery with Moses—many times my body is simply not strong enough to release what is in my soul! As I began to give myself the freedom to lift my hands in worship, I often longed to leave them up longer but my muscles simply couldn't do it. I had never realized that worship could require so much physical strength.

There are times when I have the opportunity to lift both hands and focus my heart on loving and being loved by our MotherFather God. But most of the time my body is engaged in a different kind of worship, one that also requires both hands, and more physical strength than I sometimes feel that I have. As I knead bread, carry milk home from the store, haul baskets of muddy laundry up the stairs, and pick up two crying toddlers who have both woken up grumpy and want to be held at the same time, my arms sometimes grow weary. But in these moments my body is strengthened by my soul when I remember that this, too, is worship. Sometimes my love for God can flow out through songs and lifted hands. Usually it flows out through using my hands to care for a few of God's tiny beloved children. May God give us all the strength to worship well.

The Paradise or the Presence?

> *Then the Lord said to Moses, "Go up to the land flowing with milk and honey, but I will not go with you, because you are a stiff-necked people." Then Moses said, "If your Presence does not go with us, do not send us up from here." (Ex 33:1, 3, 15, NIV)*

We just put a fence around our backyard, and I have been very excited about the prospect of letting my toddler twins play there by themselves. They love to be outside, but it's hard for me to find the time to sit out there for all of the hours that they would love to be playing there.

The day after the fence was finished, I took them out and got them all set up. They had drinks, they had bananas, they had old plastic bottles to squirt water out of, and our huge yard is a paradise for small boys, full of dirt to dig in and forests of tall flowers to explore. As always, they were overjoyed to go outside, but as soon as I went back in the house they just stood at the gate and cried! For half an hour I did dishes and watched them out the kitchen window as they ignored their paradise and mourned the absence of my presence.

Moses felt the same way. Right after the golden calf debacle, Moses was told that God would still give the Israelites the land God had promised them. They would still have their paradise. But they would have it without God's Presence. Moses declined this offer, realizing that there could be no paradise apart from God's Presence. He would rather live the rest of his life camped out in God's Presence than settled in a luxurious home without God's Presence.

> *A single day in Your courts is better than a thousand anywhere else! I would rather be a gatekeeper in the house of my God than live the good life in the homes of the wicked. (Ps 84:10, NLT)*

Whatever "paradise" or "the good life" looks like to you right now, remember that it is meaningless without God's Presence. But if those sound like empty words, if you don't feel a longing for God's Presence, or if you feel that you would quite happily accept paradise with or without God's Presence, don't take this as condemnation, and don't try to conjure up feelings of longing for God. Instead of guilt-tripping yourself or trying to manipulate your emotions, consider this.

If you're feeling content in your paradise, if you're just enjoying playing in the backyard and you don't really care if God is there or not, remember that "whatever is good and perfect is a gift coming down to us from God" (Jas 1:17, NLT). Whether we realize it or not, any good thing that delights us is only delightful because it reminds us in some way of God's Presence. Enjoying your paradise is like enjoying the smell of chocolate, and God's presence is like eating the chocolate. There's nothing wrong with loving that smell, but think about where the smell comes from. Don't try to stop enjoying the smell of chocolate—take a deep whiff and then ask God to give you a bite! Instead of trying to convince yourself to want your paradise less so you can want God more, think about how much you love your paradise and *believe that God is even better!* But you don't have to take my word for it, and neither do you have to try to conjure up feelings of longing for God. Ask God to give you a taste of God's Presence (Matt 7:7), then taste and see that the Presence of God is paradise.

Compassionate Womb-Love

> *Yahweh! The* LORD*! The God of compassion and mercy! I am slow to anger and filled with unfailing love and faithfulness. (Ex 34:6, NLT)*

During one of my pregnancies, my husband started watching the TV show *Doc Martin*. It was a fun show, but because it was about a doctor, somebody got hurt in every episode, and I found that I just couldn't handle it. While I was pregnant, I felt the pain of people around me (even fake people in movies) so deeply that sometimes it was almost debilitating.

Having a child in my womb gave me a depth of compassion that I had never experienced before, and that compassion was deepest for the baby in my womb. So it didn't surprise me when I learned that the Hebrew words for "compassion" and "womb" come from the same root! "This root refers to deep love,"[23] it is a "deep inner feeling based on some 'natural' bond"[24] and "the strong tie God has with those whom he has called as his children."[25] A compassionate God "genuinely cares about humans and holds toward them a tender attitude of concern and mercy."[26] Compassion "describes the depth of feeling a mother's love can

---

23. Harris, *Theological Wordbook of the Old Testament*, 841.
24. Harris, *Theological Wordbook of the Old Testament*, 842.
25. Harris, *Theological Wordbook of the Old Testament*, 842.
26. Stuart, *Exodus*, 715.

reach."[27] In the Hebrew language, compassion is "womb-love"[28]—the kind of love that a mother naturally feels for her children.

This is the kind of love that God says God has for us! In fact, compassion is one of God's most prominent and defining characteristics. Exodus 34:6 is one of the first times God's character is described in detail,[29] and compassion is the very first adjective used in that self-description. God defines Godself as "the God of compassion"—the God of motherly womb-love.

Moreover, God's compassion is a consistent characteristic. We don't have to wonder whether or not God is feeling compassionate today. No matter how many times we've failed or fallen, whenever God's children cry out to God, God always responds with compassion, again and again.

> Therefore you delivered them into the hands of their oppressors who oppressed them, but when they cried to you in the time of their distress, you heard from heaven, and *according to your great compassion* you gave them deliverers. But as soon as they had rest, they did evil again before you; therefore you abandoned them to the hand of their enemies. When they cried again to you, you heard from heaven, and many times you rescued them *according to your compassion*. (Neh 9:27–28, NASB)

"This is an amazing characteristic of God to depend on, that we can know what his disposition is when we cry out to him."[30] Wherever you are, no matter how many times you've turned away, God's womb-love for you will never end. "The God of compassion and mercy" hurts when you hurt, and is eager to take you back into God's arms. When you cry out to your FatherMother God, you will *always* be received with compassion.

Did I Conceive All These People?

And the people of Israel also began to complain, "Oh, for some meat!" Moses heard all the families standing in the doorways of their tents whining, and the Lord *became extremely angry. Moses was also very aggravated. And Moses said to the* Lord, *"Why are you treating me, your servant, so harshly? Have mercy on me!*

---

27. Harris, *Theological Wordbook of the Old Testament*, 843.
28. Mackie and Collins, "The Womb of God?" August 31, 2020.
29. Mackie and Collins, "The Womb of God?" August 31, 2020.
30. Mackie and Collins, "The Womb of God?" August 31, 2020.

> *What did I do to deserve the burden of all these people? Did I give birth to them? Did I bring them into the world? Why did you tell me to carry them in my arms like a mother carries a nursing baby? (Num 11:4, 10–12, NLT)*

There are times (probably more than I'd like to admit) when my children's bad behavior upsets me mostly because it inconveniences me. If I'm honest, my primary motivation for correcting them at these times is not a desire for their growth into happy and mature people; it's just a desire for them to stop annoying me.

This is not the kind of mother I want to be, but I am not the only person to fall into this selfish trap. Moses was "very aggravated" by the Israelites' complaints, but when he brought his own complaint to God about the situation, his focus was not on the Israelites' ingratitude or lack of faith. No, he was complaining mostly because he was personally tired of dealing with them.

What did I do to deserve the burden of all these people? Moses, who had been faithfully leading the Israelites since they left Egypt, was tired of his job. But the interesting thing is the way he describes his job. He does not describe himself as a leader, a teacher, a judge, or even a father—he compares his role to that of a mother!

> *Did I conceive all these people? Did I give them birth? (NIV) Why did you tell me to carry them in my arms like a mother carries a nursing baby? (Deut 11:12, NLT)*

Moses is implying that he is being asked to care for these people as if he were the one who conceived them, gave birth to them, and nursed them. His rhetorical questions suggest that Somebody did give birth to these people, but it wasn't him. Since he was not the one who conceived, birthed or nursed these people, he felt that feeding them now should not be his responsibility.

And he was right. God, as the One who did conceive, birth and nurse them (Deut 32:13, 18) was the One who would feed them now.

> *Now the Lord sent a wind that brought quail from the sea and let them fall all around the camp. For miles in every direction there were quail flying about three feet above the ground. So the people went out and caught quail all that day and throughout the night and all the next day, too. No one gathered less than fifty bushels! (Num 11:31–32, NLT)*

Everlasting Arms

> *There is none like God, who rides the heavens to your help, and through the skies in his majesty. The eternal God is a dwelling place, and underneath are the everlasting arms; and he drove out the enemy from before you. So Israel dwells in security, the fountain of Jacob secluded, in a land of grain and new wine, his heavens also drop down dew. Blessed you are, O Israel! Who is like you, a people saved by the Lord, who is the shield of your help and the sword of your majesty! God is your shield and helper and your triumphant sword! So your enemies will cringe before you, and you will tread upon their high places. (Deut 33:26–29, NASB)*

These are Moses' last recorded words, his final blessing on God's children before God took him home to the true promised land. Except for Jesus, "there has never been another prophet in Israel like Moses, whom the Lord knew face to face" (Deut 34:10, NLT). Moses knew God in a way that perhaps no other mere human ever has, and Moses' final summary of God's character is rich with motherly imagery and allusions. Moses knew, perhaps better than anyone else, that there is no God like the God of Israel.

God rides the heavens to your help, and through the skies in majesty. In Psalm 68, where God is referred to as *Shaddai*, "God of the breast,"[31] the same imagery is used. "Sing to the one who rides across the ancient heavens, his mighty voice thundering from the sky" (Ps 68:33, NLT).

The eternal God is your refuge (NIV), your dwelling place, your home. This word describes a place of utter safety and security, like the hidden den where a mother lion guards her cubs,[32] like a womb. It is the word used in Psalm 90:1, *"Lord through all the generations you have been our home!"* (NLT) and in Psalm 91:9 where God is described as our refuge and our home.

God's everlasting arms are under you. Like a mother carrying her tiny baby, like a mother eagle catching her chick on her wings, God carried Israel through the desert, letting them ride through the wilderness on the everlasting arms of God (Deut 32:11–13). Those everlasting arms are still under us, especially when we are tired from carrying babies of our own (Isa 40:11).

---

31. Ps 68:14
32. Nah 2:12

God drove out the enemy from before you, and *"The Almighty [Shaddai] scattered the enemy kings like a blowing snowstorm on Mount Zalmon" (Ps 68:14, NLT).* Like a mother guarding her children with her own life, *Shaddai* still scatters the spiritual enemies that rage against us.

So Israel will live in safety, the fountain of Jacob secluded. Apart from the womb, there is no safer, more secure place for a tiny baby than in her mother's everlasting arms, secluded, alone with her fountain of milk.

In a land of grain and new wine, while the heavens drop down dew. Deuteronomy 32:13–14 suggests that the grain and new wine come from God's metaphoric breasts, and the imagery of dripping dew is once again associated with *Shaddai* in Psalm 68:8–9. In Genesis 49:25, the heavens above and the deeps beneath are associated with breasts and the womb, respectively, in a parallel construction:

> The Almighty [*Shaddai*] blesses you with the Blessings of heaven above, blessings of the deep that lies beneath,
>
> Blessings of the breasts and of the womb. (NASB)

God has such abundance for her children that the heavens continually drip dew, like a breast so full that milk drips out even when the baby isn't actively sucking.

God is your shield and helper and your glorious sword! (NIV) God is your helper, your *ezer*. This is the title God gave to Eve when she was created; it is who women are designed to be. We are patterned after our Mother, who is our shield and helper and our triumphant sword!

God Is with You

> *Do not be afraid or discouraged. For the Lord your God is with you wherever you go. (Josh 1:9, NLT)*
>
> *Don't be afraid or discouraged, for the Lord God, my God, is with you. He will not fail you or forsake you. (1 Chr 28:20, NLT)*
>
> *Don't be afraid, for I am with you. (Isa 41:10, NLT)*

The day I came home from the hospital with my baby twins was a rough one. I got in bed as soon as I could but (tragically) wasn't able to spend much time there. When morning came and I "got up," I shuffled into the bathroom, made the mistake of looking into the mirror, and could hardly believe how terrible I looked. Green. Haggard. Old. Unbelievably awful.

I shuffled out into the living room where my mother-in-law exclaimed, "Oh, Juliann! You're looking so much better today! You were looking really awful last night." Wow.

My own mother was there too, but after breakfast she told me that she and my dad were going to go back home that day, and she and my sister would come back in a couple weeks after my parents-in-law left, to spread out the help. This had been the plan all along, the arrangement we had all agreed would be best, but when I heard my mom say, "I'm leaving today," despair washed over me. Somehow, as long as she was there, it seemed like things just might be okay. She couldn't really change anything, or remove any of my actual difficulties. She couldn't nurse the twins for me, take away the pain from my C-section, or make the older kids less emotionally needy. My mother-in-law (who I adore) would be there to do all of the practical things that would actually be helpful. It wasn't really about having her do anything for me. Just the presence of my own mommy in the house made me feel like everything would be okay.

We can take the same comfort in the presence of our heavenly Mommy. God tells us again and again that we don't need to be afraid or discouraged because *God is with us* and God will never drive away after breakfast. God doesn't promise to take away any of our difficulties, but God does promise us what we need most—just God's presence in the house.

> *A river brings joy to the city of our God, the sacred home of the Most High. God dwells in that city; it cannot be destroyed. (Ps 46:4–5, NLT)*

You are the sacred home of your Most High Mother. God dwells in you; your soul cannot be destroyed. So do not be afraid, because *God is with you!*

God's Chasing Love

> *Surely your goodness and unfailing love will pursue me all the days of my life, and I will live in the house of the Lord forever. (Ps 23:6, NLT)*

> *I can never escape from your Spirit! I can never get away from your presence! If I go up to heaven, you are there; if I go down to the grave, you are there. If I ride the wings of the morning, if I*

> *dwell by the farthest oceans, even there your hand will guide me, and your strength will support me. I could ask the darkness to hide me and the light around me to become night—but even in darkness I cannot hide from you. To you the night shines as bright as day. (Ps 139:7–12, NLT)*

"Alright, it's naptime! Everyone run to your bed!" The words are hardly out of my mouth before both small boys start running, but not to their beds. No, they're running away from me. The same thing happens when I bring out the bottle of sunscreen, or a pair of socks, or a dry shirt. Putting sunscreen on a moving target is . . . interesting. If I sat on the couch and waited for them to come to me they would live in a perpetual state of wet, sunburned exhaustion. So I pursue them with sunscreen and comfortable clothes, with good things and unfailing love.

Sometimes running is not enough and they try to spice things up by hiding—behind a curtain, behind the couch, or in the darkest depths of their closet. But I know all their tricks, all their secrets, all their best hiding places, and I always catch them in the end.

I'm so grateful that God doesn't sit passively on the couch, waiting for me to figure out what it is that I need and come ask for it. The God who knows my heart sees me even in my darkest hiding places. Before I'm even aware that I have a need God finds me and pursues me—not just around the living room but through death and back—to lavish motherly goodness and unfailing love on me.[33]

Both Mother and Father

> *Even if my father and mother abandon me, the Lord will hold me close. (Ps 27:10, NLT)*

For many of us, the idea of being abandoned by both our father and our mother seems like a ludicrous impossibility. For others, it's all too real. Some people may not have been physically abandoned, but felt emotionally abandoned by one or both of their parents. Whatever the state of your past or present relationship with your earthly parents, isn't it lovely to know that God is eager to be *both a father and a mother* to you now!

---

33. Ellie Holcomb describes this beautifully in her song, "Can't Outrun Your Love."

The Psalmist writes that if his father abandoned him, God would be there to fill that role, and if his mother abandoned him, God would be there to fill that role too! The fact that he specifically mentions each parent suggests that he relates to God as both a father and a mother. If God were only a father to him, if God were not his mother as well, there would be no reason for him to specifically mention his mother in the Psalm. Father God could fill the role of an absent father, but not an absent mother. But the Psalmist expresses his deep confidence that his Father-Mother God will always hold him close, and always be to him the best of what a father *and a mother* are meant to be!

In the very next verse, he asks God to teach him and lead him, things that Proverbs describes both fathers and mothers doing.[34]

> *Teach me how to live, O Lord. Lead me along the right path.* (Ps 27:11, NLT)

> *My son, keep your father's commandment, and forsake not your mother's teaching. When you walk, they will lead you.* (Prov 6:20, 22, ESV)

Psalm 27 is a psalm of David, and most of Proverbs was likely written by David's son Solomon. Solomon's mother was valued and respected by his father (1 Kgs 1:11–31), and I wonder if Solomon's parents taught him to love and value both his mother and his father as representatives of the teaching and guidance of the God who was and is both Father and Mother to us all.

God's Ears Are Toward You

> *The eyes of the* Lord *watch over those who do right; his ears are open to their cries for help. The* Lord *hears his people when they call to him for help. He rescues them from all their troubles.* (Ps 34:15, 17, NLT)

As a young child, I had a vague notion that my mother never slept, because she always seemed to be awake when I needed her at night. I would creep out of bed and silently glide down the hall, careful not to wake up any of my younger siblings. Without fail, as soon as I set foot in my

---

34. Jacobson and Tanner, "Book One of the Psalter," 270.

parents' room my mom would be awake, sitting up and/or asking what I needed. It seemed magical.

When I became a mother, I found that I had the same magic, at least while my children were babies. (These days my husband is halfway up the stairs to help a crying child before I even wake up!) I've never been a particularly light sleeper, but when my baby made even the tiniest squawk I would find myself instantly on my feet and at her side. Sometimes I think I got to her bed before I even woke up. Any other sound, even a louder sound, would not have woken me up so quickly, but my ears were open to my baby's cries, and when one of my twins cried out I could even tell which one was crying.

> *The eyes of the Lord are toward the righteous and his ears toward their cry. (Ps 34:15, ESV)*

God's ears are toward your cry, specially attuned to hear even the faintest cry for help from a beloved child. Your cry is unique to God, different from anyone else's, and God is ready to be at your side in an instant, to "rescue you from all your troubles." In fact, God has never left your side, but when you call out to God for help you will find that the recognition of God's presence becomes a refuge from your troubles.

Sometimes, at the end of a particularly grueling day that put the spotlight on my worst failings, it's easy to read a verse like Psalm 34:15 and think, "Well, that must be nice for the righteous. Too bad I'm not one of them." But the righteous, in Psalm 34, are not those who keep all the rules but those who recognize their deep need for God,[35] a need that is ultimately met in Jesus. The righteous, in this Psalm:

- *Boast only in the Lord (v2)*
- *Are helpless (v2)*
- *Seek the Lord (v4)*
- *Look to God for help (v5)*
- *Are desperate for God (v6)*
- *Take refuge in God (v8)*
- *Trust in the Lord (v10)*
- *Call out to God (v17)*
- *Are crushed or brokenhearted (v18)*

35. Jacobson and Tanner, "Book One of the Psalter," 328.

God's ears are toward the righteous, not those (non-existent people) who do everything right, but those who realize how much they need their Mother, and cry out for God. God will never sleep through your cries for help.

Falling Up

The LORD directs the steps of the godly. He delights in every detail of their lives. Though they stumble, they will never fall, for the LORD holds them by the hand. (Ps 37:23-24, NLT)

Tiny people fall down. A lot. One moment they're contentedly waddling along, and half a second later they're face down on the ground, and nobody really knows how it happened. But it happens frequently . . . unless someone is holding their hand. The tricky thing is that toddlers don't always like to have their hand held. They want to feel free or "big" or like they can "do it self." They tend to be less resistant if I hold out my index finger and let the tiny fingers encircle it, and then I can securely grasp the whole small hand with the rest of mine. That way the toddler thinks that she's the one holding my hand, but when she stumbles every ten seconds, it is my secure grasp that keeps her from falling headlong. Sometimes, after a particularly impressive stumble, she is literally suspended in the air for a bit, still moving in the right direction, until she gets her feet back on the ground. She can't fall down, she can only fall up, because I am holding her hand. I am directing her steps, constantly aware of what is under her feet, steering her towards whichever bit of the path will be best for her to walk on at that moment, ensuring that she is safe no matter what crazy things her tiny feet decide to do on their own.

We feel like we need to hold on to God, and that's not a bad thing to aim for. But even when you lose your grip on God's index finger: accidentally, intentionally, or because you're just plain tired, God will not let go of your hand. No matter how many times you stumble, God will make sure that you fall up, not down, and keep you moving in the right direction. Your Mother is directing your steps, delighting in every detail of your life, including details you know nothing about.

Very young children are unaware of most of the details of their lives. Food appears, and they eat it. Most of the time they feel comfortable, dry, and well. They have no idea that I pour vast amounts of time and mental energy into orchestrating the details that make that state of existence possible for them. I notice when their clothes are too small, their nails are too long, their sheets smell too stinky, their scalp is too dirty, their nose is too snotty, their water cup is too grimy, their diaper is too soggy, or their little bowl is too empty. God not only notices the intricate details of your life, but *delights* in attending to needs you may not even be aware of.

A Song in the Night

> *My soul thirsts for God, for the living God. When can I go and meet with God? My tears have been my food day and night, while people say to me all day long, "Where is your God?" By day the* Lord *directs his love, at night his song is with me. Why, my soul, are you downcast? Why so disturbed within me? Put your hope in God, for I will yet praise him. (Ps 42:2–3, 8, 11, NIV)*

My first night as a mother I spent alone in the hospital with my baby. Visitors (including my husband) had to leave at 9pm. I'd just had a C-section, and could not get up to pick up my baby without help, but we were not in our own country and the nurses on duty had said that they disliked Americans, so I was hesitant to call for them. My little daughter was in a cot beside my bed, and thankfully she slept a lot that night. Whenever she fussed, I sang to her, and many times the sound of my voice in the darkness was enough to soothe her back to sleep. Even if I didn't pick her up or feed her every time she woke up, my song in the night convinced her that I was there, and therefore all would be well.

Sometimes in the darkness, we wonder with the Psalmist where God is. We thirst for God's comfort, and have only our own tears to drink. The enemy of our soul whispers in the night, "Where is this God of yours?" and we wish we knew the answer. But God is always there, even when God doesn't change our circumstances. God sings to us through the night, even when it is too dark to see God's face. If you are in the middle of a dark and silent spiritual night, listen to "Night Song" by Ellie Holcomb and receive it as a lullaby from your heavenly Mother, a song in the middle of the night.

Be Still

> *So we will not fear when earthquakes come and the mountains crumble into the sea. Let the oceans roar and foam. Let the mountains tremble as the waters surge! The nations are in chaos, and their kingdoms crumble! Be still, and know that I am God! (Ps 46:2–3, 6, 10, NLT)*

Imagine yourself sitting in a peaceful meadow, silent except for the breeze rustling through the wildflowers, gazing at the fluffy white clouds in a brilliant blue sky. It would feel easy to be still and know God's presence in that setting. But that is not the context of Psalm 46.

No, the Psalmist asks you to imagine yourself in the middle of an earthquake so violent that entire mountains crumble into the ocean, causing a tsunami so powerful that it shakes the remaining mountains. Not only that, but there is global political and (and therefore economic) instability. It is in the middle of that chaotic upheaval that we are told to "be still, and know that I am God."

Perhaps the Psalmist uses such extreme language to let us know that there are no exceptions, no situations so drastic that we cannot experience the presence of God in the middle of it. I may feel like my world is falling apart, but God says that even if the entire world literally did fall apart, I could still be still and know that God is God.

Be still. The Hebrew root can mean "to grow slack, release, let go, stop."[36] The NASB says, "Cease striving."[37]

Some days I am caught up in a torrent of shaking, swirling emotions. God whispers, "Be still," and I want to shout back, "No! Make the storm stop first, and then I'll be still!" I feel that I cannot possibly be still until the mountains stop shaking and the oceans stop roaring and foaming. I am like my toddler—screaming, kicking, and flailing on the ground—so upset that she will not even let me take her in my arms to comfort her. Like that toddler, I tell God to fix everything first, and then I'll be still. "Take the sadness away, and then I'll know that you're God."

But that's not how it works. When I finally grow slack, release, let go, stop striving, and let God hold me with my sadness, in the middle of the storm, then I begin to truly know the God Who Is. Then I discover

---

36. *HALOT* 1277.

37. Ps 46:10

that the stillness is not dependent on the circumstances around me, but is rooted in the presence of God living within me.

> *There is a river whose streams make glad the city of God. God is in the midst of her, she will not be moved. (Ps 46:4–5, NASB)*

It is not up to me to create stillness in the middle of the storm. Whether I realize it or not, I "will not be moved" because God dwells in me. My job is simply to stop shouting and kicking, open my eyes, and notice that I am in my Mother's arms.

Tears in a Bottle

> *You have kept count of my tossings; put my tears in your bottle. Are they not in your book? (Ps 56:8, ESV)*

I remember my first baby's first tear. She had to get a hip ultrasound when she was six months old, and she was not at all pleased about the things being done to her tiny legs. When I was finally allowed to pick her up, a single tear rolled off her angry cheek and landed on the paper covering the exam table. That small, insignificant wet spot sparked a completely unexpected surge of emotion in me, and if I had been able to save it in a bottle, I am sure that I would have. All of the trauma she had just been through was represented there, packed into one tiny tear, and it felt careless and even negligent to just leave it behind as if it had no meaning.

Well, I did leave it there (of course). But your Heavenly Mother has never left behind a single one of your tears. Each tear, along with all the grief, pain, trauma, sadness, and sleepless tossing that it represents, has been seen, noticed, and lovingly collected by the God who cries when you cry. I wonder if God's own tears are kept in the same bottle?

The "bottle" that God puts these tears in is the kind of leather pouch that was used to store liquids like milk or wine.[38] It is a place to save something that will be used later. God saves your tears, not only as a way to notice and enter into your grief and pain, but also because every tear has a purpose. Not a single one is wasted; God saves them all to use later.

What could tears possibly be used for? Perhaps Psalm 84:5–6 offers a clue.

---

38. Tate, *Psalms 51–100*, 70.

> *What joy for those whose strength comes from the Lord. When they walk through the Valley of Weeping, it will become a place of refreshing springs. (NLT)*

The God who can turn water into wine can also turn your salty, bitter tears into a refreshing spring of life-giving water. Your tears are not without meaning or purpose. God is saving each one and they will one day be transformed into a source of life, both for you and for those around you.

Under God's Wings

> *[God] will cover you with his feathers, and under his wings you will find refuge; his faithfulness will be your shield and rampart. (Ps 91:4, NIV)*

Father birds care for their young alongside the mother, often bringing food for the babies to eat, but it is typically the mother bird who guards the nest, covering the eggs or the chicks with the warmth of her body and her wings. To metaphorically find refuge under God's wings and be covered by God's feathers is therefore a very motherly image. In fact, the Hebrew word for feathers has two forms—one masculine and one feminine—and it is the feminine form that is used in this Psalm.

God will cover you with his feathers. That word, "cover," means "to shut off, make inaccessible,"[39] and the word translated as "rampart" comes from a root that can mean "be encircled, be surrounded."[40] When you take refuge under God's wings, when your soul is covered by God's feathers, you are completely encircled by God's love, and you are inaccessible. When lies, fears, doubts, anxieties, or hurtful words fly at you like arrows, your soul can take refuge under the wings of your Heavenly Mother, and let God be your covering.

I don't think any of us like to feel vulnerable. To feel raw, exposed, or easily injured is not a comfortable place. But we all have vulnerable places in our hearts—tender spots that can be easily wounded by others, even unintentionally. When I am feeling particularly vulnerable, my natural reaction is to cover myself in some way—to build protective shells around my tender spots. Sometimes this looks like feigned confidence, sometimes it looks like introversion, sometimes it looks like anger, and

---

39. *HALOT* 754.
40. Clines, ed., *The Dictionary of Classical Hebrew*, 144.

sometimes it just means immersing myself in mindless distraction. But these shells, like egg shells, only seem strong at first glance. They may effectively isolate me from those around me, but their actual protection is minimal.

But when I break out of these shells and stand before God as I truly am, all vulnerabilities included, I find myself in an infinitely safer place. When I stop trying to cover myself and let God cover me with her feathers and shelter me with her wings, I find that I am no longer isolated from those around me, and yet I am much less easily injured.

In many ways, being immersed in water is one of the safest places on earth (assuming that our need for oxygen is taken care of). It absorbs a tremendous amount of shock, quenches enormous flames, and drowns out loud accusations. There is no safer place than the womb of God, where we are effectively covered, immersed in the living water of God's Spirit who fills us and surrounds us. It is God who truly covers us, within her womb and *under her wings*. Listen to Lauren Daigle's song, "Under Your Wings" and let this truth soak into your soul.

Hidden in God's Shadow

The LORD watches over you! The LORD stands beside you as your protective shade. (Ps 121:5, NLT)

We live in a small community and spend a lot of time walking. To school, home from school, to the store, to church, to a friend's house. Most of the time, my three-year-old daughter is walking along at my side, and one of her favorite walking games is to walk in my shadow. She steps in and out of the dark moving shape of me on the ground, and likes to see how long she can stay there in my shade.

I'm not usually an active participant in these shadow games, unless I've forgotten both her hat and her sunscreen and she's already spent too much time in the blazing tropical sun. Then I start to use my shadow as her sun protection, adjusting my pace so that she is always covered by my shade. Sometimes this means running, if she's decided that today the objective of the shadow game is to keep out of my shadow!

In Psalm 121, we are not advised to watch carefully where we walk so as to stay in God's shadow whenever possible. No, we are told that the Lord is watching over us! "The underlying root meaning [of the Hebrew word for 'watch'] is 'to pay careful attention to.'" [41] Our heavenly mother is paying careful attention to us, standing beside us as our protective shade and intentionally placing herself between us and anything that would not lead to our ultimate good. We can run away and (if you are like me) often do, getting a painful sunburn in the process. But even in the valley of the shadow of death, the shadow of God's goodness and unfailing love will pursue us (Psalm 23). God's unfailing, pursuing love will always win the shadow game.

When I Awake

> *It is useless for you to work so hard from early morning until late at night, anxiously working for food to eat; for God gives rest to his loved ones (NLT), gives to his beloved even in their sleep (NASB). (Ps 127:2)*

> *How precious are your thoughts about me, O God. They cannot be numbered! I can't even count them; they outnumber the grains of sand! And when I wake up, you are still with me! (Ps 139:17–18, NLT)*

> *Indeed, [God] who watches over Israel will neither slumber nor sleep. (Ps 121:4, NIV)*

Like most kids, sleeping was never something I was very interested in as a child. I've been told that as a baby I resisted sleep with a fierce vengeance, and throughout my childhood and early adult years I usually felt deeply disappointed whenever the time came to stop doing things and go to sleep. Then there was the eight-year blur of mothering babies and toddlers, which felt like one eternally long day during which sleeping was the only thing I really wanted to do and also the thing I was rarely allowed to do.

Now that I am emerging from that sleep-deprived fog, I still savor the chance to get in my bed and stay there for a good solid night, but I also find myself thinking of sleep as a necessary waste of time. Think of all the interesting, enjoyable, useful things we could do with all that time if we didn't so desperately need to sleep! But I am learning that, although I stop working when I sleep, God does not. Not only does God not sleep while I'm sleeping, but God doesn't stop working on me while

---

41. *NIDOTTE* 182.

I'm sleeping. This is why it's "useless to work so hard from early in the morning until late at night," because not only is sleep a gift from God but, as the NASB translation of Psalm 127:2 suggests, God keeps giving to us even while we're asleep.

I've spent many hours holding sleeping babies, often feeding them in their sleep. While they slept, I continued to nurture and nourish them, and when they woke up to find themselves still in my arms, they may have reached the peak of human contentment. Like a mother rocking a baby through a difficult night, God is actively engaged with us even while we sleep, feeding and singing to our souls. We can fall asleep knowing that the time will not be wasted and that, when we awake, we can say with the Psalmist, "Oh, I'm still with you!"[42]

In the Darkness of the Womb

> *I can never escape from your Spirit! I can never get away from your presence! I could ask the darkness to hide me and the light around me to become night—but even in darkness I cannot hide from you. To you the night shines as bright as day. Darkness and light are the same to you. You watched me as I was being formed in utter seclusion, as I was woven together in the dark of the womb. (Ps 139:7, 11, 12, 15, NLT)*

Maybe it's because they have each other, but my twins never cry at bedtime. I often hear them chattering or singing to each other for quite awhile, but they never cry. Never, until a few days ago, when one of them decided that standing at the door and screaming was a better plan than laying in his bed and going to sleep. For three nights in a row he cried for over an hour, for no reason that we could discover (other than a general rebellion against the concept of bed). We went in several times, checked his diaper, took him potty, sang to him and kissed him, but there came a time when he just needed to go to sleep. We knew that going in again would only delay the sleep he desperately needed, and keep his brother up as well, so we left him to cry in the darkness until he finally fell asleep.

It must have seemed so cruel from his perspective. He knew we were out there, he could see the crack of light under the door, and he knew we could easily open the door and let him out of the darkness and into the light. Why were we leaving him there in the darkness?

---

42. Ps 139:18

We might ask the same question of God during our darkest seasons of life, when it feels like we've been left alone in the darkness to cry. And being told that it's "for our ultimate good" comforts us about as much as it comforted my two-year-old to be told that he would feel better if he went to sleep. The darkness and light may be the same to God, but the darkness is still very dark to us.

We may feel abandoned in the darkness, and I think my son certainly did, but he wasn't. I was right there, listening to every cry and crying inwardly at his distress. And on the third night, when he was still crying long after his brother had fallen asleep, I couldn't bear it any longer. I quietly crept in and laid next to him in the darkness, cheek to cheek, until he calmed down and went to sleep.

God is with us in our darkness. I can't be with all of my children every moment of the day and night, but God can, and God is. No matter how dark the room is, no matter how long the night seems, God is there. And when it's too dark to see God's face, and you cannot feel God's cheek against yours, remember that one of the darkest—and safest—places is God's womb. A baby in the womb cannot see or feel her mother, and yet she couldn't be closer. Listen for God's voice in the darkness of the womb.

The Eyes of All

> *The eyes of all look to you in hope; you give them their food as they need it. When you open your hand, you satisfy the hunger and thirst of every living thing.* (Ps 145:16–17, NLT)

The kids are playing in the backyard, the dog is resting in the shade, and the cat is sleeping in the sunny spot on the porch. But the moment I open the kitchen door and step out, all eighteen eyes are immediately open and on me. The animals lift their heads expectantly, and the children come running towards the gate. Everyone is wondering the same thing. *What does she have in that dish? Did she bring something good to eat? Is it for me?* Experience has taught them all that when I come out that door, I often bring something nice for somebody. A chewed up crust of bread if you're a dog, a spoonful of abandoned tuna salad if you're a cat, cucumber peels if you're a guinea pig, or maybe even strawberries or a popsicle if you're a human child. Their eyes all look to me in hope.

It is a holy act, carrying food out to those expectant creatures. In that moment, I get to be the image of their Creator, and give them a shadowy glimpse of the God whose open hand satisfies the desires of every hungry living thing, the God who told the first human beings, "Look! I have given you every seed-bearing plant throughout the earth and all the fruit trees for your food."[43]

I go back in the house and my own soul is hungry, weary from a long day of nourishing small hungry bellies and small hungry hearts. As I finish up the day's cooking, my eyes are usually looking down the long string of tasks that still loom between me and bedtime. But occasionally I remember to turn my eyes upwards in hope, to look to my heavenly Mother and ask expectantly, "What do you have for me today? Did you bring me something good to eat?" And when I remember to ask, when I remember to look, God's hand is always open, and God's hand is always full. Full of good things to satisfy my weary soul's deep hunger and thirst.

> *Jesus replied, "I am the bread of life. Whoever comes to me will never be hungry again. Whoever believes in me will never be thirsty. (John 6:35, NLT)*

God Likes Us

> *O Israel, rejoice in your Maker. Praise [God's] name with dancing, accompanied by tambourine and harp. For the* LORD *delights in his people; he crowns the humble with victory. (Ps 149:2–4, NLT)*

> "Guest speaker at church today, dressed in a monk's habit. He said that God is nice and he likes us. Everyone looked at Edwin to see if we agreed. Difficult to tell as he was grinning like a happy little boy."[44]—Adrian Plass

I don't have much trouble believing (in my head, at least) that God loves me. Love is good, and God is good, and God is love, so of course God loves even despicable people like me. After all, God did the good, noble, self-sacrificing, loving thing and died for me, so of course God loves me. But does God *like* me? Now there's a question.

There are people I have met who I would like to think that I loved. I tried to treat them with love, anyway. But if I'm honest, I didn't necessarily like them. My heart sank when I saw them coming towards me. And for a long time I unconsciously assumed that God felt that way about me.

---

43. Gen 1:29, NLT
44. Plass, *The Sacred Diary*, 9.

Of course God would always treat me in perfectly loving ways but how could God like me? Surely God was secretly hoping that I would keep a considerate distance between God and all my smelly junk, including the junky truth about how I felt towards the people I had trouble liking.

But Psalm 149 says that God *likes* me! God delights in me, and I give God pleasure! We all love our kids and work hard to do what's best for them, but you know those moments when you stop and really look at that tiny perfect human (often when they're sleeping) and your heart overflows at how amazing they are and you just want to hug them forever? That's how God feels about you. And me. And each of us.

Psalm 149 tells us to praise God and rejoice in God. Why? Because God is good? Because God is holy? Because God loves us? Nope. Because *God delights in us!* I don't think we can truly delight in God until we believe that God delights in us. As long as we think that God just loves us because that's the good thing to do, we will be stuck on the level of praising God because that's the good thing to do. But when we notice God gazing at us with the eyes of an adoring mother, when we feel God's pleasure in holding us close to God's heart, then our praise will flow out in unstoppable delight. And from that point on the delight—both God's and ours—only gets deeper and deeper. We love God because God first loved us. But we won't like God until we believe that God likes us.

> *Even before [God] made the world, God loved us and chose us in Christ to be holy and without fault in his eyes. This is what he wanted to do, and it gave him great pleasure. (Eph 1:4–5, NLT)*

The Virtuous Woman

> *Who can find a virtuous and capable (excellent, ESV) wife (of noble character, NIV)? She is more precious than rubies. (Prov 31:10, NLT)*

It was a warm Sunday afternoon, and I was spending the hours between the morning and evening services at a friend's house, with a few other kids from church. One of the boys there was being particularly annoying and obnoxious, and after repeated provocations I could take it no longer and decided to teach him a lesson by means of physical violence. I didn't get very far into that lesson (I'd hardly begun the introduction, really) before my friend's mom rushed over and pulled us apart. Or rather, pulled me away. And what she said to me deeply impacted my view of the world and myself.

She didn't tell me that I shouldn't fight or hit people. She told me that I shouldn't fight *with boys*, "because boys are stronger than girls, and you could get badly hurt." And that was my introduction to the lesson that the church continued to teach me through the years that followed: "Girls don't fight with boys, because boys are stronger. Women don't disagree with men because men are stronger. Strong women get hurt. Being strong is not womanly."

I wasn't supposed to be strong, and I wasn't supposed to want to be strong. I was supposed to be virtuous, noble, and excellent, like the woman in Proverbs 31:10. But what nobody ever told me was that "virtuous," "noble," and "excellent" are all fancy ways to try to avoid calling this famous woman "strong." The Hebrew word that describes the woman in Proverbs 31:10 "elsewhere denotes 'competent strength.'"[45] A more straightforward translation would be "strong" or "valiant." In fact, the Greek translation of Proverbs uses a word that literally means "manly" or "courageous," a word that describes a person who does "*heroic deeds worthy of a brave person.*"[46] The Proverbs 31 woman is introduced as a strong woman!

> *She girds herself with strength and makes her arms strong. (Prov 31:17, NASB)*

> *She is clothed with strength and dignity. (Prov 31:25, NIV)*

The Proverbs 31 woman girds herself with strength. Girding is a kind of dressing that is a preparation for something.[47] Warriors gird themselves with their weapons to prepare for battle (2 Kgs 3:21). Priests gird themselves with their sacred clothing to prepare for the presence of God (Lev 8:7). Travelers gird themselves for the journey ahead of them (2 Kgs 4:29). This exemplary woman girds herself with strength, and the language used to describe her is similar to the language used to describe God's own strength.

> *Wake up, wake up, O Lord! Clothe yourself with strength! (Isa 51:9, NLT)*

---

45. Waltke, *The Book of Proverbs*, 520.
46. BDAG 76.
47. *HALOT* 291.

> *Awake, awake, put on strength, O arm of the Lord. (Isa 51:9, ESV)*

When we clothe ourselves with strength, not only are we being like the Proverbs 31 woman (the paragon of Christian womanhood), *we are also being like God*, whose arms are clothed in strength. Being strong *is* womanly; it is also godly. And strength is offered, in abundance, to *all* of God's children—boys and girls alike.

> *[God] gives power to the weak and strength to the powerless. Those who trust in the Lord will find new strength. (Isa 40:29, 31, NLT)*

The Big Blue Bucket of Grace

Between the shower and toilet in our bathroom sits a big, old, blue plastic bucket. It started its life as a diaper bucket, but it has now outlived the diaper days and exists as an Especially Gross Laundry Receptacle, for anything that needs a little extra help before it goes into the washing machine. The kids all know that if you fall in the mud, or don't make it to the bathroom in time, or spill your entire cup of milk on your shirt, you put your clothes in the big blue bucket.

Back in the days of diapers, my husband processed the blue bucket every night, and it was a magical thing. I could toss a soiled diaper in the bucket and find it later in the washing machine, rinsed and sanitized. More recently I have become the blue bucket processor, but it's still a magical thing for our little kids. No matter how filthy you get, if you throw your clothes in the blue bucket they will reappear in your drawer, clean and ready to wear again.

As I was processing the blue bucket the other night, rinsing out globs of mud, rancid milk, and even worse things in the laundry room sink, I found myself wishing for a truly magical blue bucket. Wouldn't it be nice to have a place where you could throw all your failures and mistakes and know that somebody would sort it all out after you went to bed and everything would be fresh and clean when you woke up in the morning? And then I remembered that I do have that place.

> *"Come now, let's settle this," says the* LORD. *"Though your sins are like scarlet, I will make them as white as snow. Though they are red like crimson, I will make them as white as wool." (Isa 1:18, NLT)*

> *[Jesus'] clothes became dazzling white, far whiter than any earthly bleach could ever make them. (Mark 9:3, NLT)*

> *I am overwhelmed with joy in the* LORD *my God! For he has dressed me with the clothing of salvation and draped me in a robe of righteousness. (Isa 61:10, NLT)*

Sometimes I just keep wearing my nasty old clothes, or try to clean them up myself. (My small children have tried that too, and it *always* results in an even bigger mess.) I forget that Jesus paid everything to buy me a big blue bucket of grace. Every morning, every evening, every moment, Jesus is ready to redress me in his own dazzling white clothes of righteousness, and I get to throw my old nasty ones in the bucket. That's grace. May I extend to my children the same grace that Jesus extends to me.

Until the Spirit Is Exposed

> *You complacent women, get up and listen to me! You carefree daughters, pay attention to what I say! In a year's time you carefree ones will shake with fear, for the grape harvest will fail, and the fruit harvest will not arrive. Tremble, you complacent ones! Shake with fear, you carefree ones! Strip off your clothes and expose yourselves—put sackcloth on your waist! Mourn [beat your breasts (ESV)] over the delightful fields and the fruitful vine, which [are] overgrown with thorns and briers, and over all the once-happy houses in the city filled with revelry. For the fortress is neglected; the once-crowded city is abandoned. Hill and watchtower are permanently uninhabited. This desolation will continue [until the Spirit is poured out upon us from on high (NASB)]. Then justice will settle down in the desert and fairness will live in the orchard. Fairness will produce peace and result in lasting security. My people will live in peaceful settlements, in secure homes, and in safe, quiet places. (From Isaiah 32:9-18, NET)*

These complacent women that Isaiah is addressing did not ask for this warning from God. They were feeling secure, absorbed in their comfortable pursuits, and were not pursuing God, or any word from God. But God pursued them, even in their complacency, and told them that hard times were coming. Very soon—even next year—their abundance would be gone and their homes and cities would be empty, bare, exposed. Their culturally appropriate reaction of grief is to strip off their clothes in mourning, to make themselves bare and exposed, disgraced like the land they live in.

How long will this season of sorrowful exposure last? Until they repent? Until they can rebuild? No. *Until the Spirit is exposed to us.* The word translated as 'poured out' in this passage is the same word used to describe the women's exposure to demonstrate their grief, and has an underlying meaning of being uncovered, revealed, exposed. As a mother uncovers her breast to bring comfort to a starving baby, the Spirit of God is uncovered to bring comfort to God's grieving daughters.

Once again, the women did not ask for this sign of grace—it was something they would not even have known to ask for! Nevertheless, God's Spirit promises to come, to expose Godself to end their exposure, and to clothe them and their land in justice and righteousness. Only then would they "live in safety, quietly at home" and "be at rest."[48]

Hundreds of years later, this promise was fulfilled when God, in a human body, was exposed on a cross, and God's Spirit revealed to all God's children, so that we could be clothed with salvation.

> *I am overwhelmed with joy in the* Lord *my God! For he has dressed me with the clothing of salvation and draped me in a robe of righteousness.* (Isa 61:10, NLT)

Everything Will Be Okay

> *"Comfort, comfort my people," says your God. "Speak tenderly to Jerusalem. Tell her that her sad days are gone and her sins are pardoned."* (Isa 40:1, NLT)

"It's okay. I'm here now. Everything is going to be okay." Countless moms have said these words at one time or another. After a shot, a fall, a bad dream, a scare, or a disappointment, kids want comfort—even after the pain or the unpleasant event is over. And nothing is quite as comforting to a child as being surrounded by the arms of a loving mom or dad, and hearing those tender words of reassurance. For a nursing baby, nothing is nearly as comforting as their mom.

> *Rejoice with Jerusalem and be glad for her. For you will nurse and be satisfied at her comforting breasts; you will drink deeply and*

---

48. Isa 32:18, NLT

delight in her overflowing abundance. For this is what the Lord *says: "As a mother comforts her child, so I [myself] will comfort you; and you will be comforted over Jerusalem." (Isa 66:10, 11–13, NIV)*

God comforts us like a mother comforts her child. The comfort God offers is "emphasized by adding the personal pronoun (*anoki*, 'I myself') and by describing the action twice, once from God's perspective ('I myself will comfort you') and once from Jerusalem's perspective ('you will be comforted')."[49]

Jesus, the promised Messiah, came to deliver God's comfort in a form that God's children could physically feel, hear, and see. As Jesus said himself:

The Spirit of the Sovereign Lord *is upon me, for the* Lord *has anointed me to bring good news to the poor. He has sent me to comfort the brokenhearted and to proclaim that captives will be released and prisoners will be freed. God has sent me to tell those who mourn that the time of the Lord's favor has come. (Isa 61:1–2, NLT, quoted by Jesus in Luke 4:18–19)*

"Everything is going to be okay." When I say those words to comfort my child, as my mother comforted me through my childhood, I am preaching the gospel. Jesus came to permanently establish the feeling you get when you wake up from a horrifying dream and realize that it was just a dream, and that in your real life, everything is going to be okay. One day we will wake up to our real life, where everything is okay, and the horror will be washed away forever. And even now, while we wait, and cry, and hurt, God's Spirit, our motherly Comforter, surrounds us with her arms from within our hearts and whispers, "I'm here *now*. Everything will be okay."

Messengers of Good News

You who bring good news to Zion, go up on a high mountain. You who bring good news to Jerusalem, lift up your voice with a shout, lift it up, do not be afraid; say to the towns of Judah, "Here is your God!" (Isa 40:9, NIV)

---

49. Smith, *Isaiah 40–66*, 742.

Who was this person who was told to fearlessly proclaim that God had arrived? Isaiah doesn't give us a name, but he does give us a clue that gets lost in the English translation. In Hebrew, verbs and pronouns are always either masculine or feminine, and this "you" who "brings good news" is feminine. Isaiah's messenger of good news was a woman!

Some translations assume that "Zion" and "Jerusalem" (feminine nouns) are themselves the messengers of good news, which is grammatically possible but contextually awkward. But assuming that Isaiah was referring to an actual human, and not a personified abstraction, who was the first person to proclaim that God had arrived?

> *When Elizabeth heard Mary's greeting, the baby leaped in her womb, and Elizabeth was filled with the Holy Spirit. In a loud voice she exclaimed: "Blessed are you among women, and blessed is the child you will bear! But why am I so favored, that the mother of my Lord should come to me?" (Luke 1:41–43, NIV)*

When God became human to fulfill all the promises given to Isaiah, the very first human (male or female) to verbally announce, "Here is your God!" was Elizabeth—a woman. And, as Isaiah had foretold, she made this announcement "in a loud voice," full of the Holy Spirit, with no room for fear of what the neighbors might think.

About three decades later, God arrived again, this time back from the dead. And again, the first humans to proclaim this arrival were women.

> *But very early on Sunday morning the women went to the tomb. Two men suddenly appeared to them, clothed in dazzling robes. "He isn't here! He is risen from the dead!" So they rushed back from the tomb to tell his eleven disciples—and everyone else— what had happened. It was Mary Magdalene, Joanna, Mary the mother of James, and several other women who told the apostles what had happened. But the story sounded like nonsense to the men, so they didn't believe it. (Luke 24:1, 4, 6, 9–11, NLT)*

These messengers of good news fearlessly lifted up their voices to announce God's arrival, even though their message was rejected as nonsense. May we, their daughters in the faith, follow in their footsteps and fearlessly lift our voices to announce to the world, "God is here!" And may we freely proclaim this good news to other disciples—and everyone else—even on Sunday morning.

Hands on the Doorknob

> *But, dear family of Jacob, you refuse to ask for my help. (Isa 43:22, NLT)*

It would be very appropriate (if out of context) for me to regularly quote this verse to my children (my husband's name is Jacob). My young son is deeply committed to doing things himself, and he lives out this commitment with all the passion of a two-year-old. After he uses the bathroom (all by himself, of course, but I have to stand guard to make sure he doesn't finish off by eating shampoo or toothpaste all by himself) he wants to open the bathroom door all by himself. I am fully supportive of this desire—the trouble is that he's not quite tall enough to fulfill it. On his tiptoes, he can just grab the doorknob, but he can't quite get the leverage to turn it. So he hangs there, his plump little fingers entirely covering the knob. As long as his hand is there, I can't turn it myself, not without hurting him, so we both wait there until his desire to go play with Duplos wins over his desire to open the door himself. When he finally releases the knob, I release us from the bathroom.

I wonder when I keep my hand on doorknobs I can't turn? When I struggle industriously to do something myself and instead I should be letting go and turning to my Mother for help? What metaphorical bathrooms have I been stuck in because I wouldn't let God let me out? Does God help those who help themselves, or does God help those who let God help them?

Lord, help me to be still, to cease striving, to let you open the right doors for me. Help me to let go of the doorknobs I can't turn, and wait with you until you turn the knob or give me one I can reach. Thank you that you are patient, that you wait with me, and that you are gentle even when my little hand is in the way.

Tired of Mom

> *But, dear family of Jacob, you refuse to ask for my help. You have grown tired of me, O Israel! (Isa 43:22, NLT)*

One evening, when my very extroverted daughter was still an infant, we had been planning to go to a party but she was so cranky and fussy that we nearly stayed home. We were pretty desperate to get out, though, so we went anyway, figuring we would probably have to leave early. But as soon as we stepped into that room full of new people, she stopped cranking mid-fuss and was magically transformed into a cheerful, smiling baby. She got passed around the room all evening and hardly made a sound that wasn't happy. As new parents, we were mystified for awhile until it dawned on us that she had simply gotten bored at home and grown tired of us! With new people to entertain her, she was ready to happily party all evening.

It is the fate of many mothers (and fathers who spend significant chunks of time caring for children) to be taken for granted by their kids. Moms often pour more time and energy into their children than anyone else does, and yet we are the most easily criticized when we fail and the most easily cast aside when something or someone more interesting comes along.

I think God knows how this feels. Even after God spent centuries pursuing, rescuing, delivering, feeding, and protecting God's children, they were ready to cast God aside when a new and interesting deity came along. And it's not just those ancient Israelites who treated God this way. So many times I have chosen to watch TV or scroll through Facebook instead of seeking out the presence of God.

Ironically (or perhaps logically), I think I grow the most tired of God when I feel the least connected to God. The longer I go without deeply connecting to God, or the shallower my time with God, the more wearisome it sounds to choose pursuing God over some mindless, convenient entertainment.

MotherFather God, thank you for your holy grace that pursues us even when we grow weary of you. Please delight us today with a fresh glimpse of who you are, and remind us how utterly satisfying your love is.

Before You Were Born

> *I have cared for you since you were born. Yes, I carried you before you were born. I will be your God throughout your lifetime—until your hair is white with age. I made you, and I will care for you. I will carry you along and save you.* (Isa 46:3-4, NLT)

One of my daughters was born in Australia, and one of her very first excursions was a trip to a park where we got to stand a few feet away from kangaroos in their natural habitat. We have a picture of my husband standing with our daughter asleep in the baby carrier on his chest, right next to mother kangaroos with their babies in their pouches. I am married to a stellar father, who has probably spent days, weeks, and even months of his life carrying our five babies around since their births.

Had he been able to carry them before they were born, I have no doubt that he would have. In fact, at times he expressed a bit of a longing to share the relationship that I had with our children even before birth (though I'm not sure he actually envied all that went with that relationship). But that was something only I, as their mother, was able to do. And, while I can't say I enjoyed all of it, I did enjoy being the one who got to know our children on some level even before they were born. When I was pregnant with our twins, I could usually tell which baby was moving, and had impressions about their personalities and habits even before their birth.

Like an attentive father, God carries us from the moment we are born. But as only a mother can, God carries us even before we are born. Even before we are spiritually born into an awareness of God's presence and love for us, God is there, all around us, protecting, nourishing and nurturing our souls, preparing us for the moment when we can open our heart's eyes and notice the God who birthed us. And, though our human parents may need to be carried by us when we are old ourselves,[50] the God who made us will still be there to carry us through the end of our lives on earth. And beyond.

Passionate Commitment

> *The* Lord *looked and was displeased to find there was no justice. He was amazed to see that no one intervened to help the oppressed. So he himself stepped in to save them with his strong arm, and his justice sustained him. He put on righteousness as his body armor and placed the helmet of salvation on his head. He clothed himself with a robe of vengeance and wrapped himself in a cloak of divine passion. (Isa 59:15–17, NLT)*

> *This is what the* Lord *of Heaven's Armies says: My love for Mount Zion is passionate and strong; I am consumed with passion for Jerusalem! (Zech 8:2, NLT)*

---

50. Oswalt, *Isaiah 40–66*, 231.

> *For a child is born to us, a son is given to us. The government will rest on his shoulders. And he will be called: Wonderful Counselor, Mighty God, Everlasting Father, Prince of Peace. His government and its peace will never end. He will rule with fairness and justice from the throne of his ancestor David for all eternity. The passionate commitment of the LORD of Heaven's Armies will make this happen! (Isa 9:6–7, NLT)*

There are many passionate people in the world. They are passionate about all kinds of things—some helpful, some harmful—and their passion may or may not last very long.

There are also many committed people in the world. Their commitment also has a wide range of objectives, including both worthy and destructive goals, and even themselves.

There are fewer people who are passionately committed, but if you could somehow find and interview all of them, I suspect you would find that many of them were mothers. Motherhood is one long exercise in passionate commitment. Not only are mothers utterly committed to the well-being of their children, we also feel this commitment deeply, and are emotionally engaged in the process of living out our commitment. Mother bears display passionate commitment particularly clearly.

Many Bible translations use the word "zeal" for this passionate commitment, and zeal for their children is one more way in which mothers vividly reflect the nature of God and God's love for her children. "Zeal refers to God's strong determination, his absolute commitment to accomplish what he has promised."[51] In fact, God even says that "Passionate Commitment" (also translated as "Jealous") is God's name!

> *You must worship no other gods, for the LORD, whose very name is Jealous, is a God who is jealous about his relationship with you. (Exod 34:14, NLT)*

While jealousy can have negative connotations, God's jealousy, or passionate commitment, "depicts a consuming concern for the other's best and an unwillingness that anything should hurt or destroy another."[52] Like a passionately committed mother who will go to any lengths to rescue her child from harm—even harm caused by the child's own actions—God will go (and has already gone) to unimaginable lengths to save us from ourselves.

---

51. Smith, *Isaiah 40–66*, 680.
52. Oswalt, *Isaiah 1–39*, 248.

> *I am as likely to reject my people Israel as I am to abolish the laws of nature! Just as the heavens cannot be measured and the foundations of the earth cannot be explored, so I will not consider casting them away for the evil they have done. I, the Lord, have spoken! (Jer 31:36–37, NLT)*

It was the passionate commitment of the Lord of Heaven's Armies that made it possible for us to joyfully sing, "Unto us a child is born!" And even as a sword pierced the soul of that child's mother (Luke 2:35), she herself was rescued by the passionate commitment of her Heavenly Mother.

Stirring Inner Parts

> *Look down from heaven and see, from your holy and beautiful habitation. Where are your zeal and your might? The stirring of your inner parts and your compassion are held back from me. (Isa 63:15, ESV)*

> *Is not Israel still my son, my darling child?" says the Lord. "I often have to punish him, but I still love him. That's why I long for him [my inner parts stir for him] and surely will have mercy [compassion (NIV)] on him." (Jer 31:20, NLT)*

Compassion is one of God's most prominent characteristics, and you may recall that the Hebrew word for compassion comes from the same root as the word for womb. The love and compassion that a mother feels for a child who came from her womb is a bright reflection of the love and compassion that God feels for God's children.

In both Isaiah 63:15 and Jeremiah 31:20, God's compassion is paired with another descriptive phrase, the "stirring of inner parts." These inner parts can refer to a range of locations within the body, one of which is the womb,[53] "that part of the body through which people come into existence."[54] This possible meaning for "inner parts," particularly when paired with "compassion," has led some commentators to suggest that "the exclamation is a mother's, an expression of compassion that issues in action in the same way as does a warrior's passion,"[55] and that "The

---

53. This same word describes a woman's womb in Gen 25:23; Isa 49:1; Ps 71:6.
54. *HALOT* 609.
55. Goldingay, *Isaiah 56–66*, 403–4.

Lord's actions in [Jeremiah 31:20] are motivated by powerful emotions expressed in metaphors derived from women's bodies and experiences."[56]

"Inner parts" can refer to parts of men's bodies as well as women's, so the imagery in these passages is not exclusively or necessarily feminine. Nevertheless, these verses give us a glimpse into the motherly heart of God that deeply resonates with mothers who have experienced the stirring of this kind of compassionate womb-love. Just as a mother cannot ignore or forget the stirring of her inner parts as her beloved child is birthed into the world, God will not rest until each beloved child is birthed into the Kingdom of Heaven.

Not Forgotten

> *For I will bring them from the north and from the distant corners of the earth. I will not forget the blind and lame, the expectant mothers and women in labor. A great company will return! Tears of joy will stream down their faces, and I will lead them home with great care. They will walk beside quiet streams and on smooth paths where they will not stumble. (Jer 31:8–9, NLT)*

I have been on some tough journeys in my life. I have spent a whole day climbing a muddy mountain in flipflops, with nothing to eat but half a potato and two bites of possum liver (long story, but a true one!). I have spent the night in the open jungle, spent the night in a tiny boat, been stranded on a tiny island, and run a marathon. Then I became a mother and discovered that all of that put together had simply been a warm-up for the toughest journey of my life.

Pregnancy and those early months of nursing is a tough road. You can't do a lot of the things you used to be able to do, some of them things that made you feel like you. Your world shrinks down to you and that tiny person, and it may look to others like you're "not doing anything" but you feel that you're doing more than you ever have before—possibly more than you're able to do. You no longer have time or energy for your friends, or your job, or your hobbies, and it can feel like the world moves on without you. You can feel alone (without getting the chance to ever truly be alone) and forgotten.

But you are not forgotten. God specifically mentions, and remembers, the people who are most likely to be left behind: the blind, the lame,

---

56. Keown, *Jeremiah 26–52*, 120.

and the mothers. Blind and lame people would need a lot of help on a long journey, and would not be able to contribute much to the group. In fact, "blind and lame priests were excluded from [temple] service (Lev 21:18)."[57] Moms of small kids can be similarly marginalized and excluded; during those seasons when we pour so much into our kids that we have nothing left for anyone else, we can feel left behind because we have "nothing to contribute to the group." Most days we can't even keep up with the group.

But God never leaves us behind. Not only that, God knows that the journey is already too much for us, so God leads us gently and provides for us along the way. God leads us "home with great care." With God we "will walk beside quiet streams and on smooth paths where [we] will not stumble."

> *[God] will feed his flock like a shepherd. He will carry the lambs in his arms, holding them close to his heart. He will gently lead the mother sheep with their young. (Isa 40:11, NLT)*

Even (and especially) on those days when you feel most forgotten and alone, so weary you don't know if you can take one more step, know this: God sees you. God notices you. God remembers you, and mentions you by name. God knows that you are climbing an invisible muddy mountain in flip flops, and God will provide more than possum liver (which is gross) along the way. Just take one more step on that smooth path where you won't stumble, open your mouth for one more sip from that quiet stream, and know that God's arms are supporting yours as you carry that tiny person. God will never leave you behind.

The New Covenant

> *For the* LORD *has created a new thing on the earth: a woman encircles a man. "The days are coming," declares the* LORD, *"when I will make a new covenant with the house of Israel and the house of Judah, not like the covenant that I made with their fathers. For this is the covenant that I will make with the house of Israel after those days," declares the* LORD: *I will put my law within them, and I will write it on their hearts. And I will be their God, and they shall be my people. And no longer shall each one teach his neighbor and each his brother, saying, 'Know the* LORD,' *for they*

---

57. Keown, *Jeremiah 26–52*, 113.

> *shall all know me, from the least of them to the greatest," declares the* LORD. *(Jer 31:22, 31–34, ESV)*
>
> *After supper [Jesus] took another cup of wine and said, "This cup is the new covenant between God and his people—an agreement confirmed with my blood, which is poured out as a sacrifice for you." (Luke 22:20, NLT)*

Jeremiah was given a message of hope and restoration. Although dark times lay ahead for God's people, God promised that one day there would be a new covenant for everyone, from the least to the greatest. On that day, Jerusalem would be rebuilt as God's holy city (Jer 31:38–40) and there would be rest for the weary and joy for the sorrowing (Jer 31:25). Jesus came to usher in that new covenant, and while we are still waiting for the full realization of all of God's promises, the Kingdom of God is here, now, and God is inviting us to begin making it a reality on this earth!

Jeremiah 31:22 contains an intriguing promise about God's new kingdom and covenant: "A woman encircles a man" (ESV). Nobody really knows what this phrase means, although theories abound. This word for "woman" is usually translated as "female"—its focus is on the gender of the person being referred to.[58] "Man" in this verse is also a word that specifically means "male"—often a young, strong man[59] such as a warrior. The verb has a huge range of meaning, which is part of what makes the phrase so difficult to interpret. However, in this verse it occurs in the *polel* stem, and elsewhere in the *polel* it consistently means "to protectively surround."

> *[God] found them in a desert land, in an empty, howling wasteland. He surrounded them and watched over them; he guarded them as he would guard his own eyes. (Deut 32:10, NLT)*
>
> *For you are my hiding place; you protect me from trouble. You surround me with songs of victory. Many sorrows come to the wicked, but unfailing love surrounds those who trust the* LORD. *(Ps 32:7, 10, NLT)*

Way back at the beginning, when humanity broke our very first covenant with God, one of the ways that brokenness played out was in the rule of the male over the female. But God promised Jeremiah, and promises us now, that in the new covenant, when God's ways are written

---

58. Keown, *Jeremiah 26–52*, 122.
59. *HALOT* 175.

deep within our hearts, all that was broken will be healed. Woman, created to be an *ezer* (helper, deliverer), will be released to live out her calling as a strong protector. Those who had been oppressed and trampled will be exalted to a position of strength, but instead of using that strength to become oppressors themselves, they will use it to protectively surround others, even those who used to be considered the strongest of all. The least will be greatest, and the last will be first.

We ache to see this new covenant fully expressed in Christ's Body, but we can rejoice in the confidence that it has *already been confirmed with Christ's blood!* The Kingdom of God is here—let's go live it out!

The Mother and the Husband

> *I will do this to recapture the hearts of the people of Israel, who have all deserted me for their idols. Therefore say to the people of Israel, "This is what the Sovereign* Lord *says: Repent! Turn from your idols and renounce all your detestable practices! Your father was an Amorite and your mother a Hittite. On the day you were born your cord was not cut, nor were you washed with water to make you clean, nor were you rubbed with salt or wrapped in cloths. No one looked on you with pity or had compassion enough to do any of these things for you. Rather, you were thrown out into the open field, for on the day you were born you were despised. Then I passed by and saw you kicking about in your blood, and as you lay there in your blood I said to you, 'Live!' I made you grow like a plant of the field." (From Ezekiel 14:5–6, 16:3–7, NIV)*

As God predicted long ago in Deuteronomy 32, the day came when Israel forgot the God who had given birth to them.[60] Their hearts turned to things that were not God, and they lived like the children of Amorite and Hittite gods. In a graphic parable, God describes how these new "parents" treated them. Washing a newborn, in the ancient Near East, had the legal ramifications that signing your name on a baby's birth certificate does today.[61] Whoever supervised the washing was the legal parent, and adoption could be legally accomplished by simply handing the baby over to the adoptive parents before she was washed.[62] Parents who abandoned

---

60. Deut 32:18
61. Allen, *Ezekiel 1–19*, 237.
62. Block, *The Book of Ezekiel*, 481.

a baby without washing her, as in Ezekiel's story, gave up all their legal rights as parents and could never reclaim those rights.[63]

The gods the Israelites had set up in their hearts had abandoned them, and they were as helpless as a tiny, unwashed newborn, still attached to the placenta.

Then I passed by and saw you.

The God they abandoned finds them abandoned and reclaims them, officially adopting them by taking them up in their bloody unwashed state and washing them.

I made you to grow (helped you to thrive, NLT).

This Hebrew phrase, which literally means "to make great," "in adoption contexts denotes the raising up of the adopted child by the adopter."[64] It was God who raised this abandoned child, making her grow and helping her to thrive until she reached maturity. Now, in a world where it was impossible to run to the store for some clean bottles and a can of baby formula, raising a newborn baby required a woman's presence. Only a mother could keep a newborn baby alive and allow her to thrive to the point of maturity. It was God who washed and fed this little orphan, and God could only have done so as a mother.

Later in the story, when the baby grows up and matures, the imagery changes and God becomes her husband. Is it a problem for God to be portrayed as both a mother and a husband within a single narrative? Not for God! God is revealed through so many different metaphors precisely because God is much too vast to be contained in any one of them. The God who is both Mother and Father is also Husband, Lover, Teacher, King, Friend, Shepherd, Light, and Bread. Wherever you are in your story, God knows what you need and will be that for you, whether it's Mother, Lover, both, or something else.

Running Away from Love

When Israel was a child, I loved him, and out of Egypt I called my son. But the more they were called, the more they went away from me. They sacrificed to the Baals and they burned incense to

---

63. Block, *The Book of Ezekiel*, 476.
64. Block, *The Book of Ezekiel*, 481–2.

> *images. It was I who taught Ephraim to walk, taking them by the arms; but they did not realize it was I who healed them. I led them with cords of human kindness, with ties of love. To them I was like one who lifts a little child to the cheek, and I bent down to feed them. (Hos 11:1–4, NIV)*

Recently, one of my little boys decided that his new life goal is to run away. He'll start casually walking towards the front yard, glancing over his shoulder to see if I'm watching. He continues nonchalantly as long as he thinks I'm not looking, but if I call out to him or start following him he breaks into a full-blown toddler waddle run and tries to get as far as he can before I catch him. Usually he trips over his own feet first.

It's kind of comical to watch, because our entire yard is fenced, so he really couldn't go anywhere terribly dangerous. But imagine the same scenario if he were running towards a highway, and "the more I called to him, the farther he moved from me" (Hos 11:2, NLT). This was God's sickening experience with Israel. God loved them, and saw them running towards something that God knew would destroy them. The more God called out to them, the faster their little legs ran towards their own destruction.

Ironically, it was God who taught those little legs how to walk in the first place. Teaching a baby to walk basically involves many back-breaking hours of shuffling along while bent over, so that the delighted child can hold on to your finger while she exercises her walking muscles. This is why people invented things like baby walkers. But they didn't have baby walkers when Hosea's kids were little, so it was all on the parents. Of course, either a father or a mother can help a baby walk, but when these words were written a child who was learning to walk would likely still have been breastfeeding, and most of the daily care of small children was done by their mothers. So God is using a very motherly image when God says that God is the one who "taught Israel to walk," "took care of him," "bent down to feed him," and lifted him to God's cheek. Holding a soft little baby cheek against your own is one of the sweetest human experiences. It's a moment of pure delight in the existence of that child, exactly as they are.

> *Assyria will rule over them because they refuse to repent! A sword will flash in their cities, it will destroy the bars of their city gates, and will devour them in their fortresses. My people are obsessed with turning away from me. (Hos 11:5–7, NET)*

God's sweet baby, the one God lifted to God's cheek, bent down to feed, and taught to walk, made it to the highway. Trying to find purpose or fulfillment outside of the love of our MotherFather God will always bring destruction into our lives. Nothing we could ever do will ever make God stop loving us, but each time we turn our backs and run away from God's love, instead of towards it, God's mother heart is torn.

> *How can I give you up, O Ephraim? How can I surrender you, O Israel? I have had a change of heart (My heart is torn within me, NLT)! All my tender compassions are aroused! I cannot carry out my fierce anger! I cannot totally destroy Ephraim! Because I am God, and not man—the Holy One among you—I will not come in wrath! (Hos 11:8-9, NET)*

The good news is that, when God is the mother, the highway is not the end of the story.

> *For someday the people will follow me. And I will bring them home again. I will heal their waywardness and love them freely, for my anger will turn away from them. I will be like the dew to Israel; he will blossom like a lily, he will send down his roots like a cedar of Lebanon. His young shoots will grow; his splendor will be like an olive tree, his fragrance like a cedar of Lebanon. People will reside again in his shade; they will plant and harvest grain in abundance. (Hos 11:10-11, NLT; 14:4-7, NET)*

No wound is too great for the love of God to heal. Run towards God today, and be lifted up and pressed against the cheek of your MotherFather God.

Dancing with God

> *Shout for joy, O daughter of Zion! Shout in triumph, O Israel! Rejoice and exult with all your heart, O daughter of Jerusalem! The LORD your God is in your midst, a victorious warrior. He will exult over you with joy, he will be quiet in his love, he will rejoice over you with shouts of joy. (Zeph 3:14, 17, NASB)*

There are a lot of things I do for my kids because I love them. All the hours I pour into feeding, clothing, and educating them flow out of my love for them, and I think they know that. But every once in a great while I abandon the endless stream of loving tasks, scoop a child up in my arms (or grab her hands if she has grown too big to be scooped up!), and we dance around the living room. If there's not already music on, I sing to them, improvising a silly and slightly off-key song about how very much I love them. These are the moments when they *feel* loved, the moments when their hearts are nourished with the confidence that I not only love them enough to do things for them, but also just love to be with them! Dancing doesn't really accomplish anything useful; it's just a way to enjoy being together. As they hear my song of joy and feel my delight in their existence, they shriek with delight themselves.

At other times I rock in "the big blue chair," with one of them hugged on my lap or beside me getting a back rub, and we are quiet in our love. Stopping everything just to be with them communicates the depth of my love for them, and they quietly soak it up.

God, as your mother, delights to be with you. The Bible is the story of the incredible things God has done out of love for you, but God did all those things in order to *be* with you! This is the reason for God's joy and ours: "The Lord your God is in your midst." Together with God again, as we were created to be, we "shout for joy (shriek with delight!) and rejoice with all our heart" *because God delights in us!* Listen to God singing God's love for you and let God dance you around the living room. Or stop and let God hold you, "quiet in God's love."

6

MOTHERHOOD IN THE NEW TESTAMENT

The Secret Place

> *Beware of practicing your righteousness before men to be noticed by them; otherwise you have no reward with your Father who is in heaven. Whenever you fast, do not put on a gloomy face as the hypocrites do, for they neglect their appearance so that they will be noticed by men when they are fasting. But you, . . . wash your face so that your fasting will not be noticed by men, but by your Father who is in secret; and your Father who sees what is done in secret will reward you. (Matt 6:1, 16–18, NASB)*

You know those ridiculously difficult moments of mothering, when everyone has a messy problem at the same time, and life feels outrageously hard to the point of being almost comic, and you might actually laugh if you weren't already crying? Like when the four-year-old is screaming because her little brother won't let go of her hair, but the other little brother has pooped on the floor, dinner is burning on the stove, and the cat snuck in to eat the food on the table? Well, when I've had one of these days, I don't greet my husband at the door with a kiss and a cheery smile. I want to make sure that he knows exactly how horrendous my day has been, and if I'm brutally honest, I probably hope that I look at least a little bit "miserable and disheveled" (Matt 6:16, NLT) like the fasting hypocrites. I want him to appreciate what I've been through that day, and he can't appreciate it fully if he doesn't know the full depths of the hardships I've endured.

There's absolutely nothing wrong with being honest with your spouse about a rough day, or wanting appreciation from your spouse. It wouldn't be healthy for me or for our marriage if I pretended that these hellish days were a walk in the park. But if human appreciation is the only reward I'm looking for, it's the only reward I'm going to get. And ultimately it will not be fulfilling.

The hardest and most important moments of mothering tend to happen in the secret place, alone with your kids with no other adults to applaud you or tell you what a good job you're doing (unless you snap a picture and post it on Facebook). But Jesus says that God is in that secret place, and God will reward us for what we do there. As we learn to notice God's presence with us in that secret place, God's joy in our care for "the least" of God's children will become our joy, and will be even more satisfying than a spouse's sympathy or a lot of likes on Facebook. And when we care for tiny people in a secret place, we are a brilliant reflection of God's image. Some of our MotherFather God's best work is done in the secret place too.

> *You knit me together in my mother's womb. My frame was not hidden from you when I was made in the secret place. (Ps 139:13, 15, NIV)*

Finding Life

> *If you cling to your life, you will lose it; but if you give up your life for Me, you will find it. (Matt 10:39, NLT)*

I can remember the moment I gave up my life. Or rather, the moment that I found my life. My third baby was a few days old, and I was up in the middle of the night to change and feed her. I had already lived through many nights of sleepless mothering, but I had been clinging to my life through most of them, wishing I could be asleep, feeling deeply sorry for myself every time I heard that tiny plea for milk. Now, as I launched into the venture of keeping another new tummy full through the long night hours, I thought, "Here we go again!" But this time, as I realized that I would not be sleeping much for the next year, something inside of me released, and I was freed from that feeling of desperately clinging to the sleep I knew would not be mine. I let go of the (reasonable) feeling that I deserved that sleep, and freely chose to give it up. I couldn't really have kept it if I'd tried, but in the moment when I stopped trying, I truly felt like I'd found my life, and I also found a peace and joy in that midnight mothering that I'd never felt before.

Now, don't get me wrong—I didn't enjoy every moment of being awake in the middle of the night, nor have I always been a model of joyful self-sacrifice ever since then. I've had to give up my life over and over. So many times I've lost it again by trying to cling to my own comforts and desires, and I've had to cry out for God to help me re-find it. Truthfully, that was not "the moment" that I found my life forever; it was one of many steps on my continuing journey to finding life.

Finding our life by giving it up is not a one-time discovery. It's more like an extended treasure hunt—a life-long search for life. Every time we willingly give up that hour of sleep, that peaceful cup of coffee, that clean kitchen, or that chance to pursue our own dreams and desires, we find one more piece of our lives. As mothers, it's easy to feel like we are robbed of these things, like they are taken from us whether we like it or not. But nobody can take what we freely give. As Jesus said in John 10:17–18:

> *I sacrifice my life so I may take it back again. No one can take my life from me. I sacrifice it voluntarily. (NLT)*

A word of warning is in order here. There are seasons for laying down your life, and seasons for taking it up again. There are times when pursuing *your* dreams may be the very best thing you could do for your children. And even in the middle of the most intense season of life-laying-down, you still need time to be refilled yourself. Never stop pursuing those moments of self-care—laying down a healthy life will benefit your children far more than laying down a broken one.

But with that said, if you've tried, like I have, to cling to your life through motherhood, resenting the small and large sacrifices required of you, then you know that's not a life worth clinging to. Let it go, and receive real life in exchange. May we each find our life again today.

For the Least of These

> *Whoever welcomes a child like this in my name welcomes me. (Matt 18:5, NET)*

> *And whoever gives only a cup of cold water to one of these little ones in the name of a disciple, I tell you the truth, he will never lose his reward. (Matt 10:42, NET)*

> *For I was hungry and you gave me food, I was thirsty and you gave me something to drink, I was a stranger and you invited me in, I was naked and you gave me clothing, I was sick and you took care of me, I was in prison and you visited me. I tell you the truth, just as you did it for one of the least of these brothers or sisters of mine, you did it for me. (Matt 25:35-36, 40, NET)*

I'll be honest. Today, I'm a little tired of feeding small hungry people, giving drinks to small thirsty people, putting clothes on small naked people, and wiping snot from small snuffly noses. There are so many other things that I'd rather be doing, things that feel so much more "important" than handing out snacks and sippy cups and changing muddy pants.

I need to be reminded that it's Jesus that I'm taking care of.

Jesus says that whatever I do for "the least"—the unimportant, the tiny, the short, the insignificant—I am doing for him. Jesus is hungry again, so I give him a muffin and then clean up the millions of crumbs he made before he steps in them. He's thirsty, so I fill a fresh cup with milk. When he's cold and wet because he spilled half the milk on his shirt, I get him a new one. If Jesus wants to spend his days eating muffins and drinking milk in my house, who am I to say that I have better things to do? What could be more important than hanging out here with Jesus, making sure he has dry clothes to wear?

When someone loves on my kid, I feel loved myself. There is no greater gift you could give a mother, than to show kindness to her child. And mothers feel a special burden of care for a child that is particularly vulnerable in some way. The Bible shows us that God has the same mother's heart. Over and over again God tells us to care for the smallest—the vulnerable, the poor, the outcast, the foreigners, the orphans, the widows, the homeless, the disabled, the unborn—anyone who could in any way be considered "the least." They have a special place in God's mother heart, and loving them is the very best way to love God. When we care for them, we are caring for Jesus.

And when I spend my days feeding and clothing the tiny people in my house, I am not only feeding and clothing Jesus. I am living out the mother heart of God, who cares deeply and especially for God's tiniest and most "insignificant" children.

One Thing Is Necessary

> *Now as they went on their way, Jesus entered a village. And a woman named Martha welcomed him into her house. And she had a sister called Mary, who sat at the Lord's feet and listened to his teaching. But Martha was distracted with much serving. And she went up to him and said, "Lord, do you not care that my sister has left me to serve alone? Tell her then to help me." But the Lord answered her, "Martha, Martha, you are anxious and troubled about many things, but one thing is necessary. Mary has chosen the good portion, which will not be taken away from her." (Luke 10:38–42, ESV)*

One Sunday, when I was a teenager, there was a congregational meeting immediately after an evening church service. As the service ended and the meeting began, I watched most of the women in the room quietly leave, and I knew they were going to warm the casseroles and garnish the salads for the dinner we would share afterwards. They believed that, in that moment, they could make more of an impact in the kitchen than in the congregation. And they may have been right. In a church culture where decisions are made by the men, teenage girls like me enter womanhood already knowing that our presence is not necessary when important things are being discussed, so we may as well go put olives on a salad.

In a church like this one, if only one woman had stayed in the meeting when the others left to attend to their womanly duties in the kitchen, one could imagine the comments that the olives and the casseroles might overhear.

> *Who does she think she is? Acting like one of the men. Her fruit salad is not going to be ready when dinner starts, she hasn't even sliced the bananas yet. What, she just assumes we're going to put her quiche in the oven for her?*

Martha was one of those women in the kitchen. She was doing what she was supposed to be doing, not sticking her nose where it didn't belong, in the men's world. And yet she was "anxious and troubled about many things." Was she anxious about who was going to bake the bread and slice the cucumbers? Maybe, although if she had the capacity to host Jesus and all of his disciples, she likely had quite a few servants to help her out. There may have been other, deeper concerns that were troubling her. Like the fact that her sister was bringing shame upon their household by acting like one of the men, "sitting at Jesus' feet" like a disciple. "At his feet" is the phrase Paul used in Acts 22:3 to describe his education under Gamaliel, and it didn't just mean that Mary was sitting on the floor near Jesus' toes—it meant she was learning alongside his male disciples. Women weren't supposed to do that in first-century Jewish culture—their place was in the kitchen.

So when Martha asked Jesus to please tell Mary to come help her, it was a reasonable request, not because Martha needed the help but because Mary wasn't doing what women were supposed to do. What would people think of her sister's inappropriate behavior? Perhaps Martha was even anxious about what Jesus would think. So she decided to go get Mary, perhaps to save her sister from the embarrassment of being sent away by Jesus. Rather than drawing attention to Mary's inappropriate behavior, she offers her sister a convenient, culturally appropriate escape route: "Terribly sorry to interrupt, Jesus, but I desperately need my sister in the kitchen for a moment."

I think Jesus' reply is full of empathy for Martha. He recognized that she was "anxious and troubled about many things." But only one thing is necessary, and there is only One Person's opinion we need to be concerned about. I don't think Martha left that encounter feeling rebuked, I think she left astonished that Mary had *not* been rebuked, that Mary was allowed and even encouraged to stay.

In a culture where men had virtually all of the power and respect, Jesus consistently gave up power he could have claimed, and gave respect to women. When the God who transcends gender came to dwell among us in a human body (that happened to be male), he did not limit his interactions or activities to what was considered to be culturally "manly" at the time. He stepped outside of the "men's world," began breaking down the culturally constructed barriers that limited and excluded women, and began laying the foundation of a kingdom—God's Kingdom—where creation order would be restored and men and women could once again work side by side.

Jesus made his opinion very clear that day. Mary got to stay. Women get to stay. Putting olives on the salad can be valuable Kingdom work, but only one thing is necessary, and women and men can attend to the olives together after they sit at Jesus' feet together, side by side, as they were at creation.

A Found Child

> *If a man has a hundred sheep and one of them gets lost, what will he do? Won't he leave the ninety-nine others in the wilderness and go to search for the one that is lost until he finds it? (Luke 15:4, NLT)*

> *Or suppose a woman has ten silver coins and loses one. Won't she light a lamp and sweep the entire house and search carefully until she finds it? (Luke 15:8, NLT)*

> *Do not be afraid, for I am with you. I will gather you and your children from east and west. I will say to the north and south, "Bring my sons and daughters back to Israel from the distant corners of the earth." (Isa 43:5-6, NLT)*

There have been a few times when my small daughter has found herself a cozy, hidden corner of the yard and settled down to play, blissfully unaware of the fact that I had no idea where she was. I never start to panic until I have checked all her usual haunts, but when she discovers a new one I sometimes end up in panic mode for several eternally long minutes. I can hardly bear to imagine the horror I would feel if she were truly missing, but I am certain that I would not feel able to do anything but search for her until I found her, and there would be no lengths to which I would not go to find her and bring her home.

God has the same holy mother's heart towards us, and will not stop searching for even one of God's children until that child is found. One of the greatest griefs of this broken world is that human parents are not always able to find their children, but God can always find you, and God can always find your children.

> *Where can I go from your Spirit? Where can I flee from your presence? If I go up to the heavens, you are there; if I make my bed in the depths, you are there. If I rise on the wings of the dawn, if I settle on the far side of the sea, even there your hand will guide me, your right hand will hold me fast. If I say, "Surely the darkness will hide me and the light become night around me," even the darkness will not be dark to you, the night will shine like the day. (Ps 139:7-12, NIV)*

There is no direction or distance that God will not travel to find you, and nowhere you can hide where you will not be found by your heavenly MotherFather.

The Comforter

But I tell you the truth, it is to your advantage that I go away; for if I do not go away, the Helper will not come to you; but if I go, I will send him to you. (John 16:7, NASB)

When Jesus arrived on earth, God had already been promising for hundreds and thousands of years—since sin entered the world—that a Savior was coming. God had been promising to make everything right again, and to bring comfort where God's children were hurting. Especially in Isaiah, both the coming of the Messiah and the establishment of the new heavens and earth are defined by the concepts of compassion, restoration, and motherly comfort.

> *For you will nurse from her satisfying breasts and be nourished; you will feed with joy from her milk-filled breasts. As a mother consoles a child, so I will console you, and you will be consoled over Jerusalem. (Isa 66:11, 13, NET)*

> *For the LORD comforts his people and will have compassion on his afflicted ones (Isa 49:13, NIV)*

> *The LORD will surely comfort Zion and will look with compassion on all her ruins. (Isa 51:3, NIV)*

> *I, I am the one who consoles you. (Isa 51:12, NET)*

Simeon, who was eagerly waiting for the Messiah in Luke 2:25, had obviously read his Isaiah because we are told that he was "waiting for the consolation [*literally, comfort*] of Israel" (NIV). Luke and John had no doubt heard Isaiah too, probably the Greek translation of Isaiah. They, too, were waiting for the comfort of Israel, which in Greek is the *paraklesis* of Israel. Isaiah's descriptions of God's Kingdom, defined by compassion and motherly comfort, which they had heard so many times and so deeply longed for, were all wrapped up in that Greek word: *paraklesis*.

Well, the Messiah came, and he ripped the temple curtain and tore down all the barriers between us and God's compassionate, comforting *paraklesis* that we so desperately need. And then he left, but he did not leave us alone. It was not good for us to be alone, so he left us a Helper, a Comforter—the *Parakletos*.

> *No, I will not abandon you as orphans. I will ask the Father, and he will give you another Advocate [lit. Parakletos: Comforter,*

Helper] who will never leave you. He is the Holy Spirit, who leads into all truth. (John 14:18, 15–16, NLT)

The Holy Spirit is our Helper, our *Ezer*, our comforting mother who birthed us into God's Kingdom (John 3:6) and will never leave us as orphans. This is "the Holy Spirit, who leads into all truth."

Waiting by the Tomb

Now very early on the first day of the week, while it was still dark, Mary Magdalene came to the tomb and saw that the stone had been moved away from the entrance. So she went running to Simon Peter and the other disciple whom Jesus loved and told them, "They have taken the Lord from the tomb, and we don't know where they have put him!" Then Peter and the other disciple set out to go to the tomb. The two were running together, but the other disciple ran faster than Peter and reached the tomb first. He bent down and saw the strips of linen cloth lying there, but he did not go in. Then Simon Peter, who had been following him, arrived and went right into the tomb. He saw the strips of linen cloth lying there, and the face cloth, which had been around Jesus' head, not lying with the strips of linen cloth but rolled up in a place by itself. Then the other disciple, who had reached the tomb first, came in, and he saw and believed. (For they did not yet understand the scripture that Jesus must rise from the dead.) So the disciples went back to their homes. But Mary stood outside the tomb weeping. As she wept, she bent down and looked into the tomb. And she saw two angels in white sitting where Jesus' body had been lying, one at the head and one at the feet. They said to her, "Woman, why are you weeping?" Mary replied, "They have taken my Lord away, and I do not know where they have put him!" When she had said this, she turned around and saw Jesus standing there, but she did not know that it was Jesus. Jesus said to her, "Woman, why are you weeping? Who are you looking for?" Because she thought he was the gardener, she said to him, "Sir, if you have carried him away, tell me where you have put him, and I will take him." Jesus said to her, "Mary." She turned and said to him in Aramaic, "Rabboni" (which means Teacher). Jesus replied, "Do not touch me, for I have not yet ascended to my Father. Go to my brothers and tell them, 'I am ascending to my Father and your Father, to my God and your God.'" Mary Magdalene came and informed the disciples, "I

have seen the Lord!" And she told them what Jesus had said to her.
(John 20:1–18, NET)

Why did Mary get to be the first person to see Jesus, and the person to preach the first Easter sermon, announcing the good news that Jesus was alive to the other disciples? Was she just in the right place at the right time?

Peter and John would have been the logical choices for this job. They were two of the twelve, and a prominent two at that. They were men in a culture where a woman's word was worthless as legal testimony. In fact, when Mary came with her message Luke tells us that "the story sounded like nonsense to the men, so they didn't believe it" (Luke 24:11, NLT). Why not give the message to somebody who would have been more readily believed?

Furthermore, Peter and John *were* in the right place at the right time. They were there, in the tomb, and they saw the empty wrappings lying there. It would have been a great moment for Jesus (or at least an angel) to show up and give these prominent male disciples the important message of the resurrection so they could go preach it to everyone else. But Jesus chose not to show himself to them. And it wasn't because they lacked faith. John, at least, believed. But he still didn't see Jesus. So he and Peter went home.

But Mary stayed. "Mary was standing outside the tomb crying" (John 20:11, NLT). There was nothing there for her. No Jesus, no angels, no hope. Not even a dead body. Just her grief and disappointment. But she didn't leave. She sat there, in her sadness and despair, in the place where she had last seen Jesus.

When our questions are not answered, when we find no comfort for our grief, when disappointments leave us in a place of despair, when it looks like Jesus simply isn't there, it can seem logical to leave. Leave the questions, the grief, and the absent Jesus behind, and go home. Find a new way forward without the God who isn't there anyway. We don't have to outwardly turn our backs on God or the church to make this choice. Like a broken married couple, living in the same house with no communication, we can maintain our identity as a "Christian," but gradually give up on maintaining any level of deep communication with God.

Or we can wait by the tomb. There may be nothing for us to do there but cry, and it may seem that we are alone, that Jesus isn't even there to see our sorrow. But if we wait there, like Mary, if we refuse to leave hope behind and go home, if we stay in the place where we last knew God to be, and press in to the questions, the grief, the disappointment, and even the despair in that place ... that is just the place where we are most likely to notice Jesus looking for us.

God's Helpers

> *Remember, dear brothers and sisters, that few of you were wise in the world's eyes or powerful or wealthy when God called you. Instead, God chose things the world considers foolish in order to shame those who think they are wise. And he chose things that are powerless to shame those who are powerful. God chose things despised by the world, things counted as nothing at all, and used them to bring to nothing what the world considers important. As a result, no one can ever boast in the presence of God. (1 Cor 1:26–29, NLT)*

The other day I was hiding in my kitchen, sifting flour, and desperately hoping that nobody would offer to help me. (I've never really been a sifter, but the flour in Papua New Guinea tends to come with large amounts of chaff and even small twigs. When one of my daughters declared that she wasn't going to eat any more bread because she was tired of chewing up sticks, I decided maybe I should experiment with becoming a sifter.) If I sift alone, it takes me about ten minutes to finish a sack of flour. If I have help, it takes considerably longer, and every available surface is covered in flour dust. On this particular day, I had barely started when I heard the words: "Mommy, can I help you?"

I often say no, but today I said yes, and as I stood there watching the flour dust fly mercilessly around my kitchen I asked myself (seriously) why I ever accept "help" that is not actually helpful. As my daughter chattered happily and flung a particularly impressive spray of flour onto the floor, I realized that, when I do say yes, it's for two very good reasons: I want my children to learn and develop the skills that come from "helping" in the kitchen, and I want my relationship with them to grow the way it does when we're "working" together. It's not that I need (or even want) their "help," but I do want to be with them, and I want them to learn in the process.

We can fool ourselves into thinking that the things we do and accomplish "for God" are at the heart of our relationship with God. But God doesn't need our help any more than I need flour sprinkled all over my kitchen. God invites us to "help" build the Kingdom of Heaven because God wants us to learn and grow in the process, and because God wants to be in relationship with us—God wants to be with us in the kitchen!

I recently found myself feeling very powerless and inadequate to do something that God had set before me, and I couldn't help wondering, "Why me, God? Why aren't you stirring up one of the many people who are so much more powerful and better equipped to deal with this situation?" And then it hit me. God doesn't need any of us, and a powerless person is just as nice to be with in the kitchen as a powerful one. It was my turn to help, and the important thing was for me to grow in relationship with God in the process. God would make sure the meal turned out okay in the end, even if I made a bit of a mess in the process.

Remarkably, it seems to be the powerless who are most frequently invited into the Kitchen of God to "help." It was a powerless, destitute widow who God "instructed" (1 Kgs 17:9) to feed the great prophet Elijah, though God had already been proven capable of miraculously feeding Elijah without human help.[1] It was a powerless teenage girl who was invited to birth God into the world and raise Jesus alongside her ordinary, powerless husband. It was a powerless woman (whose testimony would have been worthless in court) who was entrusted with the message of Jesus' resurrection, and powerless fishermen who were first sent out to spread the good news that the Kingdom of Heaven is now.

So if you are feeling weak, or powerless, or poor in your spirit, be glad! The Kingdom of Heaven is yours (Matt 5:3, 18:1–4)! Become like a little child in the kitchen with your mother and enjoy being with God, learning and growing in relationship with God. Dinner will turn out okay, even with your help.

Learning to See the Invisible

> *So we fix our eyes not on what is seen, but on what is unseen, since what is seen is temporary, but what is unseen is eternal.* (2 Cor 4:18, NIV)

Much of my life these days feels like an exercise in futility. I cook food that immediately disappears. I change and wash diapers that are imminently

---

1. Acknowledgement to Kristin Wright-Bettner

refilled with poop. I wash clothes that get dirty again in a few hours. I discipline for the same things, over and over, often without noticeable results. I have the same conversations every day, again and again. ("Yes, that's your shirt. No, the cat doesn't have a shirt. But you have a shirt. But the cat doesn't have a shirt. But you have a shirt. No, cows don't have shirts either. Yes, you still have a shirt.")

If you want immediately visible results, don't choose motherhood as a profession. You will spend the bulk of your time doing things that either get undone right away, or appear to have a very minimal effect on your environment. And you do these things over and over again, every single day, with no visible "product" at the end of the day. It would be a downright depressing job if the visible were all there was. But it is the invisible that is meaningful and lasting.

The visible food disappears in a flash, but invisibly it remains, building bones, muscles, and tiny brains. Clean clothes, clean floors, clean dishes, clean diapers—clean anything really—is only visibly clean for a very short time, but invisibly, young souls can flourish in the security of being consistently cared for. I may have the same one-sided conversation again and again with nothing visible to show for it, but invisibly the next generation is learning to use language.

We adults often chafe at having to do the exact same thing again and again, every day, especially if we don't see any visible results. But children don't mind at all. Neither does God. Every day God creates and sustains the same things, again and again. Planets continually whirling around in the exact same circles. Rain that falls only to evaporate, only to fall again and evaporate again. Grass and flowers that wither in a few days. Tiny flies that only live for hours. Sunrises that appear for just a few minutes and are often visible to only a few people. Have you ever wondered how many breathtaking sunrises have appeared in the Arctic and been seen by nobody at all? God's visible work may appear just as repetitive and "futile" as mine. But it is the invisible that remains. The eternal souls that are nurtured and sustained by the repetitive cycles of creation.

When I begin to feel weary of the repetitive nature of my life as a mother of small children, I am inspired by my Heavenly Mother to delight in the repetition of the visible and to believe that together we are creating an environment where the invisible can flourish. My children have already mastered this delight. In the words of G. K. Chesterton:

"Because children have abounding vitality, because they are in spirit fierce and free, therefore they want things repeated and unchanged. They always say, 'Do it again;' and the grown-up person does it again until he is nearly dead. For grown-up people are not strong enough to exult in monotony. But perhaps God is strong enough to exult in monotony. It is possible that God says every morning, 'Do it again' to the sun; and every evening, 'Do it again' to the moon. It may not be automatic necessity that makes all daisies alike; it may be that God makes every daisy separately, but has never got tired of making them. It may be that [God] has the eternal appetite of infancy; for we have sinned and grown old, and our Father is younger than we."[2]

Mud

When you're two years old, few things are as delightful as going outside in the rain, finding a ditch full of water, and covering every inch of yourself with mud. If all goes well, my twins can get several hours of solid entertainment out of a good muddy ditch, and I enjoy the experience from my observation post inside my dry kitchen. But eventually the fun ends (for all of us) when somebody gets too cold, too hungry, or too tired of his big sister rubbing mud in his hair, and the time comes for me to pay for my solitude by cleaning them up. I peel off their sodden clothing, and clumps of mud fall out. I stick them both in a warm shower, get most of the dirt out of their hair, and wash between their filthy toes. It's a messy process, and while they end up cleaner and drier, I inevitably end up dirtier and wetter. I dress their shivering bodies in dry fleece pants and hoodies, give them something warm to drink, and settle them on the couch under blankets with a book and a snack. Perhaps the only thing more delightful than getting wet and playing in the mud is the feeling of being clean, dry, and warm afterwards.

Sometimes I feel like I just need God to clean me up. After a day of getting slimed by my own sins, failures, and inadequacies, by the messy immaturity of the people under my care, and by the good but exhausting intensity of mothering, my soul feels tired, dirty, hungry, and cold and I just want Someone to take care of me. I am completely incapable of cleaning myself up, and I wouldn't even know where to start. But Jesus does.

2. Chesterton, *Orthodoxy*, 118-19.

> Christ loved the church. He gave up his life for her to make her holy and clean, washed by the cleansing of God's word. He did this to present her to himself as a glorious church without a spot or wrinkle or any other blemish. Instead, she will be holy and without fault. No one hates his own body, but feeds and cares for it, just as Christ cares for the church. And we are members of his body. (Eph 5:25–27, 29–30, NLT)

Dr. Cynthia Westfall points out that "in Hellenistic culture, [bathing, laundering and clothing] are explicit household functions that women and slaves provide for men and other women. . . . The preparation and serving of food was women's or slaves' work, as was all household care that involved nurturing."[3] The Ephesian husbands were being told to lay down the power and privileges that their culture granted them and be like Jesus, who "gave up his divine privileges; he took the humble position of a slave."[4] Since the night he wrapped a towel around himself and washed the mud off his friends' feet, Jesus has continued to do for us what only an insignificant servant . . . or a mother . . . would do for another person.

No matter how muddy I get, no matter how many times it happens, Jesus washes me, over and over again. I don't have to struggle to clean myself up before asking God to hold me in my weariness—I can rest in the arms of my Holy Mother and be cleansed by God's pure spiritual milk—washed, dressed, fed and comforted. Nothing is more delightful.

Wet, Stinky Clothes

> But now you must also rid yourselves of [take off] all such things as these: anger, rage, malice, slander, and filthy language from your lips. Do not lie to each other, since you have taken off your old self with its sinful practices and have put on the new self, which is being renewed in knowledge in the image of its Creator. Therefore, as God's chosen people, holy and dearly loved, clothe yourselves with compassion, kindness, humility, gentleness, and patience. And over all these virtues put on love, which binds them all together in perfect harmony. (Col 3:8–10, 12, 14, NIV)

Clothes are a big deal in our house. Even the toddler boys have learned that deciding what to wear is a very important part of your day. They

---

3. Westfall, *Paul and Gender*, 57.
4. Phil 2:7, NLT

don't have words yet, but they can communicate quite a lot by pointing, grunting, and shaking their heads, and they let me know if I pull out an outfit that they feel is unsuitable.

Once I've negotiated the day's apparel with one of them, he clutches it tightly and begins demanding that I instantly put the new clothes on him. Taking off his pajamas and sodden diaper is, in his mind, a completely unnecessary waste of time. As I take off layer after layer of damp, smelly jammies he uses an impressively expressive string of gibberish to say, "Mom, I've got things to do. Stop wasting my time with all this undressing nonsense and just dress me in these nice, new clothes already!" I tell him that nobody puts new wine into old wine skins, or new pants over pee-soaked diapers, but he disagrees. I also tell him that if he would just hold still, instead of struggling to put the new clothes on himself, he would end up wearing the new clothes much sooner!

Sometimes we have to take off something old before we can put on something new. It seems obvious in the context of wet, stinky clothes, but I wonder how often I holler the same string of gibberish at God. When there is something so clearly *good* that God could so easily do or give, but instead God is doing all these uncomfortable and seemingly useless things. Maybe there's something God needs to take off first, something that would only spoil the good, new gift if it were left underneath.

When my husband and I were ready to return to Papua New Guinea after he finished his Master of Theology and I finished having three babies, we were delayed for a full year by mysterious health problems. During that time, full of uncomfortable uncertainty and dozens of seemingly useless doctor visits, it was hard not to wonder why God was "wasting" a whole year. "Come on, God! We have good work waiting for us there! We're ready to get back to it! Why don't you just heal, or at least show us what the problem is?" Looking back, I think we had some old clothes that needed to come off first. The year wasn't wasted, our Mother was taking off our wet, stinky clothes so that we could fully thrive in the new clothes waiting for us. Sometimes during that process we struggled like a toddler being undressed, but I felt God calling us to "hold still" and let God do what we needed God to do.

Some mornings it takes longer than others, but I always eventually get the old pajamas off my son so he can wear the lovely new outfit he has chosen for himself. Mom always wins, and God always accomplishes God's purposes in our lives. But I think sometimes we get to choose how long it takes for the old clothes to come off. Off they will come, but it might be quicker if we hold still. This is not always the case, nor do "delays" always mean that there are old clothes to take off. But the next time you find yourself wishing that God would "hurry up" and do what is so obviously good, it might be worth holding still for a minute, and asking God if there's something that needs to be taken off of you first.

Strong Women

> *Likewise, husbands, live with your wives in an understanding way, showing honor to the woman as the weaker vessel, since they are heirs with you of the grace of life, so that your prayers may not be hindered. (1 Pet 3:7, ESV)*

I've always loved to run, whether alone or with a friend. But there's something especially thrilling about a big road race, where you're surrounded by hundreds of people all running at the same time. And at least part of that thrill comes from the opportunity to pass other runners. It's tempting to take advantage of the adrenaline burst at the beginning of a race, and start off sprinting, but I learned to resist that temptation and ration my energy so that in the second half I could pass all the people who had already used up their adrenaline. I would gradually gain on whoever was ahead of me and then, when I was a few feet behind them, sprint briefly until I was undeniably ahead of them (as my dad taught me). I'm sure they could hear me coming for quite awhile, but they couldn't see who I was until I was just ahead of them, already leaving them in my wake. If the person I was passing happened to be male, they rarely reacted when they heard my footsteps behind them, but as soon as they saw that I was a woman they would look over with a startled expression of panic and suddenly start sprinting themselves. It was usually too late by then.

Strength is generally considered to be a desirable quality but women, especially in the church, often feel a pressure not to be stronger (in any way) than the men around them. Sometimes this pressure is even preached. 1 Peter 3:7 is an explicit command for husbands to honor their wives, but it has been interpreted as an implicit command for women to be weak—at least weaker than their husbands and the men in their church. Some people feel that strong women "emasculate" the men around them and keep these men from exercising their God-given strength. There seems to be a fear that if the women were stronger, the men would necessarily be weaker.

There is a kind of "strength" that is only strong when it is surrounded by people who are weaker. And if men cannot be strong unless the women around them are weaker, we have to ask what kind of strength we are teaching our sons to have. True strength doesn't need someone else to be weak in order to make itself look stronger. True strength flows over to those around us and makes them stronger too. Jesus didn't carefully hoard his power and strength so that he could clearly be more amazing than everyone else (even though he was!). He strengthened and empowered his disciples and sent them out to do the same things he did himself. His strength was not threatened by theirs—it was magnified.

Women were designed to be *ezers*—rescuers, deliverers, protectors—in this world. That is a role that requires great strength, and when we live out that role, we are living in the image of the God who is our ultimate *Ezer*. God, as our *Ezer*, is a strong rescuer, but God also strengthens us and empowers us to be victorious ourselves.

> *[God] is your shield and helper [Ezer] and your glorious sword. Your enemies will cower before you and you will tread on their heights [stomp on their backs, NLT]! (Deut 33:29, NIV)*

God doesn't just show off God's own great strength by sending the enemies away single-handedly (though that would be well within God's abilities and rights). No, our *Ezer* strengthens and equips *us* to stomp on our spiritual enemies and send them cowering away from the strength that God extends to us. And when we, as women, use our God-given strength to empower our brothers and our sisters to use their own God-given strength, we are living out our role as *ezers* created in the image of God.

If I had politely stayed behind all those men in road races, it may have saved them some embarrassment, but it would not have made them any stronger or faster. But when I used my strength, and sped alongside them, that *did* make them both stronger and faster, as they were motivated to use their own strength more fully. Women and men should all be free to use every last bit of the strength God has given us, not to leave people behind or make others look weaker, but to strengthen our brothers and our sisters to use all of their strength as well.

> *Let us think of ways to motivate one another to acts of love and good works. (Heb 10:24, NLT)*

Weaker Vessels

> *Likewise, husbands, live with your wives in an understanding way, showing honor to the woman as the weaker vessel, since they are heirs with you of the grace of life, so that your prayers may not be hindered. (1 Pet 3:7, ESV)*

So, I've been saying that women can be strong, that we are strong, and that it's good for us to be strong. But Peter, inspired by the Holy Spirit, called us the weaker vessels. What's up with that?

First, all of Peter's instructions to citizens, slaves, wives, and husbands in 1 Peter 2:11—3:17 need to be read within the context that Peter himself specifies at the beginning and end of these instructions.

> *Be careful to live properly among your unbelieving neighbors. Then even if they accuse you of doing wrong, they will see your honorable behavior, and they will give honor to God when he judges the world. (1 Pet 2:12, NLT)*

> *Keep your conscience clear. Then if people speak against you, they will be ashamed when they see what a good life you live because you belong to Christ. (1 Pet 3:16, NLT)*

Christians are being slandered, and Peter is telling them to live in a way that brings honor to Christ. He fleshes out this command by telling specific groups of people how they can each bring honor to Christ within their particular context. For all citizens, that means respecting the authority of the government (2:13). For slaves, that means accepting the authority that the government has given to their masters (2:18). For wives, that means accepting the authority that the government has given to their husbands (3:1). For husbands, that means honoring their wives, who are powerless (weak) within the structure of the Roman empire, but are "equal partners" in the Kingdom of God.

The Greek word that describes women as the "weaker vessels" in 1 Peter 3:7 doesn't always refer to weakness as the absence of strength. It often "pertains to experiencing some incapacity or limitation" and can mean "economically weak, poor" or "without influence."[5] Sometimes it refers to the absence of power, rather than the absence of strength. Notice how the same word is used in these passages.

---

5. BDAG 142.

> *Yes, the old requirement about the priesthood was set aside because it was weak [powerless to save] and useless. (Heb 7:18, NLT)*

> *You see, at just the right time, when we were still powerless, Christ died for the ungodly. (Rom 5:6, NIV)*

The women Peter was writing to were completely powerless within their social and economic structure. "It normally was quite easy for a husband to abuse his wife physically or sexually, or, because of his social power, including the power to divorce, intimidate her emotionally. All of this Peter rules out: especially because of her vulnerability he is to be sure to honor her in word and deed; rather than exploiting his power or denying that he has it, he lends it to her."[6]

Husbands are told to *honor* their wives. Peter is not talking about condescending care—in fact, both Peter and John use the same word to talk about the honor that is given to Christ himself.

> *Yes, you who trust [Christ] recognize the honor God has given him. (1 Pet 2:7, NLT)*

> *Worthy is the Lamb who was slaughtered—to receive power and riches and wisdom and strength and honor and glory and blessing. (Rev 5:12, NLT)*

Because women were without power or honor within the structure of the earthly kingdom they lived in, Christian husbands were commanded to share their own power, and give special honor to their wives as equal partners within the Kingdom of God.

Nevertheless, even if Peter was not referring to physical weakness, it is undeniable that men generally tend to be physically stronger than women. That is one of the gifts God has given them (as he has given others to women), but it is not a gift for themselves, but a gift for them to give to those around them. Many times I have needed and been grateful for the height and muscles of my husband, my father, and my brothers! And physical strength (or lack thereof) is irrelevant to our position in God's Kingdom.

> *[God] takes no pleasure in the strength of a horse or in human might. No, the* Lord's *delight is in those who fear him, those who put their hope in his unfailing love. (Ps 147:10–11, NLT)*

---

6. Davids, *The First Epistle of Peter*, 123.

The Holy Women of Old

> *Don't be concerned about the outward beauty of fancy hairstyles, expensive jewelry, or beautiful clothes. You should clothe yourselves instead with the beauty that comes from within, the unfading beauty of a gentle and quiet spirit, which is so precious to God. This is how the holy women of old made themselves beautiful. They trusted God and accepted the authority of their husbands. For instance, Sarah obeyed her husband, Abraham, and called him her master. You are her daughters when you do what is right without fear of what your husbands might do. (1 Pet 3:3–6, NLT)*

Peter was telling women to accept the legal authority of their husbands, just as slaves were to accept the legal authority of their masters (1 Pet 2:18), so that nobody would have an opportunity to accuse Jesus' followers of doing wrong (1 Pet 2:12, 3:16). That was how first-century wives and slaves could bring honor to the name of Christ. For those of us living under governments where husbands have no legal authority over wives and slavery is against the law, bringing honor to Christ might look a bit different.

Peter told these women to make themselves beautiful like "the holy women of old." Like the first-century Christians, these ancient women lived in a patriarchal society where they had very few rights and no real options outside of accepting the authority of their husbands. And yet they navigated that world in a way that Peter says made them "beautiful." Let's take a moment to look at the way these beautiful, holy women of old related to their husbands.

"Sarah obeyed her husband, Abraham, and called him her master" (1 Pet 3:6, NLT). But their relationship was one of mutual respect and obedience. Abraham also did what Sarah told him to do (Gen 16:2, 6; 21:10–14), and on one occasion God explicitly told Abraham to follow Sarah's instructions and do whatever she told him to do (Gen 21:12). Rather than having to rely on the promise God gave to Abraham in Genesis 17:15–16, Sarah herself received the same promise directly from God and was given the opportunity to converse with God herself (Gen 18:9–15).

In the middle of a difficult pregnancy, Rebekah initiated an encounter with God, and God's plans for the future of their family were revealed to her, not her husband (Gen 25:22–23). And, while her methods may have been questionable, she was the one who engineered the fulfillment of these plans (Gen 27:5-29). Not only that, but she was also the one who initiated the sequence of events that led to her son's marriage with the women who would become the mothers of Israel and eventually the Messiah (Gen 27:42—28:5).

Jacob's wives, Leah and Rachel, arranged their husband's evening schedule for him (Gen 30:14-17), gave him advice that aligned with God's plans for him (Gen 31:14-16), and heavily influenced the men who had power over their very lives (Gen 31:32-5).

Tamar, one of the few women named in Jesus' ancestry (Matt 1:3), was married to a wicked man, cheated by one of his brothers, and deceived and abandoned by the third brother and his father, who later tried to execute her for a sin that he had committed alongside her (read all about it in Genesis 38). Cast aside with no hope or resources of her own, she single-handedly carried out a risky, elaborate, and (shall we say) unorthodox con that not only secured her own future, but also made her one of the great-great-great-etc. grandmothers of the Messiah.

These women engaged directly with God, asking questions and receiving answers, not through their husbands, but for themselves. They had ideas and carried them out, often telling their husbands what they needed to do to accomplish God's purposes, or simply doing it themselves. It's easy for us to look back and tell them that they should have done things differently, that there must have been a better way, but they are never criticized or condemned in Scripture for the choices that they made. They are remembered as beautiful, as holy, and welcomed into the family of Jesus. And we are invited to become their daughters.

Flowers for God

> *And when he took the scroll, the four living beings and the twenty-four elders fell down before the Lamb. Each one had a harp, and they held gold bowls filled with incense, which are the prayers of God's people. (Rev 5:8, NLT)*

My kids love to bring me flowers. Nearly every day I am offered a fresh-picked (though sometimes scraggly) bouquet by a beaming child, eagerly waiting to see how excited and happy it makes me. I'm pretty good at feigning excitement, which is useful because if I'm quite honest I have to say that I would prefer to enjoy these flowers outside, and keep the spiders and piles of pollen that accompany them outside too. But it makes my kids so happy to present them to me that their happiness makes me happy too, so the joy I express to them is real.

Yesterday was May Day (May 1), and when they learned about the old tradition of secretly leaving flowers outside people's doors, they could hardly contain their excitement. Sure enough, while they were playing outside I heard a loud knock on the door, and when I opened it there was a pile of mangled, stemless flowers on the ground (the two-year-olds had been allowed to participate in the fun). As I loudly expressed joy and surprise at this beautiful and mysterious gift, I could hear delighted giggles and caught a glimpse of sparkling eyes out the window.

I wonder if our worship is like these flowers. I have heard it said that worship is for God, not for us, but I suspect that it very much is for us. God needs our worship about as much as I need the flower that has been crushed by an overly excited small hand. But we very much need to worship God. When I bring my heart to a place of worship, it feels like everything has been set in order, and it feels like coming home, and I desperately need that every day. And, while God doesn't need my worship, I think it must give God joy to see the joy that it gives me.

I don't think God is very interested in having certain words said or sung, or having rituals or good deeds performed. But every time we express genuine love for God, whether it's through words, songs, feeding a hungry mouth or wiping a snotty nose, God treasures that act of worship like a golden bowl filled with incense, just like I treasure the messy, crumpled flowers that symbolize my children's love for me.

The Bread of Life

There are few things more delightful than warm, freshly baked bread, slathered in real butter. My mom baked nearly all of our bread for years, and I can remember waiting for the bread to be done, our anticipation growing as the smell filled the house. Once, when the bread baking happened late in the day, she even let us stay up past our bedtime so we could have a slice fresh from the oven. For bread to be truly fresh, you have to be right there with the person who made it for you, watching her take it out of the oven. Fresh bread, home, and my mom will always be tied together in my mind.

I love that when the God who "picks up the whole earth as though it were a grain of sand" (Isa 40:15, NLT) came here to live with us, God came to be our Bread—something simple, humble, and homey, and yet so necessary for life.

> *I am the living Bread that came down from heaven. Anyone who eats this bread will live forever; and this bread, which I will offer so the world may live, is my flesh. (John 6:51, NLT)*

When God appeared to Abram in Genesis 15:17, "Abram saw a smoking firepot and a flaming torch pass between the halves of the carcasses" (NLT). In some contexts a "firepot" is a dangerous, flaming furnace capable of great destruction, but it is also a simple clay pot used for baking bread.[7] The God of infinite power, whose full revelation would utterly overwhelm and undo us, appears as a bread oven and becomes the living Bread who gave his life to give us life.

The living Bread is always fresh. When Jesus prayed in Matthew 6:11, "Give us today our daily bread" (NIV), he was not just asking for bread for today. He was asking for *fresh* bread today. That Greek word "daily" puzzled scholars for centuries, because it's not used anywhere else in the New Testament, but it was eventually found on an ancient shopping list. "Some housewife had demanded not day-old bread but 'daily' bread. She didn't want yesterday's food."[8] Jesus was telling us to ask God every day for fresh-baked bread. Our mother doesn't hoard bread for weeks, doling out a small portion of stale bread each day. Every single day God offers you a fresh warm piece, baked just for you, to give you exactly what you need for that day.

Of course, there is nothing inherently feminine about baking bread, but within the cultures described in the Bible bread baking was generally the women's job.[9] People living in those cultures, who had grown up eating bread baked almost exclusively by their mothers, likely shared my experience of associating fresh bread, home, and their mom. When we realize that bread likely had motherly connotations for the original audiences, it's pretty cool that God appeared as a bread oven, Jesus called himself Bread, and we are told to ask God every day for fresh-baked bread. Stay close to your Mother and you'll never have to eat yesterday's food.

---

7. NIDOTTE 313.
8. Lykosh, "Daily Bread," lines 6–8.
9. Freeman, *The New Manners and Customs of the Bible*, 40.

Snacks

"Mom, do you have any snacks?" My littlest girl will ask this question anywhere—on a walk, in the car, on the way home from school. I do not always have snacks with me, but occasionally the answer is yes, so she figures it's always worth asking. Sometimes tiny tummies can't wait until the next meal for food, and they just need a snack.

As a mom, there are days when I don't have time to sit down to eat a meal. Sometimes having lunch means shoving large bites of food into my mouth in between taking people to the potty and cleaning rice off the floor. When the next meal comes and goes and you didn't get a chance to eat it, even slightly larger tummies need a snack sometimes.

More and more, I cherish the times when I can sit down with God for a leisurely spiritual meal and soak up God's love until my soul is satisfied. And I firmly believe that it's so important to find times when that can happen, whatever it takes. But it doesn't happen for me every day, and there are days when I know my soul won't last until the next "meal." I will devour somebody if I don't get fed before then. And so I shout (silently) as I rush from the poopy diaper to the sticky floor, "Mom, do you have any snacks for me?"

God knows I need proper meals sometimes, but thankfully God does snacks too: bits of truth, encouragement, and love that our souls can munch even while our bodies rush around keeping tiny bodies alive. Sometimes I ask, as I sleepily trudge up the stairs to tend to the human alarm clock that went off much too early, "What can I take with me to eat today?" And the answer always comes, though not always right away. God always has snacks for us, if we choose to notice them. Here are a few of my favorites.

- *I am the disciple Jesus loves. (see John 13:23)*
- *Satisfy me this morning with your unfailing love. (see Ps 90:14)*
- *This morning I will sing with joy about your unfailing love. (see Ps 59:16)*
- *With God's help, I will do mighty things. (see Ps 60:12)*
- *I cry to you for help when my heart is overwhelmed. (Ps 61:2, NLT)*

Happy snacking.

Monastic Motherhood

There are days when joining a monastery sounds pretty good. When five different people are all talking to me at the same time, my sink is overflowing with dirty dishes, and I trip over a plastic cow on the way to answer the phone, the thought of a solitary cell without earthly possessions becomes quite attractive.

But the monastic life has never been exclusively about solitude. It rests on the twin pillars of dedicated solitude and service to others—both to other monks and to those most in need of service. Henri Nouwen says that "prayer without action grows into powerless pietism,"[10] and Cistercian monk Thomas Keating writes that "dedication to God and service to others form the two sides of a channel," and that "service to others . . . neutralizes the deep-rooted tendency to become preoccupied with our own spiritual journey and how we are doing."[11] Solitude is readily available within a monastery, but monks might need to venture outside and search for opportunities to balance their solitude with service. I may need to leave my house to find some necessary solitude, but opportunities for service are readily available in every moment.

The goal of solitude is to experience the presence of God that transforms us to become more like Jesus. Henri Nouwen says that "Jesus consistently refuses the way of success, power, influence, and celebrity. Always, he chooses the way of weakness, powerlessness, compassion, and obscurity—the way of the poor."[12] The way of motherhood. "And so," continues Nouwen,

> "every time we choose poverty over wealth, powerlessness over power, humble service over popularity, quiet fruitfulness over loud acclaim, we prepare for our rebirth in the Holy Spirit. . . . In faith, we will no longer ignore or avoid these things, but embrace them as the place where Jesus walks with us and sends us his Spirit. Then also we will clearly see the poor around us. And out of this, a new spiritual community will be molded, not something spectacular, imposing, or world-convincing, but, on the contrary, something small, hidden, and very humble, scarcely noticed by our fast-moving world. In the midst of the world,

---

10. Nouwen, *The Only Necessary Thing*, 139.
11. Keating, *Open Mind, Open Heart*, 14–15
12. Nouwen, *The Only Necessary Thing*, 64.

but hidden from its view, something very new, very tender, and very fragile can be born."[13]

Birth is always a mystery, a miracle. It is doubly miraculous that the children I birthed into this physical world are now the very ones inviting me to embrace this "small, hidden, and very humble" world where Jesus walks with me and prepares me for my "rebirth in the Holy Spirit." I may be the only one with a plastic cow on the floor of my monastery, but it is still a holy place.

Fulfilling Motherhood

I've always wanted to be a mom. For as long as I can remember, I've loved small children, enjoyed holding babies, and dreamed of having my own kids to care for. As a teenager and young adult, I could not imagine anything more fulfilling than holding my very own tiny baby in my arms.

Well, that day came for me. Four times, and the fourth time I was holding my very own *very* tiny baby in each of my arms. And I'm so deeply grateful for each of those five amazing people, and love them with every inch of my heart. Being their mom has been one of God's deepest gifts of love to me, and I wouldn't trade these last nine years of motherhood for anything.

But what I didn't know nine years ago was that being a mom wasn't going to give me the personal satisfaction and fulfillment that I thought it would. I love my kids dearly, I love being their mom, and I honestly wouldn't change one bit of these years of being at home with them, but I figured out pretty quickly that I didn't actually love the practical, daily grind of keeping tiny people alive, especially through those very early months and years. Let's just say that caring for infants and toddlers is not a job I would seek out for the rest of my life. But even though I didn't find it to be perfectly enjoyable and fulfilling, I thought that it was supposed to be, so then I had guilt on top of the disillusioned weariness. And when I managed to drag myself and my children to the grocery store in the middle of a day that managed to be both exhausting and boring (and very full of poop) and a smiling old lady told me that I was going to miss these days, that sent me right into despair. If I was going to *miss* these exhausting, boring, poopy days, if there was nothing better than this to look forward to, that was very bad news.

13. Nouwen, *The Only Necessary Thing*, 64.

But you know what I realized? The point of motherhood is not for me to find personal satisfaction and fulfillment in being a mom, so it's okay if I don't like and enjoy every moment of momming. No, the point of motherhood, the reason why I would still choose to have five kids even knowing everything I know now, is that I get to add new lives to the Kingdom of God. It's not about me enjoying my job, it's about me getting to play a key part in building God's Kingdom, by nurturing these beautiful souls who will inherit that Kingdom. And not only do I get to keep the sweet bodies alive, not only do I get to cherish and nurture the marvelous souls who inhabit those bodies, but I get to show them who God is. And (spoiler alert) it gets more and more fun as my children grow older.

As I mother my children, crying out every day for my Heavenly Mother to transform me more and more fully into God's image, I get to be the moon reflecting the light of God's motherly love for my children. As they receive my practical love and care, I pray that it gives them a glimpse into the motherly heart of the God who loved them before they were even in my womb. And that's why I get out of bed in the morning, that's why I choose this job every day, even on the days when I don't personally enjoy all that it entails. As a woman created in the image of God, I pray that I will clearly and accurately reflect the motherly heart of God to all of God's children each day.

And I hope that I will continue to do that, even after my biological children are no longer my full-time job. I hope that I will continue to reflect God's motherly love to the future spiritual children that I long for, spiritual children who will hopefully benefit from the intense training and pruning I have received through the process of mothering my biological children. And some of you, who have not spent many of your years mothering a few biological children, probably already have far more of these spiritual children than I ever will.

> *Sing, O childless woman, you who have never given birth! Enlarge your house; build an addition. Spread out your home, and spare no expense! For you will soon be bursting at the seams. Your descendants will occupy other nations and resettle the ruined cities.* (Isa 54:1–3, NLT)

Wherever you are on your journey of motherhood, whether your children are biological, adopted, or spiritual, may our Holy Mother enlarge your house and multiply your descendants. May we each drink so deeply of God's love that we cannot contain it and it overflows onto our children. May we learn to mother as the image of our holy God. And may we find our deepest satisfaction and fulfillment not in our own mothering, but in being mothered by the Creator of our souls.

BIBLIOGRAPHY

Albright, William F. "The Names Shaddai and Abram," *Journal of Biblical Literature* (1935) 173–204.

Aldrege-Clanton, Jann. *In Whose Image? God and Gender*. London: SCM, 1992.

Allen, Leslie C. *Ezekiel 1–19*. Word Biblical Commentary 28. Dallas: Word Incorporated, 1994.

Blenkinsopp, Joseph. *Isaiah 56–66: A New Translation with Introduction and Commentary*. Anchor Yale Bible 19B. Yale University Press, 2008.

Block, Daniel Isaac. *The Book of Ezekiel, Chapters 1–24*. The New International Commentary on the Old Testament. Grand Rapids, MI: Eerdmans, 1997.

Chesterton, G. K. *Orthodoxy*. Great Britain: William Clowes and Sons, Limited, London and Beccles, 1934.

Christensen, Duane L. *Deuteronomy 21:10—34:21*. Word Biblical Commentary 6B. Waco, TX: Word, 2002.

deClaissé-Walford, Nancy et al. "The Songs of the Ascents: Psalms." In *The Book of Psalms*, edited by E.J. Young et al. The New International Commentary on the Old Testament. Grand Rapids, MI: Eerdmans, 2014. 887–909.

Clines, David J. A. *The Dictionary of Classical Hebrew*. Sheffield: Sheffield Academic, 1993–2001.

Costecalde, Claude Bernard. *Aux Origines du Sacre Biblique*. Paris: Letouzey & Ane, 1986.

Danker, Frederick William et al. *A Greek-English Lexicon of the New Testament and Other Early Christian Literature*. Chicago, IL: University of Chicago Press, 2000.

Davids, Peter H. *The First Epistle of Peter*. The New International Commentary on the New Testament. Grand Rapids, MI: Eerdmans, 1990.

De Souza, Becca. "My Body Kept Score: What Purity Culture Didn't Know about Trauma." *Mutuality* (January 2021). https://www.cbeinternational.org/resource/article/mutuality-blog-magazine/my-body-kept-score-what-purity-culture-didnt-know-about?platform=hootsuite

Freeman, James Midwinter. *The New Manners and Customs of the Bible*. Gainesville, FL: Bridge-Logos, 1998.

Geisel, Theodor S. *Oh, the Places You'll Go!* New York: Random House, Inc., 1990.

Gentry, Peter. "The Meaning of 'Holy' in the Old Testament." *Bibliotheca Sacra 170* (October-December 2013) 400–17.

Goldingay, John. *A Critical and Exegetical Commentary on Isaiah 56–66*. International Critical Commentary. New York: Bloomsbury, 2014.

Hamilton, Victor P. *The Book of Genesis, Chapters 1–17*. The New International Commentary on the Old Testament. Grand Rapids, MI: Eerdmans, 1990.

———. *The Book of Genesis, Chapters 18–50*. The New International Commentary on the Old Testament. Grand Rapids, MI: Eerdmans, 1995.

Harris, R. Laird et al. *Theological Wordbook of the Old Testament*. Chicago: Moody, 1980.

Hartley, John E. *The Book of Job*. The New International Commentary on the Old Testament. Grand Rapids, MI: Eerdmans, 1988.

Jacobson, Rolf A. and Beth Tanner. "Book One of the Psalter: Psalms 1–41," In *The Book of Psalms*, edited by E.J. Young et al. The New International Commentary on the Old Testament. Grand Rapids, MI: Eerdmans, 2014. 55–57.

Jukes, Andrew. *The Names of God in Holy Scripture*. New York: Longmans, Green, and Company, 1888. https://www.google.com/books/edition/The_Names_of_God_in_Holy_Scripture/sloXAAAAYAAJ?hl=en&gbpv=1&bsq=shaddai

Julian of Norwich. *Revelations of Divine Love*. Grand Rapids, MI: Christian Classics Ethereal Library, 2002.

Keating, Thomas. *Open Mind, Open Heart: The Contemplative Dimension of the Gospel*. Warwick, NY: A&C Black, 2002.

Keown, Gerald L. *Jeremiah 26–52*. Word Biblical Commentary 27. Dallas: Word, 1995.

Kimmerer, Robin. *Braiding Sweetgrass: Indigenous Wisdom, Scientific Knowledge and the Teachings of Plants*. Minneapolis, MN: Milkweed, 2013.

Koehler, Ludwig and Walter Baumgartner. *The Hebrew and Aramaic Lexicon of the Old Testament*. Translated and edited by M.E.J. Richardson. Leiden: Brill, 1994–2000.

La Leche League International. "Positioning." Accessed September 27, 2022. https://www.llli.org/breastfeeding-info/positioning/

Lange, John Peter. *Commentary on the Holy Scriptures: Psalms*. Bellingham, WA: Logos Bible Software, 2008.

Lewis, C. S. *Perelandra*. New York: Macmillan, 1965.

Lykosh, Amy. "Daily Bread." Accessed September 27, 2022. https://thehackpoetess.blogspot.com/2014/07/daily-bread.html

Mackie Tim, and Jon Collins. "The Womb of God," *BibleProject (August 31, 2020)* Accessed September 27, 2022. https://bibleproject.com/podcast/the-womb-of-god/

Mathews, K. A. *Genesis 1–11:26*. The New American Commentary 1A. Nashville: Broadman & Holman, 1996.

———. *Genesis 11:27—50:26*. The New American Commentary 1B. Nashville: Broadman & Holman, 2005.

Melick, Richard R. *Philippians, Colossians, Philemon*. The New American Commentary 32. Nashville: Broadman & Holman, 1991.

Modern Language Association. "How Do I Use Singular They?" Accessed September 27, 2022. https://style.mla.org/using-singular-they/

Mounce, Robert H. *The Book of Revelation*. The New International Commentary on the New Testament. Grand Rapids, MI: Eerdmans, 1997.

Nouwen, Henri JM. *The Only Necessary Thing*. St Pauls: BYB, 1999.

Oswalt, John N. *The Book of Isaiah, Chapters 1–39*. The New International Commentary on the Old Testament. Grand Rapids, MI: Eerdmans, 1986.

———. *The Book of Isaiah, Chapters 40–66*. The New International Commentary on the Old Testament. Grand Rapids, MI: Eerdmans, 1998.

Oxford Reference. "Markedness." Accessed September 27, 2022. https://www.oxfordreference.com/view/10.1093/oi/authority.20110803100134870
Plass, Adrian. *The Sacred Diary of Adrian Plass Aged 37 3/4*. New York: Harper Collins, 2005.
Smith, Aubry G.. *Holy Labor: How Childbirth Shapes a Woman's Soul*. Bellingham, WA: Kirkdale, Kindle Edition.
Smith, Gary. *Isaiah 40–66*. The New American Commentary 15B. Nashville: Broadman & Holman, 2009.
Stuart, Douglas K. *Exodus*. The New American Commentary 2. Nashville: Broadman & Holman, 2006.
Tate, Marvin E. *Psalms 51–100*. Word Biblical Commentary 20. Dallas: Word, 1998.
VanGemeren, Willem, ed. *New International Dictionary of Old Testament Theology & Exegesis*. Grand Rapids, MI: Zondervan, 1997.
Waltke, Bruce K. *The Book of Proverbs, Chapters 15–31*. The New International Commentary on the Old Testament. Grand Rapids, MI: Eerdmans, 2005.
Wambach, Karen and Becky Spencer. *Breastfeeding and Human Lactation, 6th ed.* Burlington, MA: Jones & Bartlett, 2021.
Wardlaw, Terrance Randall. "Shaddai, Providence, and the Narrative Structure of Ruth." *Journal of the Evangelical Theological Society 58, no. 1* (March 2015) 31–41.
Watts, John D. W. *Isaiah 34–66, Revised Edition*. Word Biblical Commentary 25. Nashville: Thomas Nelson, 2005.
Wenham, Gordon J. *Genesis 1–15*. Word Biblical Commentary 1. Dallas: Word, 1987.
———. *Genesis 16–50*. Word Biblical Commentary 2. Dallas: Word, 1994.
Westfall, Cynthia Long. *Paul and Gender: Reclaiming the Apostle's Vision for Men and Women in Christ*. Ada, MI: Baker Academic, 2016.

www.ingramcontent.com/pod-product-compliance
Lightning Source LLC
Chambersburg PA
CBHW051926160426
43198CB00012B/2057